# JOHN DEWEY AS EDUCATOR

# JOHN DEWEY AS EDUCATOR

*His Design for Work in Education (1894–1904)*

ARTHUR G. WIRTH

*Graduate Institute of Education*
*Washington University*
*St. Louis, Missouri*

JOHN WILEY & SONS, INC.    *New York   London   Sydney*

*To My Mother and Father*

# *Preface*

John Dewey has been the most controversial figure in twentieth-century American education. At the turn of the century, he was a leader in the criticism of traditional schooling. Sixty years later educational ideas associated with him were under heavy attack. He has suffered from uncritical adulation as well as unwarranted vituperation. In recent years, it became the mode in the popular press to identify progressive education with loose, superficial educational practice and to label Dewey as its author. There is a voluminous literature on Dewey's educational philosophy, but few efforts have been made to weigh his ideas against the practice he sponsored when an educator. After a period of unusually raucous commentary in the 1950's and early 1960's, we may be ready to seek a more rational appraisal of John Dewey's contributions to American education.

"Future thought in America must go beyond Dewey . . . , though it is difficult to see how it can avoid going through him." [1]

There is probable wisdom in this statement by Robert J. Roth, S.J., and to consider its truth, we shall need accurate knowledge of Dewey's work. The present study is based on a simple hunch: if we want accurate insights into Dewey's ideas about education, we might profit from a careful appraisal of the one period in his career when he had a direct and continuing responsibility in education. This was the decade 1894–1904 when he was at the University of Chicago as Chairman of the combined Departments of Philosophy, Psychology, and Education, and founder and director of the University Laboratory School.

The gist of the argument is that, in the Chicago decade,

[1] Robert J. Roth, S.J., *John Dewey and Self-Realization* (Englewood Cliffs, New Jersey, Prentice-Hall, 1962), p. 144.

Dewey developed a comprehensive plan for the study and improvement of education. He left the university in 1904 with the total effort barely under way and his projected goals largely unrealized. His over-all design is an indispensable source for understanding his specific ideas, then or later, in their proper intent. The failure to maintain this perspective by some of Dewey's followers in the progressive education movement, as well as by his critics, has led to unfortunate misunderstandings.

The complexity of our time gives new urgency to the need to create viable educational programs. We must have access to all responsible ideas—reasoned appraisals of our past as well as imaginative projections for the future. Without such ideas, we become foolish followers of fads and catchwords—disappointed by each in turn as it fails to produce miraculous remedies. There is no need to have so little confidence in our educational past. American education has been rich in imaginative innovations. As we mature, we should be able to build with a sense of continuity based on judicious appraisals of our experience. The kind of shallow sloganeering that has so often characterized the debate about Dewey's role in education is unworthy of a self-respecting people.

The attempt in this study is to further a realistic appraisal of Dewey's proposals by creating an account based on the sources. Liberal resort to quotations from Dewey's writings and other documents has been made to let the record speak. In concentrating on the period when he was a practicing educator, we try to avoid a mere restatement of his educational theory by checking his ideas against the practice he sponsored in the University Elementary (or Laboratory) School in Chicago. Such an approach may help to establish points of comparison between Dewey's own work and features of the later progressive education movement. In effect, we confront the question, "What did Dewey stand for when he directed a school?"

The record shows, however, that it would be an error to concentrate exclusively on practices in his Laboratory School. Dewey made it clear that his interest in experimentation in education was an integral part of his effort to work out the ideas of his philosophy of instrumentalism. In accord with the spirit of that philosophy, he needed a setting where ideas could be tested in action. Theory and practice were to move forward in continuous interaction. The Chicago decade was the period when Dewey's break with Hegelian idealism became complete, and when he and his colleagues pioneered a philosophical alternative. Because his ideas about education grew from this effort, it is impossible to understand them apart from the context of his general philosophy.

In Part I we examine, first, the emergence of pivotal philosophical concepts that influenced Dewey's educational thinking and, second, his vision of the kind of effort required to strengthen American education. Part II contains a description of the curriculum and methodology of the University of Chicago Elementary School, and an effort is made to trace the influence of the general theory on actual educational practice.

Dewey blocked out a comprehensive frame of reference for thinking about problems in education—an approach that started from such basic questions as the nature of man and man's ways of learning about his world. We shall have to create our own answers, but Dewey's work may continue to have value in serving as a model that suggests the range of questions that may be raised. Alternatives may be thrown against it for comparison. We can be challenged to make choices in terms of grounds that support one set of answers as compared with another.

It is possible to view the story to be told from another and larger perspective. The span of Dewey's life (1859–1952) points to the dramatic order of social change that transpired in the ninety-three years of American history through which he lived. He was born in 1859, at 186 South Willard Street, Burlington, Vermont, during the administration of James Buchanan. The Burlington of his boyhood might have been a model for Thornton Wilder's *Our Town*. He died in his apartment on Fifth Avenue, New York City, in June 1952, in the month when Dwight David Eisenhower was making the moves that would win him the presidency. In the intervening decades, America was transformed from a country of farms, small towns, and an open frontier into a nation of factories, sprawling metropolises, and continental superhighways. After growing to manhood in the quiet environs of Burlington, Dewey spent his mature, productive years in Chicago and New York—our largest cities.

The physical passage from the comfortable small-town round of life to the clangorous ways of the big city was a road Dewey shared with millions of his countrymen. More was involved than a change of geography. As Dewey himself was to see so clearly, such radical shifts in forms of work and community life necessarily were accompanied by modifications of mind and character. Ferdinand Tönnies, the nineteenth-century German sociologist, pointed out that the fundamental transition was from intimate, tradition-oriented communities to the massive complexities of impersonal societies ruled by law and intellectual abstractions. A prescientific view of the world was giving way before the exciting and deeply disturbing insights and consequences of modern science. Dewey was one of a multitude making the journey. We could learn something by trying to understand how any one human being reacted to the experience. Dewey's personal odyssey is especially revealing because he saw with unusual clarity what was happening—and he was one who tried to come to terms with events with above average courage and ability.

He rejected a stance of wistful nostalgia and accepted the onrush of change as a challenge to human thought and imagination. He faced the encounter head-on with a life of productive work. One of his responses was the conviction that children entering this new world needed to be prepared by a reformed kind of educational experience that would equip them for an effective, and fulfilling, go at life. He made a notable effort to stake out the features of what such an education might be.

*Arthur G. Wirth*

*St. Louis, Missouri*
*January, 1966*

# Acknowledgments

One of the most satisfying experiences in bringing a study to a close is to acknowledge the assistance of the many who contributed to the effort.

This project got under way shortly after I joined the faculty at Washington University. I found support for serious study both in the respect for free scholarship that prevails on this campus and in the high-spirited dedication to the study of education displayed by my colleagues in the Graduate Institute of Education. This investigation never would have been completed without the special encouragement and assistance of Raymond E. Callahan of the Institute, a committed scholar and teacher, who was an unfailing mentor and friend. Special appreciation is due, also, to Robert Schaefer and Judson Shaplin who provided the conditions, tangible and intangible, to sustain the labors. Timely grants from the Graduate School provided practical reinforcement at strategic points.

One of the chief delights of the research was the opportunity to interview Dr. Frederick Eby and Dr. (Mrs.) W. W. Charters, two of the few people remaining who had direct experience with Dewey's Chicago work. They searched their files and remarkably perceptive minds to recreate for the author the spirit of Dewey's Department. Professor Eby generously made available rare, unpublished materials for use in the study.

I am grateful, also, to the late Hugo Beck, who guided me with skill and good humor to the rich resources at the University of Chicago.

At critical stages of the research Erwin Johanningmeier, Carl Bewig, and Jean Pennington were imaginative and diligent in bringing to light materials to be fitted into the story. Only they and the author know the full extent of their contributions. Margaret Carmichael, Dorothy Stefany, Vicki Willman, and Ann Cohen were faithful collaborators in preparing the manuscript. They gently tried to help me write a clean sentence here and there. Miriam Sarchet and Vera Costain were careful and competent in getting the flow of words through the typewriters.

Ward Madden of Brooklyn College, Robert E. Mason of the University of Pittsburgh, Michael Simmons of the University of Buffalo, and Gail Kennedy of Amherst College read the manuscript in whole or in part, and generously offered their thoughtful reactions. I profited to the extent that I was capable of doing so.

A grant from the United States Office of Education provided financial support for research assistants and for one uninterrupted summer that could be devoted completely to writing. That grant saved, at least, several additional years of work. This book is based in large part on a research report submitted to the Office of Education entitled: "John Dewey's Ideas and Work in Education at the University of Chicago."

Finally, I am indebted to my family—to my wife, Marian, and to Vicki, Scott, and Patricia for enduring with me.

I am grateful to the following persons and publishers who generously gave permission to use quotations.

Appleton-Century-Crofts
The Association For Student Teaching, State College of Iowa
D. C. Heath & Company
Harper & Row, Publishers, Incorporated
Harvard University Press
Irving Louis Horowitz, literary executor for the works of
C. Wright Mills
*Journal of the History of Ideas*
*Journal of the History of Philosophy*
The Macmillan Company
Mrs. John Dewey
The Open Court Publishing Company
Prentice-Hall, Incorporated
G. P. Putnam's Sons, and Coward-McCann
Random House, Inc. and Alfred A. Knopf Inc.
The University of Chicago Press
Yale University Press

The comprehensive bibliography of Dewey's writings compiled by Milton Halsey Thomas, *John Dewey, A Centennial Bibliography* (Chicago: The University of Chicago Press, 1962) is an invaluable aid for all students of Dewey's work.

*A. G. W.*

# Contents

# JOHN DEWEY AS EDUCATOR

*Part* I

# THE THEORY: PHILOSOPHICAL AND PSYCHOLOGICAL

CHAPTER ONE

# Dewey's Experience in American Schools

Why would a major figure in philosophy devote so much of his energy to education, a subject passed over lightly by most philosophers? In Dewey's case, it is clear that the concern about education derived in large part from his wider intellectual interests. The purpose of this study is to analyze the relation of his general philosophy to his ideas about education. Dewey, however, would be the first to admit that men's lives are determined by their histories. Personal events as well as intellectual interests pushed him to confront problems in education. Without attempting a full-scale biographical sketch, we may be able to add to the understanding of our story by presenting a brief review of Dewey's experiences in a variety of American schools, prior to his Chicago tenure.

A child's education is well under way before he first enters a schoolhouse. Family and community are significant educators, early and late; that was a favorite theme in Dewey's writings. We begin with comments on these factors in his own life.

Dewey was born in 1859 and grew to manhood in Burlington, Vermont. He was nurtured, as child and youth, in a nineteenth-century New England town. A boy growing up in New England experiences nature in its extremes; life is a clear and dual thing: winter and summer. He and his brothers absorbed naturally the unusual beauty of the Vermont environment. Burlington looks across Lake Champlain toward the Adirondacks, and the soft, rolling Green Mountains rise behind it. The young John and his brothers explored the woods and nearby waterways, and as they grew older they came to know well the details of Lake

3

Champlain and Lake George through canoe excursions. One memorable summer, they descended the waterways connecting Lake Champlain and the St. Lawrence and, accompanied by an Indian guide, rowed up a river into French Canada. The French they learned on their trips into French-speaking territory, supplemented by the French they picked up in Burlington, enabled the boys to read simple French novels before they studied the language in school.[1]

Burlington was a busy but unhurried center for trade, agriculture, and light industry. Dewey's father, Archibald Dewey, made an adequate income as a storekeeper and the boys helped out by carrying newspapers and tallying lumber brought down the lakes from Canada. In this pre-industrial town, people were related to each other through their work and shared community activities. The tradition of direct town meeting democracy in political affairs was a fact in New England life. Differences of class and status were not emphasized, and a rough kind of human equality was taken for granted. Most of the children shared in the activities and responsibilities of the home. In the course of growing up they became aware, at first hand, of the round of simple industrial and agricultural occupations.

An uncomplicated theology prevailed in religion in both the community and the Dewey home. The whole family attended the Congregational Church. Dewey's mother, Lucina, was a convert to Congregationalism from a Universalist background. Her emphasis was on moral judgment rather than on religious dogmatism. She had strong anti-slavery sentiments, was active in philanthropic and community projects, and visited the homes of the sick and the poor. She also founded a Mission Sunday School and was active in the work of the Adams Mission. She read widely, had a quick, inquiring mind, and played an active role in the social and intellectual life of Burlington.[2]

Dewey's father was only moderately successful as a businessman but was placed in positions of responsibility and trust by his

[1] Paul A. Schilpp, ed., The Philosophy of John Dewey (New York, The Tudor Publishing Co., 1951) see Jane M. Dewey, "Biography of John Dewey," pp. 7–9, et passim.
[2] George Dykhuizen, "An Early Chapter in the Life of John Dewey," Journal of the History of Ideas, Vol. 13 (October, 1952), p. 569.

townsmen in his church, and in business, as evidenced by his selection, at one time, as treasurer of the Burlington Savings Bank. In running his grocery, he indulged a wry sense of humor, as demonstrated in his self-composed advertisements: "Hams and cigars, smoked and unsmoked"; a brand of cigars was displayed under the heading, "A good excuse for a bad habit." He had had little schooling but had acquired a taste for classical authors which he shared with his children, reciting to them passages from the works of Milton, Shakespeare, Lamb, Thackeray, and Burns. In literature, he liked the sound of words with firm modeling but he made no effort to force his children to conform to his choice. In the last year of the Civil War, when Archibald was a quartermaster with the Union Army, his wife took the adventuresome step of moving the family to Virginia to be near him. This experience of family solidarity in time of stress left a deep impression on the children. Dewey said years later that his father's character was "the larger part of [my] education in so far as any single person affected it in these early years." [3]

The young John attended traditional district schools in Burlington. Compared to the concrete learnings from family and community, work in the town school seemed a bore. The schools were overcrowded and without careful regulation of attendance. They lacked a uniform or graded course of study, and the teachers were poorly selected. A report of the superintendent declared, "Our public schools *as they now are*, are unworthy of patronage" and "a source of grief and mortification to a large majority of our citizens." [4]

A perceptive statement by Dewey's daughter, Jane, helps us see the significance of these early experiences.

"By the time he reached manhood and became a teacher himself, the growth of cities and the extension of work done by machines had interfered with the invaluable supplements to school education provided by active educational responsibilities and in-

---

[3] Frances Littlefield Davenport, *The Education of John Dewey* (unpublished Ed.D. thesis, University of California at Los Angeles, 1946), p. 22. Stated to the author in an interview with John Dewey.

[4] George Dykhuizen, *op. cit.*, p. 563. Quoting Mathew H. Buckham, *Report of the Superintendent of Common Schools*, City Documents (Burlington, Vermont, 1867), pp. 17–18.

timate personal contacts, with people in all walks of life, which occurred spontaneously in his boyhood. By this time also, reading matter, instead of being sparse and difficult of access, was plentiful, cheap, and almost forced on everyone. This had removed the significance which formal schooling in the three R's possessed in the mainly agrarian republic in which he grew up. The realization that the most important parts of his own education until he entered college were obtained outside the schoolroom played a large role in his educational work, in which such importance is attached, both in theory and practice to occupational activities as the most effective approaches to genuine learning and to personal intellectual discipline. His comments on the stupidity of the ordinary school recitation are undoubtedly due in no small measure to the memory of the occasional pleasant class hours spent with the teachers who wandered a little from the prescribed curriculum." [5]

The situation improved by the time Dewey entered the Burlington High School, which came to have a fine reputation for providing a quality education for general citizenship and for those planning to enter the University. English and classical courses were offered; the latter was undoubtedly selected by the young Dewey. [6]

Shortly before his sixteenth birthday, Dewey entered the University of Vermont. He followed the prescribed curriculum with required courses in five departments: Rhetoric and English Literature, Languages, Mathematics, Natural Sciences, and Philosophy. For the better part of the first three years he took the required courses in a routine fashion. There was little intellectual excitement on campus and Dewey, as a quiet young man, played no role that distinguished him from his fellows. Even in the staid atmosphere of the University of Vermont, students were not above testing regulations. Faculty meeting minutes indicate that students absented themselves from class; asked to have the final examination in a difficult course abolished; created disturbances in the dormitories; set the grass on fire; and brought beer into the college buildings on the day of the annual football game. Dewey was no rowdy, but the records show he had his own minor

[5] Schilpp, *op. cit.*, p. 9.
[6] Dykhuizen, *op. cit.*, p. 563.

brushes with the authorities. In 1877 he was one of nine students to receive twelve demerits for making a disturbance. The following year he earned five demerit points for absence from drill.[7]

Intellectually he was stirred by several experiences toward the end of his college career. Dewey dated the awakening of his interest in philosophical questions from the time of a junior year course in physiology. The text was Huxley's *Elements of Physiology*. In it he was introduced to the biological organism with its interdependence of parts; this gave him a sense of the possibility of a view of existence characterized by interdependence and interrelated unity. "Subconsciously, at least," Dewey later wrote, "I was led to desire a world and a life that would have the same properties as had the human organism in the picture of it derived from study of Huxley's treatment."[8] In his senior year he plunged into the study of philosophy, reading and laboring far into the night, with the result that he led his class and got the highest marks on record in philosophy.[9]

He was confronted with a philosophical problem that pre-occupied him for a lifetime: How to resolve the chasms that seemed to separate the material and moral sciences. At Vermont this issue was represented in the gap between the organic, evolutionary view of Huxley and the dominating philosophy on campus, which Dewey described as Scottish intuitionalism. The latter was standing as the champion of traditional morals and religion as against the sceptical tendencies in sensational empiricism.

"It taught that man is born with certain ultimate and unexplainable principles which are intuitively recognized as true, and which are taken for granted by common sense without any logical proof. Man is under necessity to accept them, for, lacking these self-evident intuitions, he is without starting points for his thought and without standards for his conduct. Such intuitively known principles are to be found in grammar, logic, mathematics,

[7] *Ibid.*, p. 570.
[8] George P. Adams and William P. Montague, eds., *Contemporary American Philosophy* (New York, The Macmillan Co., 1930), Vol. 2, see John Dewey, "From Absolutism to Experimentalism," pp. 13-27 *et passim*.
[9] Max Eastman, *Heroes I Have Known* (New York, Simon and Schuster, 1942), p. 282.

aesthetics, ethics, religion, and metaphysics, and supply strong evidence for the existence of God, the Soul, immortality, freedom, duty, etc." [10]

Dewey came to see this intuitionalism as typical of a New England dualist heritage that he felt a need to oppose for the rest of his life. The depth of his feeling was revealed years later when he described this tradition as representing "divisions by way of isolation of self from the world, of soul from body, of nature from God" that were felt in him as "an inward laceration." [11] The demand for a unifying philosophy to resolve these separations was experienced as an intense emotional craving. A glimpse of such an alternative had been first suggested in his experience with Huxley. In the eighties it was to lead him to Hegel, and then gradually to the elaboration of experimentalism within the evolutionary orientation.

Before embarking on what was to be a lifelong venture in philosophic speculation, he was to have another kind of experience in American education—this time as a teacher in the public schools. Upon graduating from the University of Vermont in 1879, Dewey taught high school courses for two years in South Oil City, Pennsylvania, a position he obtained through his cousin who was principal of the school. He taught a little of everything, including Latin, algebra, and natural science. His duties as a beginning teacher consumed only part of his energies, and the speculative quests that he had begun in Vermont occupied his attention. He read philosophy avidly far into the nights, and became so absorbed that he ignored the advice of two brokers living in his boarding house to invest some money in Standard Oil, the company that was at that time exciting the town.

Max Eastman reports that Dewey told him that it was during an evening in Oil City that he had a "mystic experience." It came as an answer to a question still worrying him: Whether he really meant business when he prayed. "It was not a dramatic mystic experience. There was not a vision, not even a definable emotion —just a supremely blissful feeling that his worries were over." Dewey held that such experiences cannot be described in words but in earthy language he tried to convey the feeling that came.

[10] Dykhuizen, *op. cit.*, p. 565.
[11] Adams and Montague, *op. cit.*, p. 19.

"What the hell are you worrying about, anyway? Everything that's here is here, and you can just lie back on it." [12] Many years later, we find Dewey returning to this theme in more elegant language, in a major statement on his religious orientation, *A Common Faith*. He referred to his faith as one of natural piety and contrasted it with what he called unreligious attitudes.

"The essentially unreligious attitude is that which attributes human achievement and purpose to man in isolation from the world of physical nature and his fellows. Our successes are dependent upon the cooperation of nature. The sense of dignity of human nature is as religious as is the sense of awe and reverence when it rests upon a sense of human nature as a cooperating part of a larger whole. Natural piety is not of necessity either a fatalistic acquiescense in natural happenings or a romantic idealization of the world. It may rest upon a just sense of nature as the whole of which we are parts, while it also recognizes that we are parts that are marked by intelligence and purpose, having the capacity to strive by their aid to bring conditions into greater consonance with what is humanly desirable. Such piety is an inherent constituent of a just perspective in life." [13]

After some early struggles with religious belief, Dewey gradually moved to the attitude of natural piety just described. It was a meliorist position; it enabled man to see himself as a cooperator with a supporting universe. Nature was not unqualifiedly friendly; men knew all too well its perils, but it contained enough qualities for man to grow in experience. For Dewey this came to define the task for which man was responsible; he could let the imponderables take care of themselves.

When Dewey's cousin resigned to get married, the young teacher returned to Burlington. During the winter term of the following year, he taught subjects from the alphabet to plane geometry in the nearby village school of Charlotte.[14] He took advantage of his return to Vermont to pursue a more systematic study of philosophy through tutorial work with Professor

[12] Eastman, *op. cit.*, p. 283.
[13] John Dewey, *A Common Faith* (New Haven, Yale University Press, 1934 [1961]), pp. 25–26.
[14] Eastman, *op. cit.*, p. 284.

H. A. P. Torrey, who directed him to classics in the history of philosophy and the reading of German philosophers. He now came to consider the possibility of a professional career in philosophy. The decision was reinforced by Dr. W. T. Harris, the well-known Hegelian, and editor of the *Journal of Speculative Philosophy*, who accepted several of Dewey's first articles in philosophy.

Torrey, of the University of Vermont, was a fine scholar but cautious in temperament. In his public work he stayed within the bounds of conventional thought; in private he speculated more boldly and gave Dewey a chance to stretch his mind. This included a productive encounter with Spinoza. Dewey's article "The Pantheism of Spinoza" [15] was one of two articles accepted by Harris for publication that year.

In the meantime an imaginative merchant named Johns Hopkins had founded a new kind of research university in Baltimore. The inaugural address had been given by Professor Thomas Huxley, the defender of Darwinism. The address was published and Dewey was tremendously impressed with it. Huxley's speech became the target of bitter attacks but President Gilman of Hopkins made a stout defense. On reading Gilman's reply to the critics, Dewey became convinced he had found the proper place in which to continue the search for truth.[16]

The new university was offering 20 five-hundred-dollar fellowships. Dewey tried for one and failed. (Thorstein Veblen met the same fate.) But Dewey had an aunt willing to loan him five hundred dollars. He borrowed the money and enrolled at Hopkins in the fall of 1882. The following year he won a fellowship, which permitted him to complete his doctoral study in 1884.

New intellectual worlds were opened for the budding philosopher at Johns Hopkins. There was an atmosphere of intellectual excitement at the university unmatched on any other campus of the time. A great stimulus to scholarly activity was the expectation that advanced students as well as faculty would engage in

[15] John Dewey, "The Pantheism of Spinoza," *Journal of Speculative Philosophy*, Vol. 16 (July, 1882), pp. 249–257. also, John Dewey, "The Metaphysical Assumptions of Materialism," *Journal of Speculative Philosophy*, Vol. 16 (April, 1882), pp. 208–213.

[16] Davenport, *op. cit.*, pp. 52–53.

original research. As Josiah Royce put it, "The air was full of rumors of noteworthy work done by the older men of the place, and of hopes that one might find a way to get a little working power one's self." [17] Dewey got a first-hand experience with a university as a center for advancing knowledge through disciplined inquiry. This became a guiding ideal in plans for his own later work.

In his first year, Dewey concentrated on courses in history and political theory with Herbert B. Adams. In his second year, Woodrow Wilson was a fellow student in a seminar in History and Political Science, but both were shy young men and did not become friends. He continued his interest in biology, taking a course in animal physiology by H. Newell Martin. Because he was timid and unsure as a speaker, he took a course in elocution.[18] His greatest satisfaction, however, came from his work with George Sylvester Morris, who introduced Dewey to Hegel. A close relation grew up between them and Morris got him the important fellowship for the second year.

Hegel's views of reality as an organic unity whose parts were interrelated like those of a biological organism met Dewey's deep need for an alternative to the dualisms he detested. As he himself put it,

"Hegel's synthesis of subject and object, matter and spirit, the divine and the human . . . operated as an immense relief, a liberation. Hegel's treatment of human culture, of institutions and the arts, involved the dissolution of hard and fast dividing walls, and had a special attraction for me." [19]

Dewey later found Hegel's schematism artificial and, as he put it, was to "drift away" from that philosophy over the next dozen years. Hegel's thought, however, left permanent marks, and it helped Dewey to begin the integration that he sought in his own thinking. This was evidenced, for example, in the early

[17] George Dykhuizen, "John Dewey at Hopkins," *Journal of the History of Ideas*, Vol. 22, No. 1 (January–March, 1961), p. 104, quoting Josiah Royce, "Present Ideals of American University Life," *Scribner's Magazine*, Vol. 10 (1892), p. 383. See the Dykhuizen article for fuller details of Dewey's experience at Johns Hopkins.

[18] Davenport, *op. cit.*, Ch. 5.

[19] Adams and Montague, *op. cit.*, p. 19.

formings of his social philosophy. In independent reading, he had
been impressed deeply by Comte's analysis of the disorganized
character of modern Western culture, due to disintegrative "individualism"; and by his idea of a synthesis of science that could
provide a regulative method for organized social life. He found
these same criticisms in Hegel but with a deeper, more far-reach-
ing integration.[20] This theme was to be sounded later in *Individualism Old and New* and in his many writings on a democratic
social order. Its influence was to be shown, too, in his idea that
the life of the school should be conceived as an organic community. At a more general level, Dewey's tendency to define
issues so that answers would represent resolutions of apparent
polar opposites, reminds one of Hegel's dialectic style.

In the second year, Dewey took work with Charles S. Peirce
in logic, but expressed disappointment because the approach was
mathematical and scientific rather than what he sought: a study
of the "different forms of knowledge, their origins and development, their interconnection, and their comparative value as em-
bodiments of truth." [21] This preference for a genetic rather than
a mathematical, analytic approach to logic remained a part of
Dewey's style. It was many years later, while working out his
instrumentalist logic, that Dewey recognized the significance of
Peirce's work and utilized it in his own formulations.[22]

G. Stanley Hall was another of the major minds on campus.
After studying under Wundt in Germany, Hall decided to make
the "new psychology" his primary interest. In 1882, he established two courses in physiological and experimental psychology,
and another called "Psychological and Ethical Theories." He also
gave a seminar in "scientific pedagogy" for those intending to
teach. Dewey completed work in all of these and, in addition,

[20] *Ibid.*, p. 20.
[21] Dykhuizen, "John Dewey at Hopkins," pp. 105–106.
[22] In 1903 Dewey wrote to William James about his current work in
logic, ". . . I see how far I moved along when I find how much I get out
of Peirce this year, and how easily I understand him, when a few years
ago he was mostly a sealed book to me. . . ." Ralph Barton Perry, *The
Thought and Character of William James as Revealed in His Unpublished
Correspondence and Notes together with His Published Writings* (Boston,
Little, Brown and Co., 1935), Vol. 2, p. 523.

conducted independent experiments in the psychological laboratory set up by Hall. With Hall, he encountered the genetic orientation that came by way of Haeckel and Spencer, and the idea of studying the development of children from a scientific, evolutionary point of view. His experiences with Hall resulted in two important influences: (1) a feeling of dissatisfaction with the idealist view of mind and, (2) the feeling that a philosophically oriented "rational psychology" would have to give way to experiment.[23] These ideas were to come to the surface some years later under the stimulation of reading William James. The topic of his dissertation was *The Psychology of Kant* (1884). It was never published, nor is there a copy of it in the files at Johns Hopkins.

The telling influence for Dewey's immediate career was his encounter with Hegel through his study with Morris. Dewey was now clear that his commitment was to philosophy. The choice of a career in philosophy contained more than the usual risks at that time, as most departments were staffed with men trained in theology. Dewey graduated with no job in sight. Finally, in July, 1884, he received an offer from President James B. Angell of the University of Michigan to become an instructor at a salary of nine hundred dollars. Dewey accepted with delight. With the exception of the academic year 1888–1889, when he was at the University of Minnesota, he spent a happy and productive ten years there.

In the first period, 1884–1888, he worked as a junior colleague under his friend and former mentor, George Sylvester Morris, who had been appointed Chairman of the Department of Philosophy. Morris' orientation was Hegelian, and he taught the courses in History of Philosophy, Ethics, Aesthetics, and Logic. Dewey gave the courses in psychology: Empirical Psychology; Special Topics in Psychology (Physiological, Comparative, and Morbid); Psychology and Philosophy with special reference to the History of Philosophy in Great Britain; Experimental Psychology; Speculative Psychology; and History of Psychology. In philosophy, he came to teach Formal Logic; Greek Science and Philosophy; Kant's *Critique of Pure Reason;* the Philosophy of

[23] Davenport, *op. cit.,* Ch. 5.

Herbert Spencer; and seminars in Plato's *Republic* and in Kant's ethics.[24]

George Dykhuizen has provided a detailed account of Dewey's work and experiences at Ann Arbor.[25] Several items may be noted for purposes of the present study.

The Hegelianism of Morris and Dewey was taught as compatible with traditional Christian concepts, and the religious atmosphere of the department satisfied all but the very orthodox. Morris took the lead with a position that was pietistic rather than dogmatic, but Dewey also affirmed that Hegelian philosophy "in its broad and essential features, is identical with the theological teaching of Christianity." [26] In his early years, Dewey devoted considerable energy to the Student Christian Association, for which he conducted a Bible Class on "The Life of Christ—with special reference to its importance as an historical event," and gave addresses on such topics as *The Obligation of Knowledge of God, Faith and Doubt,* and *The Place of Religious Emotion.* He was active in the First Congregational Church, where he conducted Bible Classes in 1887–1888 in "Church History." [27] Later, his ethical interests shifted from a religious to a social orientation, but his concern with the ethical dimension was constant throughout his career.

A number of publications grew out of the courses he was teaching in psychology, including his first book, *Psychology* (1887). In it he sought to combine, in a single system, the results of the new empirical physiological psychology and the concepts of Hegelian idealism. It was widely adopted as a text by many universities, but it was criticized by both G. Stanley Hall and William James for confusions introduced in its metaphysical sections.[28] Dewey himself later repudiated it.

It was during the latter part of his stay at Michigan that Dewey began to move away from Hegelianism. The growing commitment to a functionally oriented psychology with its roots

[24] From the *Calendar of the University of Michigan,* reported in George Dykhuizen, "John Dewey and the University of Michigan," *Journal of the History of Ideas,* Vol. 23, No. 4 (October–December, 1962), pp. 513–514.
[25] *Ibid.*
[26] *Ibid.,* p. 517.
[27] *Ibid.,* pp. 520–521.
[28] *Ibid.,* pp. 525–526.

in evolutionary biology was a leading factor in the shift. James's *Principles of Psychology* exerted a critical influence in leading Dewey to assign major significance to the idea of a total organism interacting with its environment and actively engaged in adjusting to it. James thought of life in terms of action. He conceived of mind not as something apart from nature, but as the process by which organisms and environment become integrated. This objective conception of mind, Dewey said, "worked its way more and more into all my ideas and acted as a ferment to transform old beliefs." [29]

Dewey's interest in primary and secondary education began while he was at Michigan. The university was an integral part of the public school system, and under the outstanding leadership of President James Angell was, in many ways, the directive force of public education in the state. Prior to 1871, the university admitted only those who could pass a formal academic examination. In 1871, however, the decision was made to admit the graduates of any secondary school whose program met the academic requirements of the university. Faculty committees were sent to high schools to see if the quality of instruction warranted admission to the university without examination. Dewey was one of these investigators, and he soon saw the need of an organization to study problems of mutual interest to high schools and colleges. He became active in the Michigan Schoolmasters Club and served as vice president in 1887 and 1888. Dewey spoke frequently at teachers' institutes and conventions, and published writings for teachers in training.[30] He became aware that the quality of the secondary school was dependent on the training the child had received in the grade schools. This led him to study programs of the elementary schools. He became convinced that work there did not coincide with the normal learning processes of young children. He came to attribute the shortcomings of the schools to ill-conceived programs and methods, and to poor coordination of the various levels. Thus, he began his search for an alternative that would integrate educational, psychological, and philosophical ideas. Within a few years, the quest was to culminate in the founding of the Laboratory School at the University of Chicago.

[29] Adams and Montague, *op. cit.*, p. 24.
[30] Schilpp, *op. cit.*, p. 27.

The Michigan phase should not be passed over without mention of another factor that also turned his interests to education. In 1886, he married Alice Chipman, a young woman who had a deep interest in philosophy. She was a charter member of the Philosophical Society and took most of the work offered by the department. Her vigorous, independent mind and strong interests in social issues were to act as an intellectual stimulant to her husband's thought. Two of their six children were born during their stay in Ann Arbor and a third during the year in Minneapolis. Both parents were concerned that their children receive richer educational experiences than those available in the routine classrooms of their day. Their children eventually became students in the Chicago Laboratory School. When Dewey was once asked what led him to turn to educational philosophy and the founding and directing of the school, he replied, "It was mainly on account of the children." [31]

In the meantime, President William Rainey Harper was assembling a brilliant faculty at the newly-founded University of Chicago. He was looking for a man to head the Department of Philosophy. James H. Tufts, a former colleague of Dewey's at Michigan and now on the Chicago staff, recommended Dewey. Dewey, at 29, had been appointed Chairman of the Department of Philosophy at Michigan upon the death of Morris. The exciting quality of the faculty at Chicago and the chance to associate with men engaged in advanced research appealed to him. Another attraction was the definition of the job, which was to have Dewey act as Chairman of the combined Departments of Philosophy, Psychology, and Pedagogy. By this time, he felt a growing need to see pedagogy given a solid grounding in psychology and philosophy. George Mead later stated that the inclusion of pedagogy was an important factor in Dewey's decision to accept the offer.[32]

[31] Katherine C. Mayhew and Anna C. Edwards, *The Dewey School* (New York, Appleton-Century-Crofts, 1936), p. 446.

[32] George H. Mead, "The Philosophies of Royce, James, and Dewey in Their American Setting," in *John Dewey: The Man and His Philosophy* (Cambridge, Harvard University Press, 1930), p. 101.

# CHAPTER TWO

# *The Philosophical Rationale*

A thorough accounting of Dewey's work in education would require not only a full biography but a mapping of the connections of his educational ideas to all the facets of his philosophy. Neither is possible within the limits of this study. Since, however, an understanding of his educational ideas is impossible without them, we cannot avoid the attempt to outline some themes that seem especially relevant.

We turn from the biographical sketch to aspects of the intellectual rationale in which his educational thought was rooted. A point from Dewey's own reminiscences about his career may serve as a transition. In a comment on his earliest philosophical articles, written before his enrollment at Johns Hopkins, Dewey noted with some humor that these articles were highly schematic and formal in character, due, he said, to the fact that he had not as yet encountered subject matter that corresponded to his deeper interests. Then he observes:

"I imagine that my development has been controlled largely by a struggle between a native inclination toward the schematic and formally logical, and those incidents of personal experience that compelled me to take account of actual material. Probably there is in the consciously articulated ideas of every thinker an over-weighting of just those things that are contrary to his intrinsic bent, and which, therefore, he has to struggle to bring to expression, while the native bent, on the other hand, can take care of itself. Anyway, a case might be made out for the proposition that the emphasis upon the concrete, empirical, and 'practical' in my later writings is partly due to considerations of this nature. It was a reaction against what was more natural, and it served as a protest and protection against something in myself

which, in the pressure of the weight of actual experiences, I knew
to be a weakness. . . . The marks, the stigmata, of the struggle
to weld together the characteristics of a formal, theoretic interest
and the material of a maturing experience of contacts with realities showed themselves, naturally, in style of writing and manner
of presentation. During the time when the schematic interest predominated, writing was comparatively easy; there were even com-
pliments on the clearness of my style. Since then thinking and
writing have been hard work. It is easy to give way to the dialectic development of a theme; the pressure of concrete experience
was, however, sufficiently heavy, so that a sense of intellectual
honesty prevented a surrender to that course. But, on the other
hand, the formal interest persisted, so that there was an inner
demand for an intellectual technique that would be consistent and
yet capable of flexible adaptation to the concrete diversity of
experienced things. It is hardly necessary to say that I have not
been among those to whom the union of abilities of these two opposed requirements, the formal and the material, came easily. For
that very reason I have been acutely aware, too much so, doubtless, of a tendency of other thinkers and writers to achieve a
specious lucidity and simplicity by the mere process of ignoring
considerations which a greater respect for concrete materials of
experience would have forced upon them." [1]

This passage is quoted at length because it deals with a theme
central to the interpretation to follow. Embedded in the basic
conviction and style of the man was the hunch that the reach
for truth must be anchored in an interplay of theory with events
in the thick stream of experience. The use of "stigmata" indicates
the personal depth of the issue and the effort. The marks of this
struggle are embedded deeply in the whole thrust of his philosophic thought and in the design for education that grew from it.

We turn first to the philosophic frame of reference to test
the idea.

"Nothing but the best, the richest and fullest experience possible, is good enough for man. The attainment of such an experi-

---

[1] George P. Adams and William P. Montague, eds., *Contemporary American Philosophy* (New York, The Macmillan Co., 1930), Vol. 2, see John
Dewey, "From Absolutism to Experimentalism," pp. 16–17.

ence is not to be conceived as the specific problem of 'reformers' but as the common purpose of men."[2]

This statement, as well as any, identifies the point of the compass by which Dewey directed the whole of his labors. It contains his definition of the paramount vocation of men. Intellectuals and educators had a special responsibility: to seek clarity about the nature of man's condition and to define and sharpen the tools for getting on with the task of human fulfillment. In the many facets of his work of a lifetime—in logic, social philosophy, ethics, aesthetics, and education—he set out to do his part. It was no small effort for one man and it became a major contribution to world philosophy.

Dewey distinguished his point of view from most philosophic systems by his acceptance of the universe as being marked by contingency as well as by order; by a dynamic process of development through the interaction of events. Man, in body, mind, self, and social life, is in and of this natural process. Nature is in the process of becoming. Experience, which in its broadest sense includes the totality of man's interaction with the universe, shares in the process. In the evolutionary scheme, experience becomes more complex, opening up new life possibilities. Man, with his special capacity for understanding and for giving direction to events, occupies a place on the forefront of the ongoing process. As Julian Huxley later put it, "In man, evolution has at last become conscious of itself." [3]

Those who charge Dewey with unwarranted optimism should be aware that he argued that the possibilities for enrichment of experience are before us, but there are no guarantees that they will be realized. With the emergence of the capacity for thinking, man is freed from the need of mere biological adjustment. The world changes as man walks and acts in it. From the beginning, the universe contains dimensions of contingency and accident that can bring tragedy. The introduction of thought frees man for a unique kind of development, but the products of thought intro-

[2] John Dewey, *Experience and Nature* (New York, W. W. Norton and Co., 1929), p. 412.
[3] Pierre Teilhard de Chardin, *The Phenomenon of Man* (New York, Harper and Row, 1959), p. 20, see Introduction by Julian Huxley.

20 *The Theory: Philosophical and Psychological*

duce new hazards too. Some feeling of this point may be conveyed by a passage from *Experience and Nature:*

"The more an organism learns . . . the more it has to learn, in order to keep itself going; otherwise death and catastrophe. If mind is a further process in life, a further process of registration, conservation and use of what is conserved, then it must have the traits it does empirically have: being a moving stream, a constant change which nevertheless has axis and direction, linkages and associations as well as initiations, hesitations and conclusions." [4]

Men might end by incinerating themselves or by generating new levels of savagery and brutality in ugly, overcrowded centers of dissonance and conflict. Experience, however, is not inevitably destined so to evolve. There will forever be new problems that demand confrontation, but there will also be new opportunities to enrich life experience. If men move in the latter direction, it will be because they deepen their understanding of their condition and muster the will, the habits of mind, the courage to preserve the tested goods, and to create indispensable innovations.

Civilization is the critical part of the evolutionary process for man. Dewey saw civilization as a junction of a stubborn past and an insistent, oncoming future. When philosophy remains alive, it does so by playing a critical role in the advance of civilized experience. Its proper role is criticism: criticism of outworn, encrusted beliefs and attitudes that blind and hobble men; but criticism, too, in the positive sense of clarifying ends and values to which men may aspire in terms of the reality they confront.

Dewey maintained that philosophic thought becomes sterile when it is preoccupied with its own abstractions and cherished, esoteric questions. The threat to its vitality is its tendency to become enamored with the "schematic and formally logical," which Dewey so strongly felt had to be resisted in his own development. Those who engage in intellectual work have a major obligation to move toward refined generalizations, but this effort can become a trap and a move toward irresponsible isolation unless these are checked against concrete events. Reality is always complex. No set of abstractions can account for it completely.

In characteristic fashion, Dewey argued for the necessity of

[4] Dewey, *Experience and Nature*, pp. 281–282.

abstraction *and* experience in fruitful interaction rather than a duality of abstraction *versus* experience. His writings are full of criticisms of philosophical traditions that violate this injunction: classical Western traditions that split man into mind and matter, and elevate the former into the instrument for winning eternal truths from the realm of pure idea; empiricist, materialist traditions that reduce men to automata, shaped by the push of stimuli and sensations. Dewey's own words may underscore the emphasis he attached to this point:

"There are two avenues of approach to the goal of philosophy. We may begin with experience in gross, experience in its crude forms, and by means of its distinguishing features and its distinctive trends, note something of the constitution of the world which generates and maintains it. Or, we may begin with refined selective products, the most authentic statements of commended methods of science, and work back from them to the primary facts of life. The two methods differ in starting point and direction, but not in objective or eventual content. Those who start with coarse, everyday experience must bear in mind the findings of the most competent knowledge, and those who start from the latter must somehow journey back to the homely facts of daily existence." [5]

One more statement, vivid in phraseology, reveals Dewey's commitment to the idea:

"Now the notion of experience, however devoid of differential subject-matter—since it includes all subject-matters—, at least tells us that we must not start with arbitrarily selected simples, and from them deduce the complex and varied, assigning what cannot be thus deduced to an inferior realm of being. It warns us that the tangled and complex is what we primarily find; that we work from and within it to discriminate, reduce, analyze; and that we must keep track of these activities, pointing to them, as well as to the things upon which they are exercised, and to their refined conclusions. When we contemplate their fruits we are not to ignore the art by which they are produced. There is a place for polishers of stones and for those who put the stones

[5] John Dewey, *Experience and Nature* (1925 ed.), p. 2.

together to make temples and palaces. But 'experience' reminds us that a stone was once part of some stratum of the earth, and that a quarryman pried it loose and another workman blew the massive rock to smaller pieces, before it could be smooth-hewn and fitted into an ordered and regular structure. Empirical method warns us that systems which set out from things said to be ultimate and simple have always worked with loaded dice; their premises have been framed to yield desired conclusions." [6]

Dewey's hunch that he needed a point of view that would keep ideas in touch with the world led gradually to his disenchantment with the nebulous abstractions of Hegelian idealism. This trend quickened sharply in the years immediately preceding his departure from Ann Arbor for Chicago. In 1894, he was referring to his point of view as "experimental idealism." [7] This turn was given a strong push by the increasing dominance in his thinking of evolutionary biology and functional psychology. As we have seen, James's *Psychology*, which he was using as a text in the early 1890's, forced on him the idea of an organism actively engaged in seeking an adjustment to an environment. Accompanying this was the revolutionary idea of mind as an emergent function of organism–environment interaction. This brought mind down from the lofty realm of Hegel's Absolute Spirit.

At this time Dewey was being stimulated by his colleagues George H. Mead and Alfred Henry Lloyd, whose work in psychology was moving rapidly in a similar direction. In Mead's courses in psychology and in his course, "The Philosophy of Evolution," the effort was made to determine the bearings of evolution for scientific psychology. In concentrating on seeing mental processes as functions of the interaction of a total organism to a total environment, he was laying the groundwork for the social component of mind that he clarified later. Lloyd, too, worked with the interactionist concept and declared that "ideas are plans, and consciousness is always a planning." [8] In a 1903 letter to William James in which Dewey explained the

[6] *Ibid.*, pp. 13–14.

[7] George Dykhuizen, "John Dewey and the University of Michigan," *Journal of the History of Ideas*, Vol. 23, No. 4 (October–December, 1962), p. 539.

[8] *Ibid.*, p. 536.

emergence of the pragmatic point of view at the University of Chicago, Dewey wrote, "As for the standpoint, we have all been at work at it for about twelve years. Lloyd and Mead were both at it in Ann Arbor ten years ago." [9] Thus, Dewey and his colleagues shared the exciting task of creating a theory of the functional role of thought. Closely related was their concern with how to employ effective thinking to the end of enriching human experience.

At the same time, Dewey saw a new urgency for philosophical reform. Science, which was so full of promise, was also the source of disruptions. One of these was the creation of a technological-urban social order with novel complexities of tempo and texture. Old community forms were disappearing and viable alternatives were not in sight. Dewey later described the last two decades of the nineteenth century as a turning point in American history. These decades marked the close of the pioneer period. The aftermath of the Civil War led the United States into an industrialized and commercial age. As early as 1888 in *The Ethics of Democracy*,[10] Dewey was describing the stakes at issue for a free society. Years later, in *Individualism: Old and New*, he stated the crucial question with powerful directness: "Can a material, industrial civilization be converted into a distinctive agency for liberating the minds and refining the emotions of all who take part in it?" [11]

In Chicago, Dewey encountered the raw realities of a burgeoning megalopolis. His associations with Jane Addams deepened his awareness of the miseries of the exploited. The corruption of municipal politics and the political apathy of the impoverished masses sharpened his sense of threats to free institutions. The new urbanism could increase human tribulation and manipulation as compared with the restricted but more humane community life Dewey had known in New England. Miss Addams' idealism and democratic faith whetted his interest in social problems. They both held that the task was to formulate the conditions necessary

[9] *Ibid.*

[10] John Dewey, *The Ethics of Democracy*, University of Michigan Philosophical Papers, Second Ser., No. 1, 1888.

[11] John Dewey, *Individualism: Old and New* (New York, G. P. Putnam's Sons, 1930), p. 124.

to make democratic ideals function in huge, amorphous industrial settings.[12]

Intellectual and spiritual crises, as well as social disorders, were generated by the advent of science, and men needed help.

"Modern science, modern industry and politics, have presented us with an immense amount of material foreign to, often inconsistent with the most prized intellectual and moral heritage of the western world. This is the cause of our modern intellectual perplexities and confusions. It sets the especial problem for philosophy today and for many years to come." [13]

Evolutionary theory was the great source of intellectual ferment at the time. It exemplified the changing insights about man and the universe that scientific inquiry was producing. In its broad scope, it encompassed more than innovations in biology; geology and astronomy were advancing within an evolutionary framework, and it was exerting a profound influence on the newer sciences of sociology, anthropology, and psychology. It was one source of the excitement on the Chicago campus as the vigorous thinkers that Harper assembled saw the need to ask new questions and create novel intellectual formulations.

Dewey was to embrace the evolutionary point of view and assign it a pivotal place in his thought, because reality demanded it. At the same time, he was much aware of its disturbing effects as the disjunctions between prescientific and scientific traditions

[12] See, for example, the letter of John Dewey to Jane Addams in the Swarthmore College Library, Peace Collections (January, 1896). It was written in regard to her paper concerning the Pullman strike.

Jane Addams was motivated by goals that went far beyond the desire to establish settlement houses. The pressing need as she saw it was to reduce the degrading influences of harsh urban life by instituting a series of social changes in industrial practices, housing, recreation, education, etc., that would humanize industrial society. See, for example, Jane Addams, *The Spirit of Youth and the City Streets* (New York, The Macmillan Co., 1909) and *Democracy and Social Ethics* (New York, The Macmillan Co., 1902).

Jane Dewey attested to the influence of the social views of Miss Addams on her father when she said, "Dewey's faith in democracy as a guiding force in education took on both a sharper and a deeper meaning because of Hull House and Jane Addams." (See Schilpp, *The Philosophy of John Dewey*, pp. 29–30.)

[13] John Dewey, *Experience and Nature*, p. ii.

became more acute. He felt that a primary task of intellectuals was to help effect a new integration, consistent with the findings of science, but in a way that would enable man to live with a sense of purpose and commitment to the human adventure. In retrospect, in 1939, Dewey stated that this had been one of the persistent problems in his philosophical inquiry:

"The problem of restoring integration and cooperation between man's beliefs about the world in which he lives and his beliefs about values and purposes that should direct his conduct. . . . Philosophy's central problem is the relation that exists between the beliefs about the nature of things due to natural science to beliefs about values. . . . The other main problem . . . is the problem of the relation of physical science to the things of ordinary experience." [14]

Dewey insisted that philosophers and intellectuals have a special responsibility when civilization is in a time of revolutionary change. The duty of philosophy is to *comprehend* and *articulate* the critical elements in the emergence of civilized experience; and beyond that, to make imaginative projections for the future. It is to clarify factors in man's condition that help or hinder the possibility of his growth. It must refer its conclusions back into experience.

Dewey made dogged and imaginative efforts to work in this way in all aspects of his thought. It was in the stimulating atmosphere of the Chicago campus that his instrumentalism blossomed and took shape. Intellect was to be put to work. Foremost was the need to understand the nature of thought itself. Scientific investigation was giving new insights about the nature of thinking. Dewey's logic and psychology combined to explain the natural evolution of effective thought, the conditions that give rise to it, the possibilities for refining and extending its application, and the hindrances that block resort to it. His conception of reflective thinking was rooted in a biological model and the methods of scientific inquiry. The primary idea was William James's notion of living things falling out of adjustment with their world and

[14] Paul A. Schilpp, ed., *The Philosophy of John Dewey* (New York, The Tudor Publishing Co., 1951), see John Dewey, "The Philosopher Replies: Experience, Knowledge and Value: a Rejoinder," p. 523.

needing to restore equilibrium. In thinking, the counterpart was the encounter with troublesome, problematic situations that needed resolution before advances could be made.

In social philosophy, he argued that institutions had to be understood historically with reference to critical factors of adjustments that led to change. Their functioning had to be judged in terms of their results in enriching or demeaning lives caught up in them.

Moral and ethical theory was to be rescued from the uttering of soothing but ineffectual truisms. Emphasis, instead, was to be placed on the analysis of concrete conditions which was needed to realize moral goods.

Aesthetics was to be brought out of the museums and the private collections of a cultured elite. The aesthetic was envisaged as the consummatory quality of heightened experience that could be present in everyday living, in the expressive work of children, in the form of cities, or in sophisticated abstract thought as well as in canvases on the walls of marble buildings.

Finally there was education. Dewey's central conviction, that theory and abstract thought must interact with the world of nature and the problems of men, provided the key to understanding the attention he gave to education—a feature of his work that professional philosophers found difficult to take seriously. He once observed that for many years *Democracy and Education* was the one book in which his philosophy was most fully expounded—and then wryly remarked that his critics in philosophy refused to read it.[15] If philosophy was to provide the insights to help men find their way, then educating the young, in accord with needed attitudes and understanding, was as critical a social task as any. In Dewey's view, educational problems were to act as a testing ground in which philosophical ideas had to prove themselves.

The demands to think through the concrete consequences of his philosophy for educational practice worked as a factor in integrating his thought. In the 1930 essay in which Dewey reflected on aspects of his intellectual development, the first point he referred to was the importance that the practice and theory of education had for him. "This interest fused with and brought together what might otherwise have been separate interests—that in

[15] Adams and Montague, *op cit.*, pp. 22–23.

psychology and that in social institutions and social life." He came to believe, he said, that philosophizing about education was the supreme human interest in which "other problems, cosmological, moral, logical, come to a head." [16] He added that his special ←· interest was in the education of the young, "for I have never been able to feel much optimism regarding the possibilities of 'higher education' when it is built upon warped and weak foundations." [17]

He concluded with the comment that this appraisal of the pivotal role of education in his thought is a "handle offered to any subsequent critic who may wish to lay hold of it." [18] This invitation provides the occasion to turn to Dewey's work as educator at the University of Chicago.

[16] *Ibid.*
[17] *Ibid.*
[18] *Ibid.*

# CHAPTER THREE

# Dewey's Plan for Work in Education

The opening sentence of Dewey's first lecture in pedagogy in 1896 reads as follows:

"The philosophy of education has the problem of discovering what the value of education is in human experience, of discovering, that is to say, the place which it occupies in the larger whole of life." [1]

In his fourth lecture of that year, he added:

"Education consists either in the ability to use one's powers in a social direction, or else in ability to share in the experiences of others and thus widen the individual consciousness to that of the race." [2]

Dewey's plan for work in education received its character from a broad overarching directive: to conserve, transmit, and advance civilization in such a way as to make it a functioning part of individual, responsible selves. One can defend the idea that his concern with civilized experience, the nature of its evolution and its role in the fulfillment of individuals, provided the unifying theme that gave direction to his various proposals for education.

He stressed, time after time, the joint responsibility of intellectuals in philosophy, scholarship, and education. Civilization is

[1] John Dewey, *Lectures for the First Course in Pedagogy*, unpublished, No. 1 (1896), p. 1. Copy made available to me by Professor (emeritus) Frederick Eby, University of Texas.
[2] *Ibid.*, Lecture No. 4, p. 1.

a process of growth in human experience. Philosophy's task is to work out the conditions that lead to human fulfillment within the conditions emerging in the specific civilization in question. It should illuminate the course that experience has taken, and it should make imaginative projections for the future.[3] It needs intellectual co-partners. On the one hand, it must keep abreast of advances in knowledge coming from research in the natural and social sciences, and in literature and religion in order to keep in contact with man's real situation. On the other hand, work in psychology and education is required to assure that knowledge will function fruitfully in men's lives.

In *Democracy and Education*, Dewey affirmed that it was impossible for philosophy

"to have any success in these tasks without educational equivalents as to what to do and what not to do. . . . By the educative arts philosophy may generate methods of utilizing the energies of human beings in accord with serious and thoughtful conceptions of life. Education is the laboratory in which philosophic distinctions become concrete and are tested." [4]

Contrary to a popular stereotype that Dewey wanted to indulge children, it is clear that his goal was to create a reformed and vital liberal education, appropriate for a democratic society. He once said:

"The more one appreciates the intrinsic esthetic, immediate value of thought and science, the more one takes into account what intelligence adds to the joy and dignity of life, the more one should feel grieved at a situation in which the exercise and joy of reason are limited to a narrow, closed and technical social group and the more we should ask how it is possible to make all men participators in this inestimable wealth." [5]

The kind of person who should emerge from a truly liberalized education would be one prepared to learn throughout his

[3] See, for example, John Dewey, *Democracy and Education* (New York, The Macmillan Co., 1916), p. 378.

[4] *Ibid.*, p. 384.

[5] John Dewey, *Philosophy and Civilization* (New York, Minton, Balch and Co., 1931), p. 35.

life, capable of acting in his natural and social world effectively, and with a sense of obligation to human society—past, present, and future. His criticisms of educational practice grew from the conviction that the schools of his time were not seriously concerned with such goals.

Dewey pinpointed some of the shortcomings in a famous chapter on "Waste in Education" in *School and Society*.[6] He charged the schools with being wasteful in that they failed to make any significant difference in the lives of their students or their communities. The waste was due to the isolation of work done in school. There was the isolation of activities of the classroom from the out-of-school activities of the child; there was the bits-and-pieces approach of presenting object lessons or ill-coordinated, self-contained lesson plans under the illusion that the child's mind could be shaped by "scientific" insertions. There was the isolation of one set of studies from another and a lack of unified connections of lower, middle, and higher parts of the system. Dewey pictured the system as a patchwork in which the different levels represented borrowing from various centuries and traditions. For example, the universities were from the medieval scholastic tradition, the kindergarten from romantic, moralistic philosophies of the eighteenth century, and the primary school a response to practical needs to teach reading when printing was invented. Since coordination had never been effected, the whole system suffered from discontinuities.

In addition, school approaches were based on false prescientific psychologies of learning that led to rote and ineffective learning.

Related to these criticisms was the charge that the content of studies was not only irrelevant and disjointed but thin and out of touch with the wellsprings of scholarship.

"There is much of utter triviality of subject matter in elementary and secondary education. When we investigate it, we find that it is full of facts taught that are not facts, which have to be unlearned later on. Now, this happens because the 'lower' parts of our system are not in vital connection with the 'higher.'

---

[6] John Dewey, *The School and Society*, revised ed. (Chicago, University of Chicago Press, 1923), Ch. 3.

The university or college, in its ideal, is a place of research, where investigation is going on; a place of libraries and museums, where the best resources of the past are gathered, maintained, and organized. It is, however, as true in the school as in the university that the spirit of inquiry can be got only through and with the attitude of inquiry. The pupil must learn what has meaning, what enlarges his horizon instead of mere trivialities. He must become acquainted with truths, instead of things that were regarded as such fifty years ago or that are taken as interesting by the misunderstanding of a partially educated teacher. It is difficult to see how these ends can be reached except as the most advanced part of the educational system is in complete interaction with the most rudimentary." [7]

The result, from Dewey's point of view, was a pitiable waste of human life. He was angry about it. His bill of particulars helps to explain the specific features of the program he did advocate. He treated his denunciation of the *status quo* as a personal challenge to create an alternative.

In the years since, sharp criticisms have been directed against the "new education" launched by reformers like Dewey and Colonel Parker. The fact that a great number of their proposals have been absorbed and are now taken for granted has sometimes been overlooked. It is difficult to measure the revolution the reformers wrought in thought and practice without reference to the school situation they fought to change. Where education is concerned, the habit has been to describe schools in white or black, according to one's preferences. The reformers shared this tendency. Their pictures of traditional schools undoubtedly were overdrawn and they ignored the fine teaching that did exist. On the other hand, those who yearn nostalgically for the educational virtues of the good old days when grandfather went to school are deluding themselves.

There is a report of American education in the 1890's by Joseph Mayer Rice, *The Public-School System of the United States*,[8] which helps explain the zeal and dedication of the reform-

[7] *Ibid.*, pp. 70–71.
[8] Joseph Mayer Rice, *The Public-School System of the United States* (New York, The Century Co., 1893).

ers. Dr. Rice was a physician with an interest in pediatrics, which led him to study European schools, particularly those in Germany. What he discovered about teachers, normal school preparation, and the quality of educational theory and research in the universities awoke him to the backwardness of American education. Walter Hines Page, editor of the lively, controversial journal *Forum*, invited Rice to write a series of articles on American schools, based on extended observations. Rice had a scientific temper and training and spent over five months observing twelve hundred classrooms in major schools in the East and Midwest. He supplemented these by attending teachers' meetings and sessions of boards of education. Rice concentrated on city systems, and he tried to see at least twenty-five to thirty-five teachers in each in order to obtain a fair sampling. His reports were first issued in a series of articles in *Forum* and then published as a book in 1893. One does not have to accept his findings as the definitive statement of the condition of American schools, but the care and energy devoted to the preparation of these reports by a well-trained mind gives one confidence that there is truth in them. It was not a pretty picture.

He expressed shock at the poor preparation of teachers, many of whom lacked even normal-school training. Often they were intimidated by high-handed methods of school officials who had received their positions as political handouts. The low quality of educational thinking represented in school boards depressed him. Compared to Germany, there was a relative lack of effort to build educational theory on the basis of research and relevant findings from sciences related to education. He found instances of good practice, but all too often classrooms were conducted in the manner he described as typical in New York City.

In New York he chose to visit schools and teachers that had been rated high by their supervisors. Typical preparation consisted of arranging long lists of questions with fixed answers. The goal was to set forth in concise form most of the facts prescribed in the course of study. The assumption was that children knew nothing as they came to class and had to be taught specifics by the teacher.

"The instruction throughout the school consists principally in grinding these answers *verbatim* into the minds of the children.

To reach the desired end, the school has been converted into the most dehumanizing institution that I have ever laid eyes upon, each child being treated as if he possessed a memory and the faculty of speech, but no individuality, no sensibilities, no soul." [9]

The chief maxim was "Save the minutes." The method was to see how the greatest number of answers could be given in the smallest number of minutes. Techniques to expedite the goal were developed. A student was taught to pop up and say quickly and loudly, "A note is a sign representing to the eye the length or duration of time." As he was sitting down, the next child arose for a similar performance. Variations on the theme were developed to coincide with "modern methods" of sense training. Children, for example, were given little flags with geometrical forms in different colors on them. This led to: "A square; a square has four sides and four corners; green." (Down). "A triangle; a triangle has three sides and three points; red" (Down), etc.[10]

In such schools, even the teachers who had received preparation that gave them some insight into the needs and behavior of children were reduced to the level of assembly-line tenders.

Rice included in his itinerary visits to Chicago schools. He was observing them shortly before Dewey's arrival to the city. He found a few excellent schools which, he said, were exceptions, but in the main, he found Chicago schools not in advance of those in New York and Philadelphia. "Indeed the schools of that city may be justly regarded as the least progressive of the three." [11]

With conditions like these and with the kinds of values and philosophical interests Dewey had developed by 1894, it is not surprising that he welcomed President Harper's invitation to become Chairman of the combined Departments of Philosophy, Psychology, and Pedagogy. It gave him an unparalleled opportunity to put his ideas into action. A major opportunity to make education a subject of detailed study was now being provided.

Dewey needed to create a program adequate for the size of the problem as he defined it. It included:

1. A plan to create education into a disciplined area of inquiry. The university, through this new discipline, working in

[9] *Ibid.*, p. 31.
[10] *Ibid.*, p. 38.
[11] *Ibid.*, p. 166.

continuing cooperation with other academic departments, was to provide leadership, through research and development, for the whole system of American schools from the kindergarten through higher education.

2. A decision to found a laboratory school where research would be conducted and where a liberal education would be developed that would function in character and behavior. Eventually it was to embrace all levels and was to be characterized by unity and coherence in curriculum and methodology.

3. A conceptual frame of reference, derived from the intellectual work of Dewey and his collaborators, to give direction to the total effort.

The three parts of the plan were organically related. They provide the frame of reference for understanding Dewey's ideas about education.

# CHAPTER FOUR

# Education and
# the University Disciplines

In the last decades of the nineteenth century, the emergence of a complex industrial society and a mushrooming public school system created a demand for more highly trained teachers. Large numbers were needed in a hurry. One response was the rapid expansion of normal schools and teacher training programs. This was accompanied by a quickened interest in the theory and practice of education. Dewey's personal experiences and his mode of philosophizing had led him to be deeply concerned with problems in education.

President Harper of Chicago shared with Dewey an interest in coming to terms with the problems that related the lower schools with higher education.[1] Dewey's proposals for a fresh approach won ready support from Harper.

The general thrust of Dewey's proposal was that the institution of education and the process of learning should become major areas of inquiry within the university; that the scholarly research facilities of the campus should be brought to bear on the problems of education.

In the present chapter we propose to examine: (1) Dewey's case for including education as a university discipline, and (2) his proposals and efforts to use an interdisciplinary approach in the study of education.

---

[1] See William R. Harper, "Ideals of Educational Work," *Journal of the Proceedings and Addresses of the National Education Association* (1895), pp. 987–998. Professor Frederick Eby, who was a graduate student in education and a member of the staff of the Laboratory School for a time, emphasized this point in an interview with the author.

EDUCATION AS A SUBJECT OF UNIVERSITY INQUIRY

In four articles Dewey set forth his ideas on the proposition that education should be a matter of university inquiry. He explained the reasons for such a proposal and recommended an outline for the work. The first two articles are closely related in title and content: a two-part article, "Pedagogy as a University Discipline," [2] appeared in 1896, the year in which the Laboratory School was founded; "Education as a University Study," [3] was published in 1907, just three years after Dewey had left Chicago and had had a chance to reflect on his experience. The latter essay amplifies some ideas touched on earlier.

He argued for a division of labor in the science and art of education. There was a need, he said, for one set of schools to prepare the great army of teachers for the insatiable demands of the expanding public schools. These training schools were to put to use tested knowledge and practice. Programs parallel to these were to be directed toward the leaders of American education—teachers of the normal schools, professors of pedagogy, school administrators, and educational innovators. Such offerings should be made available at the graduate level. Dewey, it turned out, was describing his own plan for the Department of Pedagogy at Chicago.

The need stemmed from the near absence of opportunities for graduate study of education in American universities. Dewey described the kind of students who would be attracted as those who had completed college study of high quality and who had served apprenticeships in the schools. They probably would be repelled by the routine content of the normal schools; if they wanted to pursue investigation of further problems in education, their only recourse seemed to be to enroll in German universities.

It is likely, Dewey said, that such leaders would be discontented with the shortcomings of the *status quo*. They would be seeking new ideas, new perspectives. But, at the same time, they

[2] John Dewey, "Pedagogy as a University Discipline," *University Record*, Vol. 1, Nos. 25, 26 (September, 1896), pp. 353-355, 361-363.
[3] John Dewey, "Education as a University Study," *Columbia University Quarterly*, Vol. 9, No. 3 (June, 1907), pp. 284-290.

needed an opportunity to study education under the disciplines of research and experimentation, which only the universities could provide.

Dewey pursued the point with additional reasons:

1. The traditions of localism militated against centralized planning and supervision of American education, yet there was an undeniable need for direction. In the absence of a National Ministry of Education, the universities were natural and proper centers for producing leadership and organization. They could substitute the authority of science and philosophy for that of bureaucracy.

"It is for them to gather and focus the best that emerges in practices of the present; it is for them to experiment in the development of more adequate conceptions of subject matter, and to issue the results to the schools with the *imprimatur* not of officialdom but of intelligence." [4]

2. Rapid intellectual advances in the closing decades of the nineteenth century posed another problem for the schools. Dewey described this trend as having a disintegrating effect on the curriculum at all levels:

"The pressure began in the college and high school. It is now finding its way into the primary grades, partly from the continued pressure from above for such training below as will relieve the difficulties of the situation above. It is as nearly certain as any education expectation may be that if the increased demands as regards number of languages, range of literary study, of history and of physical and biological sciences are to be met, even halfway, in the college and high school, the response must proceed from changing the methods in the lower grades, and by beginning work along those lines in the primary school—yes, and in the kindergarten. It is not a mere question of local expedience, whether it is advisable here and there to modify the traditional 'three R's' curriculum. It is a question of the right organization and balance of our entire educational system and in its adjustment to the existing social environment." [5]

[4] *Ibid.*, p. 290.
[5] Dewey, "Pedagogy as a University Discipline," *University Record*, p. 354.

The pressures to introduce new content at each level were heavy and varied. The danger was that the schools would lurch along, responding to one interest group after another, grasping at fads to ward off criticisms. Chaos and waste could result. An agency was needed to bring order into meeting the problems deriving from what later was referred to as "the knowledge explosion." Dewey held that the universities should serve in this task:

"This reconstruction may go on in a haphazard way . . . now trying this scheme, now abandoning it for that, without consciousness of the ends to be reached . . . and with all the waste of time, money and human life involved in such change. Or it may go on with some clear, if flexible, consciousness of the nature of the problem, of the ends to be met, and with some adaptation of means to these ends. The latter conditions ought to be most clearly met at a university where psychology and sociology are most systematically pursued: where scientific inquiry is at its height and where methods of work are most fully developed. In addition it is at the university where there is the accumulation of the quantity and quality of knowledge which is trying to break through into the secondary and primary school systems. That is to say, the experiment of the introduction of science matter as well as method. It is reasonable to suppose that it can most fruitfully and efficiently be attempted where this subject matter is most adequately and accurately represented. . . . Where specialists abound, where the laboratory and the library are thoroughly equipped, is, if anywhere, the place where such requirements are met." [6]

Having affirmed that problems of both method and content deserved the attention of university scholars, Dewey then sketched the outlines of a program for the study of education. In the 1907 article, while Professor of Philosophy at Columbia, he attacked those "Bourbons of Culture" who dismissed education as a subject of university study. Their tiresome habit, he argued, was to equate educational theory with the peddling of trivial techniques and spurious panaceas. Others, more fair-minded, seldom gave thought to the significance of the scope of education as a field of inquiry. Dewey saw the matter differently:

[6] *Ibid.*, pp. 354–355.

"It may be asserted, without danger of successful challenge, that no subject touches life on so many sides and brings with itself such a wealth of materials combined with such stimulating outlook upon the past and present humanity." [7]

He found it paradoxical that education should be made a subject of near reverence in American life, while political scientists and sociologists neglected the study of it. In bringing education into the framework of the university, he saw two major areas of inquiry deserving attention—the administrative, and the scholastic.

In the "administrative" area Dewey included the range of questions about the school as a social and political institution. In order to create an awareness of the intricate relation of education to other institutions and to social ideals, he suggested comparative studies of other cultures. This should include a historical dimension that would encompass the school systems of the ancient Egyptians, Hebrews, Greeks, and Romans, as well as more contemporary systems. Another facet would bring the economics of education and school politics within the range of scholarly research. American education was plagued, he argued, with serious financial problems. In a time of school expansion there was an inadequate school plant, teachers demanded better salaries, students were on part-time schedules, and there was a need for a more rational way of classifying teachers for rates of pay. Dewey also found it very difficult to understand why the universities would offer such systematic study to help their students think intelligently about other social and political questions but would leave them in ignorance where the institution of education was concerned. There were other urgent administrative problems, such as the relations of local, state, and federal agencies; the need of a rationale for consolidation of schools; and the definition of the functions and proper relations of boards of education and school administrators. "Unless such matters somewhere are made the objects of systematic study, they will continue to be settled in the future as in the past, by clamor, rule of thumb and the interests of ward politicians." [8]

Dewey also included hygienic and aesthetic questions in the

[7] Dewey, "Education as a University Study," p. 285.
[8] *Ibid.*

"administrative" area. American schools were drab factory-like structures, spruced up with castle-like turrets, and busts of Julius Caesar. Could not more viable designs, appropriate for educational purposes, be created? The matter of how to provide good light, heat, ventilation, sanitary facilities, educational equipment, and play space also deserved careful thought. Architects would be required for technical details, but answers should not be formulated in isolation from ideas of well-conceived educational theory.

Dewey maintained that the scholarly or academic side of education also needed to be developed. Just as education as a social institution can be understood only in the context of related institutions, so, too, educational thought must be understood in relation to the general history of ideas—to ideas in philosophy and religion, among others:

"No reason can be given for neglecting this that would not apply with equal, or greater force to the history of science or philosophy. The theoretical study involves the generalization of this historic material, the various systems of pedagogy which have emerged, together with a thorough discussion of psychology and sociology in their bearings upon the selection, arrangement and sequence of the studies of the curriculum and the methods required to give them their full efficiency." [9]

He thought, too, that it would be only a matter of time until a set of topics concerned with the sociology of the child, now scattered in areas such an penology, law, economics, and medicine, would be brought together under the head of education, or "some other rubric." As he put it, "each society has continually to maintain its life by renewing it through the immature." [10] Specific concerns become vital to society, such as child education, compulsory education, reform schools, the training of children with various handicaps, after-school programs, and evening schools. There was no valid reason why the university should fail to make these matters subjects of research and inquiry.

3. Dewey described a third set of questions that needed to be investigated. These included problems of how to teach children

[9] Dewey, "Pedagogy as a University Discipline," p. 362.
[10] Dewey, "Education as a University Study," p. 286.

effectively and how to understand and direct behavior in the classroom. He argued against the concept of methods as tricks of the trade. Method and subject matter could not validly be divorced from each other. Method had to be approached in terms of examining how the abstractions of a given subject matter could be "put into its concrete connections with the rest of the world of knowledge and culture and with the life of man in society."[11] Then, projecting an idea he had put to work in his own Laboratory School, Dewey said, "There is opportunity and demand here for the most progressive psychology in determining the relation of studies to the mind in its various stages of development."[12]

In the 1907 article, he stated that psychology was in its scientific infancy, but that the problems involved in the teaching of the whole range of subjects—reading, writing, arithmetic, foreign languages, or manual training—were either proper topics for systematic investigation or dependent on uninformed habits.

Finally, he maintained that philosophy itself could be revitalized by being forced to re-examine some of its time-honored questions in terms of practical issues in education; that theories of knowledge could attain significance when examined in terms of the relation between intellectual training and the control of conduct, or when the educational problem of the relation of science to the arts was considered. The long debate over mind and matter could be given renewed impetus when the respective claims on the school by liberal culture and by the demands of serviceable skills were made subjects of scrutiny.

Dewey reminded his readers that a university discipline comes into being, in part, when the study of a sector of the world by systematic investigation and research is undertaken. Thus, psychology broke away from philosophy; political science became the study of political institutions when it was separated from history and philosophy. He maintained that education deserved as much attention as economics, politics, or religion, especially as education occupied a new level of significance in an era of science and technology. The way to introduce a serious intent into

[11] Dewey, "Pedagogy as a University Discipline," p. 362.
[12] Ibid.

the study of problems in education was to employ the techniques and findings of allied disciplines. He said of educational administration, for example:

"It is not a matter of crude speculation nor of doling out arbitrary empiric devices, but of getting together a definite sphere of historical, sociological, and economic facts, and of combining these facts with others drawn from physiology, hygiene, and medicine, etc., and of effecting a working synthesis of this great range of scientific data." [13]

Interdisciplinary cooperation was an important part of his plan for the work at Chicago.

A further important step was required in order to bring education within the framework of university graduate study. Those whose work is in a university discipline do more than gather information about the attainments of the past and systematize it. They are expected, also, to evaluate these accomplishments with reference to contemporary needs, and to make contributions to knowledge. Researchers need a setting that contains problems into which they can inquire. Dewey drew the conclusion that investigators of pedagogical questions needed a laboratory school "which shall test and exhibit in actual working order the results of the theoretical work." [14] For this reason he founded the Laboratory School at Chicago. We shall study the work pursued there in the following chapters. First we wish to examine in more detail how he tried to implement his recommendation for interdepartmental collaboration in the study of education.

INTERDISCIPLINARY COLLABORATION

We cannot discuss the interdisciplinary features without first considering the setting for Dewey's work in Chicago.

The University of Chicago campus in the 1890's was an exciting place. Backed by money and land gifts from Rockefeller and Marshall Field, the university opened in 1892 with a burst of energy and activity. Its President, William Rainey Harper, was one of the most dynamic and creative university presidents this

[13] *Ibid.*
[14] *Ibid.*, pp. 354–355.

country has produced. He had determined at the beginning that the university was to be a leader in graduate studies. That kind of goal required great scholars, and with Rockefeller money as an instrument Harper assembled a collection of world-famous research professors in remarkably short order. He had no compunction about raiding other campuses to secure them.[15]

Clark University, headed by G. Stanley Hall, was one of the first to feel the effects of Harper's search for talent. From Clark came men who provided the nucleus of leadership in the natural sciences for the University of Chicago; for example, Albert Michelson in Physics, who, in turn, later secured Robert A. Millikan. Michelson devised the experiments that measured the speed of light and proved that the "ether" did not exist; Millikan became a Nobel Prize winner in Physics. Henry Donaldson, Chairman of the Department of Neurology, was the author of *The Growth of the Brain* and *Physiology of the Nervous System*. He supervised the doctoral dissertation of John Watson, the founder of behaviorism in psychology; Charles Otis Whitney became Chairman of Zoology but continued his great work as Director of the Marine Biological Laboratory at Woods Hole, Massachusetts, after coming to Chicago; and John U. Nef headed the Department of Chemistry. These men from Clark were joined by others: the German physiologist, Jacques Loeb, an authentic genius in research, who identified the machine-like reactions of plants and animals, which he called "tropisms," and who opened the field of artificial parthenogenesis by causing the unfertilized egg of a sea urchin to begin development; John Coulter, Chairman of Botany, a co-founder with Loeb of the principal scholarly journals in physiology and botany, and supporter of the research of Henry C. Cowles, who was developing the new field of ecology. Thomas C. Chamberlin resigned as President of the University of Wisconsin to chair the Department of Geology. He founded the *Journal of Geology*, and framed a theory of the origin of the solar system.

Ferdinand Schevill in History and Paul Shorey in Greek illustrate the kind of quality Harper obtained in the humanities. Harper himself was a Professor of Hebrew and Semitic Studies.

[15] Ray Ginger, *Altgeld's America* (New York, Funk and Wagnalls Co., 1958), pp. 307–313, *et passim*.

The standards were equally high in the social sciences, where University of Chicago scholars were to open fresh trails. In political economy, J. Laurence Laughlin was obtained from Cornell, and he brought with him his student and protégé, Thorstein Veblen. Albion W. Small resigned from the presidency of Colby College to found the Department of Sociology—the first such department in an American university. Like so many of his other colleagues, he founded a journal, the *American Journal of Sociology*, which he edited for thirty-one years. He was known for his rejection of a "value-free" sociology and for his insistence that all investigations must relate to the improvement of society and the enhancement of human life. He also bolstered his department with scholars who became luminaries in the field: W. I. Thomas and George Vincent, and Frederick Starr, who conducted pioneer field studies in anthropology.

The Chicago campus had the quality of an intellectual frontier. This was one of the attractions that drew Dewey to the city.[16] Another was his friendship with Jane Addams. Dewey had lectured at Hull House while at Michigan, and through Miss Addams had made acquaintance with social reform groups in the city. These contacts fitted the plans he was to develop. He met, for example, wealthy reformers like William Kent, George Crane, and George E. Cole. Kent was a member of the famous Committee of Nine of the Civic Federation, which Lincoln Steffens in *The Shame of the Cities* characterized as a model reform organization. Under the prodding of Jane Addams, he established the first children's playground in Chicago. Cole was a courageous executive of the Municipal Voters League. Crane donated a nursery to Hull House, helped start Robert La Follette's magazine, and later was vice chairman of Woodrow Wilson's finance committee. The Dewey School was dependent mainly on private financing; the Kent and Crane families sent their children to the school, and became its financial mainstays. Men like these did battle against municipal corruption and urged improvement. They were also active in the struggle over public education. At the

[16] The section that follows is based largely on the careful scholarship in Robert L. McCaul's "Dewey's Chicago," *The School Review*, Vol. 67, No. 2 (Summer, 1959), pp. 258–280, *et passim*.

center of the storm was Colonel Francis W. Parker, head of the Cook County Normal School and the staunch supporter of the "new education," who fought annual skirmishes with the Board of Commissioners. The running debate over issues in education provided an alert audience to which Dewey could present his own ideas. One problem with which Dewey did not have to contend was an atmosphere of apathy or indifference. Chicago was an arena where a series of battles was under way which he was ready to join.

The young Dewey joined forces with the old warrior Colonel Parker on a number of specific issues, and they often worked from the same podium. A newspaper account of one of their meetings describes the contrast of their platform styles and also the personality of Dewey.

"It was my privilege recently to be present at the last one of a series of lectures on psychology by Dr. Dewey. . . . His course of lectures was delivered at the Cook County Normal School. If one had been deaf, the interest in watching the 'personnel' of the two famous men, Dr. Dewey and Col. Parker, the psychologist whose fame is not confined to his own country, would have been enough to repay one for coming. Dr. Dewey is one of the quietest and most modest appearing men imaginable. He appears like a gentle young man who is studious and willing to learn. To see him on the platform in his gray sack coat, drooping moustache, hair parted in the middle and his 'excuse me for intruding' air, as opposed to Col. Parker, with his massive bald head, his impressive and aggressive personality and his 'you had better not get in my way' air one would never dream that the quiet man with his level eyebrows and pleasant gentle voice was the lion, and the great Colonel Parker was the lamb.

"Such, however, is the case. Col. Parker sits at one side of the platform, listening, often with closed eyes, as is his wont, to the agreeable voice of Dr. Dewey, as he quietly utters those radical ideas which simply remove the bottom from all existing forms of educational effort, excepting those scattered instances, here and there, or those who are applying the right methods, or those who, natural teachers, apply them unconsciously. Col. Parker, in his aggressively earnest way, has been lustily pounding for years, on the same thing. Dr. Dewey does not pound. He quietly loosens the hoops, and the bottom insensibly vanishes.

"Dr. Dewey is worshipped by his hearers. There is a charm about his personality which is simply irresistible. He is as simple in his language as in his manner, and the ease with which even the great unwashed can comprehend the principles he lays down, is proof of his grandeur.

"At the close of the lecture—which in itself is artistic, for instead of sending off a literary skyrocket at the end, he simply turns away from the board and melts into the nearest chair—one of the bright girls of the training-class stepped up and handed him a beautiful bouquet of pink and white carnations. . . .

"He rose, and true to his nature, uttered just the right thing, in about six words, thanking his listeners for the stimulus they had furnished him, which was all a man could desire.

"Col. Parker then arose, and in an unnaturally tame voice, which indicated to those who know him best a mighty surging torrent of emotion within, said: 'Ladies and gentlemen, if what Dr. Dewey has been telling you is true, the millions upon millions which are expended upon our public school system is not only spent in the wrong way, but we are dulling bright intellects and doing incalculable harm to the future generations . . .' " [17]

There was another factor that made Chicago the right place for Dewey to work. President Harper and the University of Chicago faculty were unusually responsive to Dewey's interest in education.

Even before Dewey arrived, Harper had begun to advance a personal goal of trying to relate the university to the lower schools in order to effect a better articulation between primary, secondary, and collegiate training. One of his administrative inventions was the division of affiliated high schools and academies. Through this division he hoped to raise standards by sending

[17] George Dykhuizen, "John Dewey: The Chicago Years," *Journal of the History of Philosophy*, Vol. 2, No. 2 (October, 1964), pp. 246–247, quoting from Ellen Eames DeGraff, "Chicago Happenings. Of Interest to Evansvillians—Something about Psychology." This is a newspaper account appearing in a Chicago or Evansville paper sometime in late 1894. The clipping is to be found in Colonel Parker's Scrapbook, University Archives.

University of Chicago examiners into the public and private secondary schools, and by planning regular campus conferences for the school faculties. This coincided with one of Dewey's ambitions. The two of them joined in planning many meetings that brought together university scholars and personnel from the schools. Some examples of the nature of such occasions were: lectures by Colonel Parker on the art of teaching; a campus meeting of the Illinois Society for Child Study; a joint meeting of the Mathematical and Philosophical Clubs on the teaching of arithmetic; separate conferences for Latin teachers, for teachers of chemistry, and for manual training instructors; a conference on nature study in elementary education, and still another for teachers of high schools or academies cooperating with the university. Some of these were attended by five, six, or seven hundred persons. Harper, Dewey, and other members of the faculty became directly involved in educational questions through arranging these programs and preparing speeches. There was a lively give and take in discussions between teachers and university professors. The department also had a Pedagogical Club devoted to the reading and discussion of original papers by faculty and graduate students, to book reviews, and to reports on current happenings in education.[18]

Harper himself had a continuing concern with problems of public education. In the midst of his tremendous task of building the university, he served a term on the Chicago Board of Education. As a university president, he was anxious to prepare superior teachers and develop pedagogy into a discipline that would occupy a place of distinction on the campus. To a university trustee who intimated that it was below the university's dignity to sponsor *The School Review*, Harper replied bluntly, "As a university we are interested above all else in pedagogy." In the year that Dewey launched the experimental elementary school, Harper stated, "It is our desire to do for the Department of Pedagogy

[18] Dykhuizen, *op. cit.*, pp. 241–242. That efforts like these to advance the cause of education were appreciated by people in the field is evidenced by a resolution adopted by summer school students in 1897. It praised the university for seeking to make the Pedagogical Department "one of the essential features of a great university" and particularly commended Dewey for the quality of his lectures in Educational Psychology.

what has not been undertaken in any other institution." In his *Report* for 1898–1899 he expressed esteem for Dewey and the conviction that the work of the Dewey School was "in the truest and highest sense University work . . . no work can commend itself more heartily to the attention of the investigator than the study of the growth and development of the mind of the child and the adaptation of educational theories to such growth." [19] Although Harper and Dewey sometimes had differences over budget items, Harper made personal efforts to help the Laboratory School in several periods of financial crisis. Generally, they agreed on how to go to work on problems in education. It was only in the later years of Dewey's stay that bad feeling developed between the two which eventually led to Dewey's resignation.

When Dewey assumed the chairmanship of the combined Departments of Philosophy, Psychology, and Pedagogy, he followed Harper's lead in assembling an able faculty. James Tufts, a member of the faculty when he arrived, eventually collaborated with Dewey in elaborating the ethical theory of instrumentalism. Tufts also collaborated in a course for the parents of the elementary school. James Angell was a co-partner with George H. Mead and Dewey in developing functional psychology. By his work in his experimental laboratory he made important contributions to the effort to give a scientific base to psychology. Dewey fought on a number of occasions to get Angell the financial help needed to support his research.[20] Some of the stalwarts in education were Julia E. Bulkley, Charles H. Thurber, Ella Flagg Young,[21] Frederick W. Smedley, Wilbur Jackman, and the

[19] McCaul, *loc. cit.*

[20] See John Dewey's letter to Harper, The President's Papers, University of Chicago (May 13, 1897; December 21, 1899; February 3, 1900).

[21] Ella Flagg Young became Dewey's supervisor of instruction in the Laboratory School. Dewey relied heavily on her and his wife, who became principal, for advice on the practical operation. Jane Dewey wrote that her father regarded Ella Young as "the wisest person in school matters with whom he has come in contact in any way." (Schilpp, *op. cit.*, p. 21.) Dewey once said, "I would come to her with these abstract ideas of mine and she would tell me what they meant." (Max Eastman, *Heroes I Have Known*, p. 300) Ella Young had served as District Superintendent in the Chicago schools prior to joining Dewey's staff.

Herbartian leaders Charles De Garmo and Frank and Charles McMurry as visiting lecturers.

Within Dewey's department, George Herbert Mead undoubtedly had the most influence on Dewey's thought. Dewey brought Mead from Michigan. For many years, the Meads and Deweys lived in the same building in Chicago. Dewey said his friendship with Mead was one of the most valued in his life. In a later tribute,[22] Dewey called Mead the chief force in the United States in turning psychology from introspection to an alignment with biological and social data and concepts. While describing him as a scholar with a remarkable range of competence in literature and the sciences, Dewey said Mead's professional thought was unified by a central problem: the relation of the individual mind and consciousness to the world and society. Mead's ideas on the social origin and nature of mind and self caused a revolution in Dewey's thought. Dewey said it was only over a period of time that he began to see the full implications of Mead's thesis that "the individual mind, the conscious self was . . . the world of nature first taken up into social relations, and then dissolved to form a new self which then went forth to re-create the world of nature and social institutions." [23] Mead provided a depth to the concept of mind and thinking that was at the heart of Dewey's philosophical and educational writings. In more specific terms, Mead's study of the psychology of the act in its biological origins, and his analysis of the educational components in the play and role-playing of children, influenced the approaches to early childhood education in Dewey's School.[24] Scholars of this mettle could hold their own even on Harper's star-studded campus.

Students in pedagogy were required to take introductory courses in psychology, logic, and ethics given by Mead, Angell, and Addison A. Moore. Dewey himself gave a number of courses in education over the years, including Educational Psychology,

[22] John Dewey, "George Herbert Mead as I Knew Him," *University Record*, Vol. 27, No. 3 (July, 1931), pp. 173–177, or, John Dewey, "George Herbert Mead," *Journal of Philosophy*, Vol. 28 (June, 1931), pp. 309–314.
[23] *Ibid.*, p. 176.
[24] George Herbert Mead, "The Relation of Play to Education," *University Record*, Vol. 1, No. 8 (May, 1896), pp. 141–145, and "The Child and His Environment," *Transactions of the Illinois Society for Child Study*, Vol. 3, No. 1 (April, 1898), pp. 1–11.

Philosophy of Education, Educational Methodology, Evolution of Educational Theory, Elementary Education, Logical Methods in Relation to Education, and the Evolution of the Curriculum in the Fifteenth to Seventeenth Centuries.[25]

Finally, Dewey was warmly supported in his work in education by many members of the general faculty. Many of the professors had been, earlier in their careers, teachers or administrators in schools. Of the thirty-seven full professors in the arts, literature, and science departments, sixteen had had previous experience at subcollegiate levels. Two of the sixteen had taught in normal schools, and one had been a lecturer in pedagogy at a state university.[26] Consequently, many of them had an interest in pedagogical problems and could see the implications of their field of scholarship for school curriculum and methods. Many were willing to address conferences on campus or to make speeches to groups like the National Education Association and other teacher organizations.

Dewey adopted a style of work that involved him in lively interaction with many of his colleagues on campus. He later said that his personal contacts in this period had more influence on his thinking than reading books had, and that contacts formed through the Laboratory School were among the most important.[27]

He often could be seen in lively, informal discussion with one or more colleagues from his own or other departments.[28] Many of the leading scholars and departmental chairmen were genuinely interested in educational problems of the lower school. One could see evidence of their influence and participation in many of the features of the Laboratory School.[29]

John M. Coulter, Chairman of the Department of Biology, planned and guided the experiments in the Laboratory School on

[25] Dykhuizen, *op. cit.*, p. 240. For a complete listing of courses taught by Dewey see the *Register* of the University of Chicago, 1894–1905.

[26] McCaul, *op. cit.*, p. 264.

[27] Paul A. Schilpp, *The Philosophy of John Dewey* (New York, The Tudor Publishing Co., 1951), p. 28.

[28] Reported in conversations with Dr. (Mrs.) W. W. Charters and Dr. Frederick Eby, who were graduate students in the department at the time.

[29] Katherine C. Mayhew and Anna C. Edwards, *The Dewey School* (New York, Appleton-Century-Crofts, 1936), pp. 4 and 10.

plant relations; he wrote a series of important articles on the teaching of science at the various levels of education.[30] Thomas C. Chamberlin, Chairman of Geology, made available to teachers and children ideas from his studies, and directed the construction of a geological mock-up table. Dr. (Mrs.) W. W. Charters, who was doing doctoral work under Angell at the time, recalls seeing Dewey in animated conversations with Frederick Starr, the anthropologist. Her recollection is that Starr stimulated Dewey to see the significance of the evolution of social life, and that the units on the primitive stages of development in the Dewey School and the approach to the study of Greek civilization were influenced, in part, by Starr's ideas.[31]

Scholars from other departments who are mentioned in the school records as helpful collaborators were Albert A. Michelson in physics, Jacques Loeb in physiology, Charles A. Whitman in zoology, Rollin Salisbury in geography, and George Vincent in sociology.[32]

Further evidence of interdepartmental cooperation is furnished by the cross-listing of courses in other departments in the *Register* of the University of Chicago in these years. Some examples from the bulletins for 1896 and 1897 illustrate the point: Under sociology–anthropology, W. I. Thomas is listed for "The Child in Folk Psychology," "Sex in Folk Psychology," and "Primitive Art"; Albion W. Small [33] for "Outlines of Constructive Social Philosophy" and "Philosophy of Society." Professor Goodspeed's course on the "History of Greece" is listed with others on Greek language and literature; also a variety of courses in zoology, physiology, and neurology, including one on "Theories and Facts of Heredity and Evolution." Included in the 1902 *Register* as Advisory Members of the School of Education are

[30] Series of articles by John Coulter, "Some Problems in Education," *University Record*, 1. "The Act of Teaching" (May 21, 1897), pp. 65–67; 2. "Science in Secondary Schools" (May 28, 1897), pp. 77–80; 3. "Over Production of Teachers" (June 11, 1897), pp. 90–91; 4. "The School and the University" (June 4, 1897), pp. 97–99.

[31] Interview with Dr. (Mrs.) W. W. Charters.

[32] Mayhew and Edwards, *op. cit.*, p. 10.

[33] See also Albion Small, "Some Demands of Sociology upon Pedagogy," *American Journal of Sociology*, Vol. 2, No. 6 (May, 1897), pp. 839–851.

Coulter, Chamberlin, Vincent, Salisbury, William Garner Hale, Head of the Department of Latin, and William D. MacClintock, Professor of English.

As educationists and their academic colleagues are once again establishing some rapport, they may recall, with profit, the tradition in Chicago at the beginning of the century.

# CHAPTER FIVE

# An Image of the Teacher
# and the Dynamics of the Classroom

Having examined the nature of Dewey's rationale for educational work, we may appropriately turn our attention to the school, to see what happened to his philosophy when it was put to work. We offer first, however, a transition chapter.

The goal of the School of Education was to provide teachers with a fresh vision of the work of their profession, and to equip them with the insights and skills to realize ideals in practice. What image of the teacher did Dewey propose for the reform of the teaching profession in America?

First, we shall examine Dewey's portrayal of the teacher as a scholar and as a student of the psychology of the learning process; next, we shall consider his analysis of the dynamics of the classroom; and finally, we shall review his plan for implementing his ideas at the University of Chicago.

## THE TEACHER AS SCHOLAR AND STUDENT OF
## THE LEARNING PROCESS

A paper that Dewey published in 1904, "The Relation of Theory to Practice," [1] which purports to deal with the narrow subject of practice teaching, in fact contains the essence of his

---

[1] John Dewey, "The Relation of Theory to Practice in Education," *Third Yearbook* of the National Society for the Scientific Study of Education, Part I (Chicago, University of Chicago Press, 1904), now available in reprint form as Bulletin No. 17 in a series published by the Association for Student Teaching, State College of Iowa, Cedar Falls, Iowa (quotations are from this second edition).

vision for transforming "school-keeping" into the profession of teaching.

His basic concern both in his approach to education and in his general philosophy was how to relate idea and action toward the end of enriching experience. On this occasion he raised the question again in confronting the problem of how best to prepare teachers. The task of teacher education requires one to conceptualize the kind of teacher he would hope to create, and to propose a program that might produce such a person.

Dewey began by defining the kind of school experiences that would help children to grow intellectually, ethically, emotionally, aesthetically, and spiritually. Teachers were needed who were sensitive to the conditions that could either foster or thwart such growth in their students. To assist them, they needed the valuable knowledge that could be gained only by personal professional experiences. They had to acquire the attitudes and skills that would enable them to continue learning about teaching even after they had become professionals. They needed, in short, to become permanent students of education. This required the habits of mind that characterize work in the modern laboratory.

Dewey thus assumed that theory and practice both have a place in the education of teachers. But how were they to be related? He contrasted two approaches: (1) the apprentice idea versus (2) the laboratory idea. They lead to different kinds of teachers, he argued.

The apprentice idea, he said, has wide and understandable appeal. The pressures are great to secure large numbers of new teachers who can move into classes of thirty to sixty children; who can keep order and proceed with a definite plan of work. The apprentice scheme concentrates on equipping teachers immediately with as many details of the craft as possible. They are asked to learn the techniques of a master teacher; they are equipped with detailed lesson plans designed by experts and guaranteed to produce results. Dewey did not try to dismiss with ridicule either the pressures or the well-intentioned efforts to meet them. He acknowledged the trying difficulties for the new teacher in confronting large classes of restless youngsters. Pleas for help were justified. Nevertheless, he questioned the efficacy of the approach. The apprentice model aims at turning out finished masters of the craft through extensive and detailed practice. The laboratory idea, on the other hand, aims at *control of the intellectual methods* required for personal and independent mastery, through "typical and intensive" experiences in the training period.[2]

An apprenticeship model, Dewey said, is based on the false assumption that a finished teacher can be produced in training. Instead, the short time available should be used to gain insights that can continue to be used for professional growth. If these are missed during training, it is difficult to acquire them later, whereas increased proficiency in technical skills can be learned on the job. More specifically, he argued that the emphasis on attaining proficiency in teaching skills tends to turn the attention of the student-teacher to the wrong concerns and therefore militates against a really productive learning experience.

A basic fact that every true teacher knows, he said, may well be obscured for the neophyte by the sheer complexities of the classroom: pupils have *external* and *internal* levels of attention. The external behavior consists of the conventional responses children learn to make to please the teacher. The teacher who mistakes these for the genuine response will never get the class to go beyond the level of "teacher-talk." The true teacher knows, however, that another order of reality is present: the inner play of thoughts, images, and emotions in response to the subject matter. Dewey called this

". . . a fundamental condition of mental growth. To be able to keep track of this mental play, to recognize the signs of its presence or absence, to know how it is initiated and maintained, how to test it by results attained, and to test *apparent* results by it, is the supreme mark and criterion of a teacher. It means insight into soul-action, ability to discriminate the genuine from the sham, and capacity to further one and discourage the other." [3]

When student teachers are pressured simply to teach "good lessons," they can miss what is at the heart of the work.

Fixing attention on secondary matters can have another consequence, he said: *"the formation of habits of work which have*

[2] *Ibid.,* p. 3.
[3] *Ibid.,* p. 6.

*an empirical rather than a scientific sanction.* The student adjusts his actual methods of teaching, not to the principles which he is acquiring, but to what he sees succeed and fail in an empirical way from moment to moment." [4] Thus, habits of teaching are formed without relation to psychological, sociological, or philosophical principles or theory. This relates to one of the chief evils of the profession. "There is an enthusiastic devotion to certain principles of lofty theory in the abstract—principles of self-activity, self-control, intellectual and moral—and there is a school practice taking little heed of the official pedagogic creed. Theory and practice do not grow together out of and into the teacher's personal experience." [5] This dichotomy enfeebles teaching.

The question at issue is critical for the profession: What habits of mind are to be brought to the job? Dewey argued that a healthy profession requires teachers who have learned to apply the habits of critical thought to their work. To do this, they must have a full knowledge of their subject matter, and observe and reflect in terms of psychological and philosophical concepts. Teaching becomes a profession only when it is composed of thoughtful students of education.

The apprentice approach may appear to be superior as its products operate with smooth efficiency during their first weeks. This accomplishment means little if they have not been equipped with the professional habits required for self-generating growth.

"Such persons seem to know how to teach, but they are not students of teaching. Even though they go studying books of pedagogy, reading teachers' journals, attending teachers' institutes, etc., yet the root of the matter is not in them, unless they continue to be students of subject matter and students of mind activity. Unless a teacher is such a student, he may continue to improve in the mechanics of school-management, but he cannot grow as a teacher, an inspirer and director of soul-life." [6]

We may note, with special care, several items in this statement: A real teacher is one who continues to be a student of *subject matter* and of *mind activity*. This theme pervaded the

[4] *Ibid.*, p. 7.
[5] *Ibid.*, pp. 7–8.
[6] *Ibid.*, p. 8.

whole of the Laboratory School enterprise, and recurs again and again in his writings on education, from *The Child and the Curriculum* (1902) to *Experience and Education* (1938).

In the article before us, he explicated the role of psychology in education. We shall forego the details of his argument and reach for the heart of it.

There is the need, first, to distinguish educational psychology from psychology in general. He stressed two distinctions: (1) Educational psychology is concerned with the goal of human growth—with the conditions that foster or arrest it, (2) it pays special attention to social interaction and to the interplay of minds. General psychology has other goals. It is concerned with understanding all aspects of mental life. An important consequence is that *"no educational procedure nor pedagogical maxim can be derived from pure psychological data. . . .* It is the subordination of the psychological material *to the problem of effecting growth and avoiding arrest and waste* which constitutes a distinguishing mark of educational psychology."[7]

For the preparation of teachers, this distinction has a bearing on the differences in approach of the apprentice and laboratory methods. When student teachers are assigned to classroom observations the apprentice approach would have them concentrate on the methods and instruments used by a good teacher in teaching a subject with the hope that they would accumulate a store of techniques. The laboratory hypothesis stresses a different idea. The prospective teacher should be taught to observe the pattern of interaction of teacher and students—how mind answers mind. To help overcome the tendency to mere imitation, the student needs most, at this stage, practice in seeing "what is going on in the minds of a group of persons who are in intellectual contact with one another. He needs to learn to observe psychologically —a very different thing from simply observing how a teacher gets 'good results' in presenting any particular subject."[8]

There remains the matter of subject matter, or scholarship. Dewey tried hard to show that, in his laboratory model, the psychological and methodological aspect is a companion of the content and subject matter. This is so because they are simply

[7] *Ibid.*, p. 13. (My italics.)
[8] *Ibid.*, p. 12.

different dimensions of mind at work. As Dewey put it, "There is . . . method in subject matter itself—method indeed of the highest order which the human mind has yet evolved, scientific method." [9] Any subject matter represents the ordering of some aspect of the world that man encounters. The generalizations, classifications, interpretations contained in it represent the arduous efforts of human minds to bring order out of a welter of phenomena. It represents the need of the human being to see the world with more meaning—and with that meaning attained, to explore the world and self still further. Scholarship itself, therefore, may be an effective tool in training good teachers; it can be an "object lesson" of the finest type of mental growth, which is to say, of the educative process. By recognizing science and literature as modes of thought activity, students can gain psychological insights into the processes of effective thought in general.

Dewey argued that this applied with equal force to elementary school teachers as well as to those working at higher levels.

"Otherwise, the current traditions of elementary work with their tendency to talk and write down to the supposed intellectual level of children will be likely to continue. Only a teacher thoroughly trained in the higher levels of intellectual method and who thus has constantly in his own mind a sense of what adequate and genuine intellectual activity means, will be likely, in deed, not in mere work to respect the mental integrity and force of children." [10]

Teachers who have been taught to see their subject matter as a product of thought in action, who understand the disciplines that led to the advance of knowledge as well as the end products in textbooks can be more sensitive to signs of intellectual activity in children of four or youths of sixteen. We have here, he said, the clue to genuine teachers, whether they follow favored methodological techniques or not.

"They are themselves so full of the spirit of inquiry, so sensitive to every sign of its presence and absence, that no matter what they do, nor how they do it, they succeed in awakening and

[9] *Ibid.,* p. 15.
[10] *Ibid.,* p. 16.

inspiring like alert and mental activity in those with whom they come in contact." [11]

The concept also contained implications for ways of conceiving problems of the curriculum. Approaches that center on stringing together well-packaged but isolated lesson plans, or that teach the teacher to snatch at items that may be fitted into a cookbook formula, are harmful.

"What is needed is the habit of viewing the entire curriculum as a continuous growth, reflecting the growth of mind itself. This in turn demands . . . consecutive and longitudinal consideration of the elementary and high school rather than a cross-sectional view of it." [12]

## THE DYNAMICS OF THE CLASSROOM: THE INTERACTION OF TEACHER, STUDENT, SUBJECT MATTER

In order to clarify further Dewey's concept of the teacher's role, we turn to one of his most famous essays, *The Child and the Curriculum* (1902).[13] Here he elaborated his views on the dynamics of the classroom. The fundamental factors are the *teacher*, the *subject matter*, and the *students*. The critical pedagogical question is, how are these to be related to obtain the most fruitful educational results? Dewey said that the history of education reveals two educational sects: one, with *The Child* emblazoned on its banner; the other, with *The Subject* as its slogan. A set of related catchwords are used by the followers of each camp. Those championing the cause of *Subject Matter* stress the importance of discipline, guidance and control, law, and conservation of the heritage. The advocates of *The Child* present the case for interest, spontaneity, freedom and initiative, and the importance of innovation and progress. Charges of inertness, dull routine, and tyrannical authoritarianism are met with countercharges of chaos and anarchism and neglect of the sacred authority of duty. Dewey said that those who are adherents of common-sense practice have

[11] *Ibid.*, p. 17.
[12] *Ibid.*, p. 19.
[13] John Dewey, *The Child and the Curriculum* (Chicago, University of Chicago Press, 1902).

avoided following the extreme leaders of either side. But the continued existence of such divisions points to a genuine problem: that legitimate values for education are represented in both schools of thought. Typically, Dewey deplored the tendency toward an either/or dualism. He then attempted to define the educational task in a way that would resolve the opposites.

Dewey held that both the student and the studies share something basic in the human situation. They represent different aspects of the human drive to see the world and self with greater meaning, and to develop capacities to live more effectively—to realize experience more fully. The teacher may approach work in the classroom so that his relations to his students and to subject matter are defined in constructive, mutually helpful ways, or in ways that subvert the educative process.

The teacher may see the child as an individual human being, actively engaged in trying to understand his world and to come to terms with it. The child's experience, as he comes to school,

"contains within itself—elements—facts and truths—of just the same sort as those entering into the formulated study; and, what is of more importance, . . . it contains within itself the attitudes, the motives, and the interests which have operated in developing and organizing the subject matter to the plane which it now occupies. From the side of the studies, it is a question of interpreting them as outgrowths of forces operating in the child's life, and of discovering the steps that intervene between the child's present experience and their richer maturity." [14]

His argument is that the child's experience is partial and fragmentary but not different in kind from that of the human race which culminated in creating fields of knowledge and disciplined tools of thought.

Dewey argues that the various studies, such as mathematics, language, science, "are themselves experience—they are that of the race. They embody the cumulative outcome of the efforts, the strivings, and successes of the human race generation after generation. They present this, not as a mere accumulation, not as a miscellaneous heap of separate bits of experience, but in some

[14] *Ibid.*, p. 16.

organized and systematized way—that is, as reflectively formulated." [15]

From a pedagogical point of view, however, both the child and the subject matter may be incorrectly treated. The subject matter in the textbooks tends to contain the logically organized *end products* of inquiry. The teacher who insists that students merely recite this organized body of knowledge is cheating his students of insight into the exciting processes of inquiry and questioning that went before. The child who asks the worker in the stone quarry how it is that one finds fossils of fish on a mountain is asking the kind of question that spurred geologists to create their science. Yet geology may be taught so that students see it merely as a matter of giving right answers in listing the geological layers: Silurian, Devonian, Mississippian, etc.

On the other hand, Dewey warned that proponents of the "new education" can mistakenly regard the child's present interests as finally significant in themselves.

"In truth his learnings and achievements are fluid and moving. They change from day to day and from hour to hour.

"It will do harm if child-study leaves in the popular mind the impression that a child of a given age has a positive equipment of purposes and interests to be cultivated just as they stand. Interests in reality are but attitudes toward possible experiences; they are not achievements; their worth is in the leverage they afford, not in the accomplishment which they represent. . . . Any power, whether of child or adult, is indulged when it is taken on its given and present level in consciousness. Its genuine meaning is in the propulsion it affords to a higher level." [16]

What is the meaning of this for the teacher or educator? As we saw earlier in this chapter, it means that he has certain obligations both to the subject matter and to his pupils—and that he must be a student of each. The teacher's effectiveness depends on his ability to interpret the meaning of his subject and to develop insights into the processes of inquiry that led to its creation. The teacher who truly understands the significance of his subject may help students, through acts of appreciation,

[15] *Ibid.*, pp. 16-17.
[16] *Ibid.*, pp. 20-21.

to share the sense of discovery of the creators of knowledge.[17] Some years later, Dewey elaborated the point when he considered the question of what is required for a teacher to become the intellectual leader of a group.

"The first condition goes back to his own intellectual preparation in subject matter. This should be abundant to the point of overflow. It must be much wider than the ground laid out in textbook or in any fixed plan for teaching a lesson. It must cover points, so that the teacher can take advantage of unexpected questions or unanticipated incidents. It must be accompanied by a genuine enthusiasm for the subject that will communicate itself contagiously to pupils.

"Some of the reasons why the teacher should have an excess supply of information and understanding are too obvious to need mention. The central reason is possibly not always recognized. *The teacher must have his mind free to observe the mental responses and movements of the student members of the recitation-group.* The problem of the pupils is found in *subject matter;* the problem of teachers is *what the minds of pupils are doing with this subject matter.* Unless the teacher's mind has mastered the subject matter in advance, unless it is thoroughly at home in it, using it unconsciously without the need of express thought, he will not be free to give full time and attention to observation and interpretation of the pupils' intellectual reactions. The teacher must be alive to all forms of bodily expression of mental condition—to puzzlement, boredom, mastery, the dawn of an idea, feigned attention, tendency to show off, to dominate discussion because of egotism, etc.—as well as sensitive to the meaning of all expression in words. He must be aware not only of *their* meaning, but of their meaning as indicative of the state of mind of the pupil, his degree of observation and comprehension." [18]

Dewey's insistence that the teacher be a serious student of his subject is clear enough; but the quotation illustrates, too, his

[17] See Jacob Bronowski, *Science and Human Values* (New York, Harper and Row, 1959), especially pp. 30–32.

[18] John Dewey, *How We Think*, revised ed., 1933 (Boston, D. C. Heath and Co., 1910), pp. 274–275.

forceful insistence that the teacher's obligation to advance the learning experiences of his students was the real task. It is not enough to cover ground skillfully. Dewey stressed a point that has since been proved by studies in perception—that what goes on in a classroom will be perceived with some uniqueness by each individual. This uniqueness will vary with the range and quality of each person's experiences. In the final analysis, the ordering of the world represented in geology, for example, is comprehended by specific individuals only when they absorb it for themselves. Ideas become most effectively incorporated when they are seen and felt through personal efforts. As Dewey put it, in one of his less elegant expressions, the subject matter must be "psychologized."¹ The more the teacher is aware of the interests of his students and of the factors in their experience, the more imaginative he can be in establishing situations, raising questions, and suggesting activities that might engage students in an effort to make sense of things for themselves. This increases the chances of effectively "reconstructing experience."

There is no question that this general rationale was represented in Dewey's analysis of the task of teaching. In setting forth this conception of content and method, Dewey, however, did not cover many of the problems to be met in realizing the goal. Furthermore, the differences among his followers on where to place emphasis may be traced to certain ambiguities in his own position. For example, although Dewey did make clear statements about the significance of subject matter, other passages leave room for doubt as to what was intended in handling it. In *The Child and the Curriculum* he described subject matter as providing the end toward which the teacher is to lead students but said, "To see the outcome is to know in what direction the present experience [of the child] is moving, provided it move normally and soundly." [19] What does moving "normally and soundly" mean? It may mean that if a teacher knows his subject, and sees the child raising certain questions, he will be able to detect where the child's queries *could* lead—to what concepts, etc. Then he could set up certain situations or provide materials to help the child reach the goal. But the notion that

[19] Dewey, *The Child and the Curriculum*, p. 18.

experience would move "normally" to such ends is unconvincing or unclear.

Toward the end of the same essay, there is a frequently quoted passage in which Dewey made the case for the subject matter.

"Now, the value of the formulated wealth of knowledge that makes up the course of study is that it may enable the educator *to determine the environment* of the child, and thus by indirection to direct. Its primary value, its primary indication, is for the teacher, not for the child. It says to the teacher: Such and such are the capacities, the fulfilments, in truth and beauty and behavior, open to these children. Now see to it that day by day the conditions are such that *their own activities* move inevitably in this direction, toward such culmination of themselves. Let the child's nature fulfill its own destiny, revealed to you in whatever of science and art and industry the world now holds as its own." [20]

From the point of view of classroom strategy, subject matter has a twofold value. It provides the teacher with the significant ideas, meanings, and concepts he can help his students to understand; it provides the teacher with a sense of direction. Mastery of the significance of his subject also equips the teacher to set up situations that will move the student to gain insights on his own. Part of the strategy of teaching is to "determine the environment of the child." Dewey seems to have meant this in two senses. Sometimes the teacher would place the student in situations that would lead to a conclusion considered significant by the teacher; on other occasions the student would be confronted with less neatly structured conditions which would lead him to novel combinations or outcomes that might not be fully anticipated by either the student or the teacher. Dewey refused to reduce to a neat pedagogical formula the matter of deciding when and how to employ one emphasis or the other. The creative professional would have to develop his own sense of appropriateness.

But puzzling items remain in Dewey's style. For example, what is the meaning of the phrase "their own activities" will

[20] *Ibid.*, pp. 39–40.

move *inevitably* in the direction of truth, beauty, etc? Although Dewey himself clearly warned against pedagogical approaches that placed undue emphasis on the child and his immediate interests, it is clear that the more child-centered followers of the progressive education movement could point to phrases in Dewey's writings that seemed to support their case.

There were other problems of implementation that Dewey did not discuss in detail. He did not indicate, for example, the minimum level of intellectual ability and training that would enable teachers to work in the way he advocated. Clearly teachers of the "scholar-teacher" category would be required. In his writings, he did not treat the details of how academic scholars and educators could cooperate to organize the meanings and concepts of subject matter fruitfully. He did not clarify how often, in the daily round of teaching, it would be possible to relate the key concepts of organized subject matter to the range of experience in the lives of children in large classes.

On the other hand, it is not fair to say that Dewey avoided these questions in practice. The whole effort in the Laboratory School was to create a program consistent with the dicta he described. His main responsibility as philosopher of education was to define the task of the teacher—to clarify the goals and the elements in the teacher-learning situation that could be utilized to achieve them. He never claimed that the means or methods were easily available in some foolproof formula that could be universally employed. His position, in fact, held that specific means had to be developed for differing situations. He was modest about the claims he could make for results obtained in his own school.

## THE PLAN TO REALIZE THE GOALS IN THE LABORATORY SCHOOL

Dewey did expect the Laboratory School to offer a challenge to limited and stereotyped conceptions of teaching. He turned to the idea of the classroom as a laboratory for educational experimentation in order to shift the thinking about education from several *cul-de-sacs* that hindered the formulation of the critically grounded theory required of a true profession.

Earlier in this chapter, we saw him rejecting as inadequate the detailed-training or apprenticeship approach—the practice of having veteran teachers pass on to beginners their accumulated *ad hoc* wisdom as a simple common-sense appeal. He also held that the ideological warfare represented in the competing champions of The Child and The Subject Matter has conclusively demonstrated the limitations of extremists in both of these camps. The victories won by skilled, witty, and vicious argumentation are seen to be temporary and disillusioning. They merely lay the ground for still another round of battle.

In his address as President of the American Psychological Association (1899), "Psychology and Social Practice," [21] Dewey sketched a model for creating a more firmly established theory upon which to build educational practice.

In his opening remarks, Dewey acknowledged that the title revealed his original intention to consider fundamental questions relating psychology to the social sciences—and through them to social practice. He said, in fact, that he was prepared only to treat a more restricted subject—the relation of psychology to education, a phase "with which I have been more or less practically occupied within the last few years." [22]

Dewey said that school practice of the day had a psychological basis. Teachers proceeded on the basis of psychological assumptions that controlled theory and practice, but a painful gap existed between actual theory in psychology and that which governed school practice. His argument involved the point that psychology recognized certain continuities and discontinuities in the psychology of children as compared with that of adults. Practice among educators showed that they misunderstood and confused these points. Since we shall be following Dewey's psychological theory in detail in subsequent chapters, we shall not analyze the specifics of his argument in this instance. The main point of the article concerns recommendations for working relations between psychologists and educators, and it is to this that we shall devote our attention.

[21] John Dewey, *Psychology and Social Practice* (Chicago, University of Chicago Press, 1901). I am indebted, too, for the summary and interpretation of this paper by Charles J. Brauner, *American Educational Theory* (Englewood Cliffs, New Jersey, Prentice-Hall, 1964), pp. 97–101.

[22] Dewey, *Psychology and Social Practice*, p. 7.

The school provides an excellent setting, he said, for exploring the relations between psychological theory and social practice.

"[It] . . . stands in many respects midway between the extreme simplifications of the laboratory and the confused complexities of ordinary life. Its conditions are those of life at large; they are social and practical. But it approaches the laboratory in so far as the ends aimed at are reduced in number, are definite, and thus simplify the conditions; and their psychological phase is uppermost—the formation of habits of attention, observation, memory, etc.—while in ordinary life these are secondary and swallowed up. . . . While the psychological theory would guide and illuminate the practice, acting upon the theory would immediately test it, and thus criticize it, bringing about its revision and growth. In the large and open sense of the words, psychology becomes a working hypothesis, instruction is the experimental test and demonstration of the hypothesis; the result is both greater practical control and continued growth in theory." [23]

Dewey proposed a triumvirate of workers to implement the laboratory idea: psychological theorists, educational theorists, and classroom teachers. School practice cannot be changed in a sounder direction, he argued, unless it is based on an accurate understanding of psychological principles. At the level of practice, the key figure is the teacher. He cannot be expected to be a wholehearted and intelligent partner in effecting reforms unless he understands the scientific basis and necessity of the changes.[24] Yet Dewey shared the view of William James that it was a mistake to think that "psychology . . . is something from which you can deduce definite programs and schemes and methods for immediate schoolroom use." [25] What is needed is a middle level theorist, an educational conceptualist, who will take hold of psychological conclusions and organize them into ideas for educational practice. "He should put the matter into such shape that the teacher may take the net result in the form of advice and rules for action. . . ." [26] The educational theorist will be most

[23] Ibid., pp. 33–34.
[24] Ibid., p. 12.
[25] Quoted in Brauner, op. cit., p. 98.
[26] Dewey, Psychology and Social Practice, p. 15.

conscious of the psychological basis and equivalents of the educational work. He will suggest the pedagogical aspects of psychological facts and principles. The teacher can profit, but when trained as a student of psychology he has his own important professional role. The teacher is not to be a mere passive recipient of "obligatory prescriptions." He will be trained to see the reasons for and the import of the suggestions. But also he will treat them as ideas to be tested. He will be in a position to report the results of his experience. As Brauner summarizes it, "Dewey sought to join the objective science of psychology with the subjective consciousness of the practitioner through the agency of a linking science or philosophy of education." [27]

Having general psychology as a model for inquiry and scientific generalization, Dewey saw the possibility of building a second discipline of educational theory, which would involve descriptions and generalizations about the behavior of students and teachers in the classroom. Then,

". . . through the imaginative mind of a conceptualist, psychological science could be translated into principles, if not predictions, about how to improve practice. This body of educational theory could be tested in the classroom, not by a disinterested third party, but by a very much interested practitioner. Reports gathered from many practitioners would confirm some principles and refute others. This body of somewhat confirmed principles would help build a linking science, not so objective as psychology, but not so subjective and personal as one teacher's belief as to what worked and what did not." [28]

Dewey created the Laboratory School in order to demonstrate the new possibilities. One of its distinctive features was that it was part of a university. It should take advantage of that connection to exploit the opportunities available. Other school systems would have to recognize which of the experiences created at Chicago might be adapted to their own situations.

There was, as we have mentioned, the opportunity for the school's staff to establish cooperative relationships with the bril-

[27] Brauner, *op. cit.*, p. 99.
[28] *Ibid.*

liant scholars on campus. The school that functioned as a laboratory where people were interested in inquiry and investigation
provided a milieu in which scholars were willing to collaborate.
Mayhew and Edwards, who were on the staff, report that many
of the professors, upon encountering teachers with genuine
intellectual concerns, responded with their own pedagogical interests and gave constant help to the teachers of the school.[29]
Dewey took seriously his injunction that elementary school
teachers should be constantly engaged in genuine intellectual
activity, and sought ways to get them into research investigations.

At the end of the third year of the school, the administrative
arrangements for the curriculum were given a departmental form
analogous to that of the university. The staff, which was small,
was organized into the following departments: Kindergarten,
History, Science and Mathematics, Art, Music, Languages, Domestic Sciences and Industry, Manual Arts, and Physical Culture. Each department was headed by a director qualified by
social and technical training, as well as by experience, to utilize
his special field to deal intelligently with the problems met in
carrying on activities in the classroom.[30]

Although the teachers at the school had their main responsibility to their students, it was assumed that some among them,
trained in research techniques, would also work with university
colleagues in advancing knowledge. The director of the department, for example, was a trained investigator

". . . who realized that her intelligent reports of the results of
testing certain educational theories in the actual practices of her
classroom were to constitute scientific findings for study and
revision by other teachers, administrators, and students of educational science. As an investigator she had no fixed or final set of
objectives, but each day of teaching enabled her in the light of
her successes or failures to revise and better these objectives.

"The reports made weekly in typewritten form, furnished the
data of the problems for study and discussion in the weekly in-

---

[29] Katherine C. Mayhew and Anna C. Edwards, *The Dewey School*
(New York, Appleton-Century-Crofts, 1936), pp. 3-4.
[30] *Ibid.*, p. 374.

formal conference of teachers, as well as in the more formal seminar groups and larger pedagogical club meetings. Thus all the teachers in actual daily contact with children of all ages furnished, in these reports, the data for further inquiries and conclusions. The value of such material to the Department of Pedagogy of the University, engaged as it was with the problems of educational science, became almost like the systematic and cumulative clinical records of medical science." [31]

Needless to say, a teaching profession, conceived in this fashion, would have attractions for very able young men and women. Certain conditions, however, are required to make them actually respond. One of these is a limitation on class size and teaching load that can make the job something other than the processing of large numbers of children. This involves the problem of school finance, which Dewey personally confronted. During the hard and continuing battle of the budget in the early years, President Harper, at one time, exerted pressure on Dewey to increase class enrollments to augment revenue from tuitions. This forced Dewey to take a position. In a letter to Harper of June 23, 1898, he wrote,

"As for your point regarding the size of groups, I can only repeat what was said that day, that continuous and earnest attention has been given to the matter, and that as it now stands, it is a matter of principle and not of detail. I think that any increase forced in this direction simply for the sake of additional revenue would involve such a complete change in the ideals and methods of the School as profoundly to modify its whole character—so profoundly indeed, that it would lose whatever reason for existence it now possesses as an educational undertaking." [32]

Another condition required to attract the kind of persons capable of building a profession involves the concept of adminis-

[31] *Ibid.*, pp. 373-374. The weekly reports were never published but are available in the Archives of the University School at the University of Chicago. They vary in scope and quality, but constitute a fascinating record of work pursued there. Detailed excerpts in notebooks are on file at Teachers College, Columbia University.

[32] John Dewey, "Letters to William Rainey Harper," The President's Papers, University of Chicago (June 23, 1898).

tration. Teachers trained as Dewey recommended would be self-reliant and proud of their profession. They would not be tolerant of small-minded or paternalistic administrators who would deny them the chance to work with imagination and integrity. Dewey was not the perfect administrator. He was far from blameless in the wrangles with Colonel Parker's staff, particularly with Wilbur Jackman,[33] but the record is clear that, generally, he gave considerable freedom of initiative to creative teachers, and encouraged a free give and take of ideas in a lively intellectual climate.[34]

More than six decades later, Dewey's ideal is more relevant than ever, yet still remains to be realized. A full accounting for the limited progress to date constitutes one of the sorely needed studies about twentieth-century American education. It may be that the pressures of an expanding educational system were just too great. An imaginative use of new technology may bring the ideal closer to our grasp. One thing is certain; such an ideal will never be realized without the necessary money and personnel, without vision, and without struggle.

[33] See Robert L. McCaul, "Dewey and the University of Chicago," *School and Society*, Vol. 89, Part 2 (April 3, 1961), pp. 179–183, and Part 3 (April 22, 1961), pp. 202–206.

[34] Mayhew and Edwards, *op. cit.*, pp. v–vi.

# CHAPTER SIX

# The Psychological Theory
# for Experimentation in Education

In 1896, Dewey's dream of a University Laboratory School became an actuality. Even though the school began humbly with only sixteen students, it quickly grew in numbers and won the loyal support of the parents and friends who shared Dewey's educational vision. Our purpose is to reflect on aspects of the theoretical rationale that lay behind Dewey's general plan for work in education.

Dewey's position was that teaching would become a profession only as it contained members who were "students of subject matter, and students of mind activity." Thus universities had the responsibility to create, through research, a theory and a philosophy of education upon which work in the profession could be based. This could not be done without an educational equivalent to the laboratories in the sciences. For Dewey this meant the creation of an actual school where ideas growing out of the psychological-philosophical theory of his staff would be tried and tested.

As the Director of the University Elementary School, he had to state its special purposes on many occasions. There is a high order of consistency in these expositions. He emphasized that as a Laboratory School of the university, its most important function was to contribute to the progress of scientific thought in education.[1] He acknowledged that its program had to be effective to justify its existence for parents and supporters; but they, too,

[1] John Dewey, "The Psychology of the Elementary Curriculum," *The Elementary School Record*, Vol. 1, No. 9 (December, 1900), p. 221.

had to understand the school's primary purpose. He made clear that it was not intended to be a normal school for the training of teachers, nor a model school offering specific answers for the immediate problems of the public schools. He hoped that it would eventually influence teaching practice through creating a more firmly grounded theory and demonstrating its applicability in action.[2] Such work required a climate of free investigation where well-considered hypotheses could be tried and examined in terms of factual results without being fettered by long-standing traditions or being pressured for quick results. In order to accomplish this, the school would set up conditions to provide rich educational experiences—conditions that could never be used as a basis for rationalizing failures on the grounds of inadequate resources. This meant that no effort was made to present the situation of "normal" classrooms.

"If it is advisable to have smaller classes, more teachers and a different working hypothesis than is at present the case in the public schools, there should be some institution to show this." [3]

The values and ideas characterizing the ideal of university research were to prevail.

What was to be at the center of the effort? Dewey, in his ninth and final monograph in a series about the school, (1900) envisaged it as a laboratory for psychology applied to education:

"A place for the study of mind as manifested and developed in the child, and for the search after materials and agencies that seem most likely to fulfil and further the conditions of normal growth." [4]

We find a restatement here of themes previously discussed: (1) Educational psychology was to be concerned with the conditions that foster growth, and (2) the school as a research center was to be concerned with the study of the learning process and of the organization of subject matter; both were to be seen as aspects of "mind activity"; both involve questions that must be

[2] John Dewey, "The University School," *University Record*, Vol. 1, No. 6 (November, 1896), pp. 417-418.
[3] *Ibid*.
[4] Dewey, "The Psychology of the Elementary Curriculum," pp. 221-222.

answered by anyone starting a school. What is to be taught? How is it to be taught?

The description of the school as a psychological laboratory gives the impression that the emphasis was to be on learning theory and method. Such an interpretation would fail to acknowledge Dewey's repeated insistence that questions regarding content and method could not be considered in isolation from each other. This, in turn, was related to the conviction that the central educational problem was that of the evolution of mind or "minded" behavior. The social-psychological side of the problem dealt with an analysis of the processes of mental life that facilitated the growth and emergence of effective thinking in human experience. As for the curriculum side, the subjects were to be seen as examples of disciplined thought processes that, by extending human knowledge and experience, had gradually enabled man to understand the nature of his world. Dewey's definition of educational psychology required that it be as concerned with the problems of curriculum content and sequence as with questions of methodology. In this sense, the term *laboratory*, as applied to his school, must be interpreted as a laboratory for educational psychology.

Having underscored Dewey's point about the importance of treating problems of subject matter and method in conjunction, we must now consider them separately. Dewey is a thoroughgoing contextualist. Every item in experience is related to a network of supporting factors; yet, in exposition, the human mind is required to work in linear fashion. Not all things can be discussed at once. Before completing our analysis of the Dewey school, we shall try to show the intimate relation between its "psychological" and academic features. Because each needs special treatment, we shall begin with the psychological side of the continuum and later consider the subject matter.

THE PSYCHOLOGICAL THEORY

A crucial question at the time Dewey was formulating his views of education was that concerning the evolution of the mind of man. Surely this was the great question for him also, and the response his work received indicates that he was speaking to a deep and widely felt need. The challenge was coming from science—more specifically from evolutionary theory, broadly conceived. Evolution contained dimensions that were exciting and, at the same time, frightening. On the one hand, there was the picture of emerging life and experience with man as a participant; on the other hand, man seemed diminished by the loss of his special place outside nature and by his reduction to a minute entity in the immensities of space and time. Was it possible to have a philosophy that coincided with reality as revealed by scientific investigation but that still preserved an image of man as possessing dignity and purpose? There was, and still is, a great hunger for the answer to that question.

Dewey himself knew the need in a deep and personal way. He found that in the problems of education the most profound philosophical questions were brought to focus. How does an infant, entering the world helpless, achieve an awareness of his existence on a planet that revolves about a star in a universe of infinite galaxies? How is it that man can lift himself from a state of nakedness to become the creator of civilizations stocked with plenty, yet can be dogged by the war of man against man? How can we account for the existence of savagery and cruelty alongside the emergence of ideals of justice, equality, and charity? Can children be educated to nourish their positive potential and to control their destructive proclivities? These are ancient questions. Evolutionary theory required the formulation of new answers. Dewey was one of those who set out to create an image of man that would coincide with the new perspective. To the end, he was aware of the limitations of his efforts.

Philosophical questions led him to consider education. The process of educating the young into their humanity was dependent upon an answer to the question, What is involved in the process of learning, or, in traditional terms, what is the nature of man's mind? Dewey was convinced that the traditional answers were undermined by the new advances in science. In our biographical sketch, we saw the young Dewey resisting the disjunctions inherent in the tradition that defined man in terms of dichotomous substances of mind and body. We saw his initial response to the theory of organic holism of Huxley's *Physiology*. Although he was attracted to the Hegelian alternative to dualism, he gradually felt bound to relinquish it as he could not reconcile it with scientific findings. During the last two decades of the nineteenth century, many of his inquiries pivoted around the effort to create a convincing psychological accounting of mind. He taught and wrote about psychology at Michigan and Chicago. Psychology was in the process of disengaging itself from philosophy in order to become an autonomous branch of science. The physiological movement in psychology, with its emphasis on laboratory research, urged him in that direction. Within limits, he was a supporter of the movement. Dewey and his colleague James Angell argued that psychology, broadly conceived, was the "natural history of the various attitudes and structures through which experiencing passes." [5] As such, it was indispensable in both method and content for work in philosophy. Dewey played a leading role, in collaboration with his colleagues George H. Mead and James Angell, in creating a biosocial conception of mind. In psychology, this was functionalism; in philosophy it was instrumentalism or experimentalism. These were related aspects of a single point of view.

The educational program of the University School can be understood only in terms of the concepts of this position, as they furnished the intellectual support for the theory and practice of the school. The working out of the details of this rationale—Dewey's major preoccupation before and during his residence in Chicago—was largely responsible for his turning to education.

## The Philosophical Source of Dewey's Interest in Psychology

A bio-social alternative to traditional psychological theories of "mind activity" and to Hegelian idealism was formulated gradually over a period of years.

Dewey's concept of mind and self obviously contained a strong biological component. This first feature to emerge is understandable in terms of the exciting developments in biology. We have noted that Dewey's encounter with William James's *Principles of Psychology* had oriented him to consider a biological

---

[5] John Dewey and others, *Studies in Logical Theory* (Chicago, University of Chicago Press, 1903), pp. 15–16. See also, John Dewey, "Psychology and Philosophic Method," *The University of California Chronicle*, Vol. 2 (August, 1899).

origin of "minded activity." James broke free from the tendency to describe life structurally and emphasized the concept of life in action. The psychological dimensions of mind and thought were brought within this orientation. The processes of thought, such as discriminating, abstracting, and generalizing, were viewed as more elaborate functions of adjustment. The traditional view of mind as an entity apart from nature was replaced by seeing mind, or "minded behavior," as an objective process of interaction of organism and environment, like breathing and walking.[6] Dewey himself acknowledged the revolutionary influence of James's work on his thought. Actually James acted as a catalyst in bringing clarity to ideas Dewey had been pursuing for some time.

As early as 1884, Dewey wrote an article, "The New Psychology," [7] in which he wrestled with the impact of the new physiological approaches to psychological problems. In it he was already reaching to make the discriminations that were to characterize his mature thought of later decades. He applauded the effort of a physiological psychology that challenged the tendency to treat psychical life as consisting of "distinct ideas which are separate existences." He termed this the eighteenth-century approach, as typified by James Mill's "calculating man," whose behavior is neatly determined through his efforts to increase pleasure and avoid pain.

"We know better now. We know that the life of man whose unfolding furnishes psychology its material is the most difficult and complicated subject which man can investigate. . . . We see that man is somewhat more than a neatly dovetailed psychical machine who may be taken as an isolated individual, laid on the dissecting table of analysis and duly anatomized. We know that his life is bound up with the life of society, of the nation. . . ." [8]

He contrasted this with the movement of nineteenth-century psychology and physiology "back to the mother soil of experi-

[6] George P. Adams and William P. Montague, eds., *Contemporary American Philosophy* ( New York, The Macmillian Co., 1930), Vol. 2, see John Dewey, "From Absolutism to Experimentalism," pp. 24–25.

[7] John Dewey, "The New Psychology," *The Andover Review*, Vol. 2 (September, 1884), pp. 278–289.

[8] *Ibid.*, pp. 278–279.

ence." [9] The turning of psychological investigation from a concern with abstract "ideas" toward an effort to discern the physiological aspects of psychic phenomena was salutary; but he challenged the notion that demonstrating "some or all of the events of our mental life are physically conditioned upon certain nerve structure" *ipso facto* proves that psychic life can be explained completely in physiological terms.[10] He refused to accept materialistic reductionism as the answer to the problem of mind. We see foreshadowed here his criticisms of British empiricism and the physiological behaviorism represented in John Watson.

He did applaud biology for its introduction to psychology of the conception of organism and its employment of experimental methods.

His encounter with James's *Principles of Psychology* took place before he left Michigan. He used it as a text for a course in psychology—a course taken by James Angell, who shared the excitement of his teacher and became a co-founder of the Chicago School of functional psychology.

In 1896, the year of the founding of the Laboratory School, Dewey wrote "The Reflex Arc Concept in Psychology." [11] Here the organismic view became full grown and his break with Hegelian idealism was definitive. It became a landmark among the psychological writings that have influenced education.

In it he took up the attacks on dualist positions old and new, and tried to present a unifying psychological principle to supplant these positions. This time, however, he concentrated his fire not on the older body-soul dualism but on misinterpretations of stimulus-response (S-R) psychology. He argued that stimulus and response were not treated as the continuing, coordinated acts of an organism, and the reflex arc had become a "patchwork of disjointed parts, a mechanical principle of unallied processes." [12] Dewey's argument was not with the reflex arc concept itself, which had been borrowed from physiology, for he saw in it a potential for uniting a multiplicity of facts around one principle.

[9] *Ibid.*, p. 281.

[10] *Ibid.*, pp. 281–282.

[11] John Dewey, "The Reflex Arc Concept in Psychology," *The Psychological Review*, Vol. 3, No. 4 (July, 1896), pp. 357–370.

[12] *Ibid.*, p. 358.

But old notions were being read into the concept. Sensation was taken for stimulus and movement for response. Each was treated as a discrete element having its own independent existence. Thus they were related in a causal–mechanical, "push–pull," chain.

Dewey argued that the trouble lay in the concentration on the stimulus-response unit of psychological activity. His position was that S-R units are products of the psychologist's analysis, not the basic existential material in human experience. The fundamental factor was the total act of the organism. The child's reaching for the candle flame or pulling away from it were not responses "caused" by the sight of the flame. They were functions within the action of the organism and were determined by prior experience with candle flames as well as by mere exposure to the flame itself. In this sense, they had to be seen as functions in a well-coordinated series of acts. The psychologist who focuses merely on observation of stimulus and response reactions apart from the complete act breaks the total experience into artificial, isolated entities.

Dewey defined two situations from which distinctions of stimulus and response could be functionally derived. The first deals with ordinary habitual behavior which constitutes the bulk of experience. The second kind of situation arises when there is a break or disruption in habit.

In the first situation, habits are working in a well-coordinated pattern in the activity of the organism. Stimulus can be distinguished from response, in such an orderly sequence of acts, only if we see man's activities as leading to some objective end.

"It is only when we regard the sequence of acts as if they were adapted to reach some end that it occurs to us to speak of one as stimulus and the other as response. Otherwise we look at them as a mere series." [13]

In such a series of acts, one act is designated as a response and acts as a stimulus to the next act (response), and so on. Each act leads into another; each serves as both stimulus and response. By so designating them, we are simply analyzing aspects of finely coordinated behavior.

The second kind of situation in which functions of stimulus

[13] *Ibid.,* p. 366.

and response may be derived concerns a more important aspect of Dewey's theory. In his view, experience is generally continuous; most of the time habitual ways of behaving work well. But there are occasions when experience is disrupted. Then there is the need to restore continuity.

When the habitual modes no longer work, man is confronted with what Dewey later was to call a problematical situation. Any discontinuity means that stimulus and response are no longer functioning in a well-coordinated series of acts leading to some objective end. In such situations, it is necessary to isolate the disturbing factor in order to determine the stimulus. The determination of the course of action needed to restore continuity is the response.

Dewey was rejecting the reflex arc as being composed of a chain of isolated stimulus-response entities. The proper view, he argued, was to see experience as a continuous whole. Even when this continuity of experience is disrupted, it is repeatedly restored. The existential matrix was the ongoing experience of a living, acting organism. Stimulus and response, then, were to be seen as functions, dependent on each other, within a total act. They had meaning in terms of the act but not in themselves. The acts or functionings of the organism—reaching, seeing, hearing, remembering, purposing in order to attain ends—were the essential units of psychological activity. The effort in psychology to analyze these apart from their context in experience was to resort to artificial "pigeon-holing."

At about the same time, Dewey elaborated related themes in a briefer article, "The Psychology of Effort." [14] He was concerned with the conscious sense of effort. Stimulus and response have meaning only within the total act; effort is part of this act when discontinuity of experience occurs. Conscious effort was described as awareness of the necessity to select a mode of action (response) after the source of the disruption (stimulus) had been determined. An act is concluded by selecting a course of activity.

". . . [The] process of execution, the use of means, is the process of integrating acts hitherto separate and independent, and

[14] John Dewey, "The Psychology of Effort," *Philosophical Review*, Vol. 6, No. 1 (January, 1897), pp. 43–56.

putting together the result of fragments, into a single piece of conduct." [15]

Here, experience is not merely restored to its previous state, but is reconstituted.

"To make a new coordination the old coordination must, to some extent, be broken up, and the only way of breaking it up is for it to come into conflict with some other coordination; that is a conflict of two acts, each representing a habit, or end, is the necessary condition of reaching a new act which shall have a more comprehensive end." [16]

In conclusion, Dewey continued his functional treatment of psychological material by a brief reference to the role of *attention*. Attention, he said, arises in a conflict situation when a choice of actions has to be made and a new coordination effected. "Attending" is the continual selection of observations and ideas that can be combined toward some end.

Even those with but a cursory knowledge of Dewey's thought will recognize in these articles conceptions fundamental to his whole instrumentalist theory. The basic model is biological: the living organism seeks to maintain itself in its environment. There is a basic continuity of experience, occasionally disrupted by conflict or the breakdown of habit. This is accompanied by the need and drive to reconstitute adaptive, continuous behavior. Out of these disjunctive or "problematic" situations experience may be reconstructed. Functionalist psychology concentrated on how the organism functions, how it maintains activity. It paid special attention to behavior in troublesome situations.

By the time these articles were written and the Laboratory School was getting under way, Dewey had rejected mind-body dualisms. The organism was seen as the fundamental actor—not the mind or the body, but the organism in its total range of interaction with its environment.

## The Social Dimension of Learning

This emphasis on organism reflects the biological emphasis of instrumentalism. One must hasten to emphasize, however, that it

[15] *Ibid.*, p. 54.
[16] *Ibid.*, p. 55.

was a bio-*social* concept of mind developed by Dewey and his colleagues. Man's distinctive capacity to think reflectively in dealing with a problematic environment was dependent on the use of language, meanings, and fine tools of thought that had grown out of long human experience.

The social dimension of thinking and learning is emphasized, for example, in the 1900 monograph on "The Psychology of the Elementary Curriculum." [17] The idea stressed here and elsewhere is that to be human is to be socialized. The growth of individuals or of societies is dependent upon incorporating accumulated knowledge and thought processes, and upon bringing them to bear on life situations. The social element is critical for human development. Processes of learning and thinking are advanced modes of adaptation and are continuous with evolutionary development.

Dewey again criticized approaches in psychology that considered mind to be an individual entity in direct contact with an external world that shaped it. This theory maintained that mind would have been the same had there been only one in the universe. The psychology represented in the Laboratory School, on the other hand, conceived

"individual mind as a function of social life—as not capable of operating or developing by itself, but as requiring continual stimulus from social agencies, and finding its nutrition in social supplies. The idea of heredity has made familiar the notion that the equipment of the individual, mental as well as physical, is an inheritance from the past and held in trust by him for the future. The idea of evolution has made familiar the notion that mind cannot be regarded as an individual monopolistic possession, but represents the outworkings of the endeavor and thought of humanity; that it is developed in an environment that is social as well as physical, and that social needs and aims have been most potent in shaping it—that the chief difference between savagery and civilization is not in the naked nature which each faces, but the social heredity and social medium." [18]

[17] Dewey, "The Psychology of the Elementary Curriculum," pp. 221–232.
[18] *Ibid.*, p. 223.

Physical nature itself is transformed by social experience. Physical stimuli of light, sound, and heat are furnished by nature, but the *significance* attached to these depends on the interpretations given to them by the society in which the person lives and acts.

"The bare physical stimulus of light is not the entire reality; the interpretation given to it through social activities and thinking confers upon it its wealth of meaning. It is through imitation, suggestion, direct instruction and even more indirect unconscious intuition, that the child learns to estimate and treat the bare physical stimuli. It is through the social agencies that he recapitulates in a few short years the progress which it has taken the race slow centuries to work out." [19]

The biological base was supplemented by social meanings, skills, values, and attitudes. The theoretical conceptions of each were to have direct effects on the program developed by the University School. We shall return to this later.

## Dewey's Logical Theory

A special aspect of the social dimension requires attention: the nature and role of *reflective thinking* in the growth of experience. The extension of the psychological analysis into logical theory was required to incorporate the critical role of thought in reconstructing experience. Dewey undertook this expansion of his philosophical work in several important writings on logic during the Chicago period.[20] They are of interest because they constitute the ground from which his later expanded treatments

[19] *Ibid.*

[20] Two of these are essays: John Dewey, "Psychology and Philosophic Method," *University of California Chronicle*, Vol. 2 (August, 1899); reprinted with slight variations under the title "Consciousness and Experience," it appears in John Dewey, *The Influence of Darwin on Philosophy* (New York, Holt, Rinehart and Winston, 1910). Also, Dewey's important essays on "Thought and Its Subject Matter" in John Dewey and others, *Studies in Logical Theory*, Vol. 12 (Chicago, University of Chicago Press, 1903); and "Some Stages of Logical Thought," *Philosophical Review*, Vol. 9 (September, 1900), pp. 465–489; reprinted in *Essays in Experimental Logic* (1916), pp. 183–219.

of logic emanated. They also contain concepts that were incorporated into the educational theory and practice of the University School. We shall attempt a summary of points that bear most directly on matters affecting the school.

In the psychological writings, Dewey developed the concept of organic continuity of experience, of its disruptions, and of the need to restore or reconstitute it. Experience is viewed, then, as continuous and capable of expansion; however, the function of reflective thinking in the reconstitution of human experience was not specifically treated.

Dewey saw the critical role of thought, and made his essays on logic studies of the nature of effective thinking. His analyses were a continuation of his earlier treatment of the biological and psychological phases of experience.

The early article, "Psychology and Philosophic Method," set the stage for the transition from psychology to logic. He began by clarifying the division of labor between biology and psychology. Both are concerned with experience. Biologists and physical scientists deal with the *content* of experience, with what might be experienced. The experience that zoologists, chemists, mathematicians, and historians deal with is that of the psychologist also, but he has to make a special kind of inquiry.

"What characterizes his specialty is not some data or existences which he may call uniquely his own but the problem raised —the problem of the course of experiencing as such as distinct from its special contents." [21]

Being concerned, first and foremost, with the workings of experience, he is

"really after the process of experience, the way in which it arises and behaves. He wants to know its course, its history, its laws; its various typical forms; how each originates; how it is related to others; the part it plays in maintaining the inclusive, expanding, connected whole of experience." [22]

His problem as psychologist is to learn its *modus operandi*, its method.

[21] Dewey, "Psychology and Philosophic Method," p. 169.
[22] *Ibid.*, p. 164.

Dewey then underscored a point he had made in the "Reflex Arc" essay. The primary concern of the psychologist is experience, but he cannot deal with it directly. He needs tools, and the tools he creates are states of consciousness.

"I conceive that states of consciousness (and I hope you will take the term broadly enough to cover all the specific data of psychology) have no existence 'as such' . . . before the psychologist begins to work. He brings them into existence. In asking a certain question, he operates to secure the media of answering it, and this medium is 'consciousness' as the psychologist treats it." [23]

Just as stimulus and response in the reflex arc were defined as having no independent existence, so states of consciousness are seen as methodological products for the purpose of psychological analysis.

*Acts* of perceiving, remembering, intending, and loving constitute real experience. In trying to understand these experiences, the conditions under which they arise, and the effects they produce, the psychologist analyzes and categorizes them into states of consciousness. But to mistake the psychologist's abstractions for the actual experience of another person is the "psychological fallacy": "the confusion of experience of the one experiencing with what the psychologist makes out of it with his reflective analysis." [24]

Psychology tries to understand the expanding, connected whole of experience. Experience itself consists of the complex of events in the life activity of human beings. Psychology's task, as Dewey saw it, was to study "how experience becomes here and now in some uniquely individualized life." [25]

This had important consequences for education. We note in passing that they bore directly on his argument that subject matter had to be "psychologized." The abstractions and generalizations in subject matter represent efforts to order and make generalizations about aspects of experience. But, he argued, "geometry, geography, history never had any existence except in

[23] *Ibid.*, pp. 163–165.
[24] *Ibid.*, p. 165.
[25] *Ibid.*, p. 179.

somebody's consciousness." [26] Those who do the logical ordering must realize that the meanings in subject matter only become educational experiences when they are incorporated into the experience of a specific individual child and are put to work in his life. Educational psychology had to understand the processes by which abstract meanings could become functioning parts of the child's experience. This was to "psychologize" subject matter.

One aspect of the functioning of experience is "thinking." Dewey treated this specifically in *Studies in Logical Theory* (1903). There is obvious continuity between his approach to logic as the analysis of effective thought and his work in psychology.[27]

Dewey asserted that the whole significance of the evolutionary method in biology and social history is that it has caused us to see all aspects of life—organic structure, behavior, and institutions —as instruments for adjusting to particular environmental situations. The meaning of each can be understood only in terms of its role in meeting specific conditions. Psychology, which may be defined as the study of the natural history of the processes through which experience passes, is indispensable to logic, when logical theory is treated as an account of thinking as a mode of adaptation.

The occasion for thinking occurs when the flow of experience is disrupted. Thinking is a way of removing obstacles and reconstituting experience. "Thinking is a kind of activity which we perform at specific need, just as at other needs we engage in other sorts of activity; as converse with a friend; draw a plan for a house; take a walk; eat a dinner . . . etc." [28]

[26] Dewey, *Lectures for the First Course in Pedagogy*, No. 3, p. 4.

[27] In an enthusiastic review of the studies by William James—"The Chicago School," *Psychological Bulletin*, Vol. 1, No. 1 (January, 1904)— James acknowledges that Dewey's work in psychology led to the *Studies in Logic*. We have already seen how, in turn, James's organismic approach to psychology acted as a "ferment" in Dewey's thought. He pays tribute to James in the preface to the *Studies*.

Jane Dewey, in the biography of her father, says that Angell's functional psychology "played a part developing the logical theories of Dewey and in making a bridge from his logical to his moral theory." (Schilpp, *op. cit.*, p. 32.)

[28] Dewey, *Studies in Logical Theory*, pp. 2–3.

He maintained that there is relationship between the thinking of the plain man and the processes of thought involved in the more sophisticated methods of scientific inquiry. Both the plain man and the scientist are controlled by practical difficulties; both are attempting to solve problems; both then move on to other spheres of experience. There are no limits to the material of thought. Whether it be the plain man or the scientist:

"He knows no two fixed worlds—reality on one side and mere subjective ideas on the other. . . . He assumes uninterrupted, free and fluid passage from ordinary experience to abstract thinking, from thought to fact, from things to theories, and back again. Observation passes into development of hypothesis; deductive methods pass to use in description of the particular; inference passes into action with no sense of difficulty save those found in the particular task in question. The fundamental assumption is continuity in and of experience." [29]

The test of effective thinking is whether it leads to the resolution of difficulties. Ideas and processes of thinking are to be instruments for reconstructing the unity of experience. A study of the conditions when thinking is effective or ineffective is a major part of the subject matter of logic. Logical theory, for Dewey, was critical reflection upon thought itself. It included study of the genesis of thinking in human experience and the evolution of those modes of thought that have served or hindered man's growth. The Chicago decade was a period of creative activity when pivotal concepts in Dewey's instrumentalism were formed. From the rationale then emerging he tried to generate ideas for directing educational practice that could be tested in the Laboratory School.

[29] Ibid., p. 10.

# CHAPTER SEVEN

# The Laboratory School:
# Hypotheses and Conceptions

We have seen that the critical problem for Dewey was to understand the processes in the evolution of mind and experience. His goal was to formulate a unified theory that would avoid traditional dualisms. He became convinced that within the evolutionary frame of reference, broadly conceived, such a unity could be found.

The problem of growth of experience was significant at two levels: in the emergence of the civilized experience of mankind, and in the life of each child who would be born and come to maturity in the world. Education provided the setting for bringing these two together.

In his *Plan of Organization of the University Primary School* in 1896,[1] he stated his conception of the basic educational task in the opening paragraph:

"The ultimate problem of all education is to coordinate the psychological and social factors. The psychological requires that the individual have the free use of all his personal powers; and, therefore, must be so individually studied as to have the laws of his own structure regarded. The sociological factor requires that the individual become acquainted with the social environment in which he lives, in all its important relations, and be disciplined to regard these relationships in his own activities. The coordination demands, therefore, that the child be capable of expressing *himself*, but in such a way as to realize social ends."[2]

[1] John Dewey, *Plan of Organization of the University Primary School* (unpublished, University of Chicago, 1895 (?)).
[2] *Ibid.*, p. 1.

Dewey was prepared to found a school designed to work on the educational problem thus defined. Since it was conceived as a laboratory school, its specific practical problem needed to be defined. On various occasions, he presented its problems somewhat differently, but the definition that he provided in the ninth monograph is representative, comprehensive, and carefully considered:

"In its practical aspect, this laboratory problem takes the form of the construction of a course of study which harmonizes with the natural history of the growth of the child in capacity and experience. The question is the selection of the kind, variety, and due proportion of subjects, answering most definitely to the dominant needs and powers of a given period of growth, and of those modes of presentation that will cause the selected material to enter vitally into growth. . . . We cannot admit too freely the limits of our knowledge and the depth of our ignorance on these matters." [3]

It is clear from this statement that his definition of the educational problem is concerned with how to bring together two aspects of the growth of mind or experience.

On the one hand, there is the evolution of the experience of the human race. Gradually the skills of more effective thinking (or "minded behavior") emerged as man dealt with the challenges posed by nature and by complex social realities. Included in these skills are the products of mind: artifacts, inventions, and technical skills; institutions and values; and the whole range of knowledge and meanings about the world, accumulated in the various subject matters. This aspect is critically important. It includes the wealth of experience without which the development toward mature humanness is impossible; it contains the ingredients upon which growth of experience, individually or socially, is dependent. Scientists and scholars work arduously to organize and advance knowledge. Educators properly focus on the problem of how to organize it for instruction. But Dewey never ceased to point out a danger involved—the danger that the abstractions will remain, in Whitehead's term, "inert knowledge." While concentrating

[3] John Dewey, "The Psychology of the Elementary Curriculum," *The Elementary School Record*, Vol. 1, No. 9 (December, 1900), p. 222.

on how to organize, divide, and cover the content of knowledge, one may make the mistaken assumption that this, of itself, will ensure that learning will automatically be absorbed by the students.

This leads to the other side of the educational problem. Experience is existentially real only in the lives of specific human beings. *The* problem for education is how to organize the meanings, the insights, the habits of mind into a functional pattern that will eventually become a part of the life and character of each student. Dewey wrestled constantly with the question of how to relate the logical *and* the psychological; the curriculum *and* the child.[4] He never stopped opposing educational approaches that pitted the two elements against each other in an either/or fashion.

In turning from his psychological-philosophical theory to the practical problems of education, he had to come up with concepts and hypotheses that were more specifically pedagogical in nature. Two examples of these were: (1) his treatment of interest, and (2) his ideas about the stages of development in child growth. Before we examine how these fit into his plan, a side comment is in order.

It would be poor history to state that the ideas Dewey projected for his Laboratory School sprang, full-blown from his own head. Dewey was deeply immersed in the history of educational thought and in the vital educational movements of his time. He was stimulated and influenced by the ideas of others, and borrowed and adapted as he saw fit. He had great admiration for the early dialogues of Plato, and knew well the work of educational reformers such as Rousseau, Pestalozzi, Froebel, and Spencer. His involvement in the contemporary educational scene is illustrated by the fact that he was one of the sponsors of the Illinois Child Study Association. He was also on the Executive Board of the Herbart Society, and a participant in its publications and meetings. Charles De Garmo and the McMurry brothers, leaders in American Herbartianism, were brought into his department as visiting lecturers. The Herbartian movement was a dynamic force in educational thought of the time. Its leaders had

[4] See, for example, John Dewey, *The Child and the Curriculum* (Chicago, University of Chicago Press, 1902); and his rewrite of it in *Experience and Education* (New York, The Macmillan Co., 1938).

studied in Germany; they helped define the dynamic educational concerns of the period. They sponsored studies on child development and on the use of interest in educational practice. Major attention was given to the question of correlation: how to correlate studies with the stages of child growth, how to formulate unifying principles that would give direction to the sequence of studies, relate studies to each other, and provide greater internal coherence. The Herbartians were intrigued with various uses of the culture-epoch theory and with its role in building ethical character. Their forums for study were characterized by a generous spirit in which free debate with a minimum of rancor prevailed.[5]

It is a matter of record that ideas like these, prevalent at the time, were those to which Dewey directed attention. Herbartian features appear in the program of his school. However, because he insisted on searching for the educational implications of the psychological-philosophical theory he was constructing, Dewey worked out answers that had the stamp of his own distinctive orientation. A surface similarity in Dewey's terminology and that of the Herbartians far from indicates a neat congruence. He learned from them, but he was also discriminating in what he adopted or rejected.

The concept of interest is a case in point. A good deal of attention was being paid to the role of interest in educational reform movements. The study of the child had been presented in the writings of Rousseau, Pestalozzi, and Froebel. The Herbartians and G. Stanley Hall, with his efforts in child study, had given additional impetus to the study of the role of interest in educating children. Dewey took up the subject in some memorable articles but again insisted on his own interpretation.

In "The Psychological Aspect of the School Curriculum" [6] in 1897, Dewey stated that "the crying evil in instruction today is that the subject matter of the curriculum, both as a whole and in its various stages, is selected and determined on the objective or logical basis instead of on the psychological." Here he was

[5] See, for example, *Publications of the Herbart Society (1895–1900)* (Chicago, University of Chicago Press, 1908).

[6] John Dewey, "The Psychological Aspect of the School Curriculum," *Educational Review*, Vol. 13 (April, 1897), pp. 356–369.

concentrating his fire, in familiar fashion, on the overly formal, routine coverage of material.

Searching for an alternative that would be more sound psychologically, he wanted to employ a concept of interest and an organization of school work appropriate to several stages in the growth of children. Both of these ideas were current in Herbartian circles. In an article for the Herbartian Society in 1895, "Interest as Related to [the Training of the] Will," and in an amplification of it in *Interest and Effort in Education* [7] some years later, he set forth some of his major pedagogical principles.

In the 1897 article, Dewey made note of the current popularity of the role of interest in education; he criticized several theories of interest and then clarified his own view, which treated interest as related to will, effort, and discipline. He was critical, for example, of positions that state the issue in terms of interest *or* effort. This, he said, is characteristic of a faculty psychology approach, which argues that the will is trained when one is forced to exert an effort to do necessary life tasks; the use of interest merely serves to divert the child from the tasks of intellectual discipline. Equally futile is a compromise approach of trying to sugarcoat routine material with tricky motivational methods. They are deceptions and, as such, cannot lead to genuine results. He also found the Herbartian concept of interest faulty. The basic weakness in Herbartian psychology is its habit of giving ideas a kind of existence of their own. Interest emerges as a product of the action and reaction of ideas in the apperceptive mass. Interest is a feeling of pleasure that results at the juncture of a new idea and an old one.

These theories exemplified the "psychological fallacy" discussed in Chapter Six. Items like will, effort, and interest, which are products of psychological analysis, are transformed into independent entities. They are products of psychological analysis that are mistaken for the actual content of experience.

Dewey proceeded to give his own definition of interest, its

[7] John Dewey, "Interest as Related to [the Training of the] Will," Second supplement to the Herbart *Yearbook* for 1895 in *Publications of the National Herbart Society* (*1895-1900*) (Chicago, University of Chicago Press, 1908), pp. 5-34. Also, John Dewey, *Interest and Effort in Education* (Boston, Houghton Mifflin Co., 1913).

origins, and its applications in educational practice. Interest was described as arising from the activities of human organisms interacting with their world. The primitive condition of spontaneous activity is the source of *natural interest*. Men have needs to be met and are interested in moving in one direction rather than another. They seize on objects to satisfy needs. At this level, action is *direct* and immediate. There is no gap between ends and means. Dewey offered play as an illustration. In play, doing and enjoying come together and there is no demand for goals beyond them.

But not all ends have this direct and immediate quality. It is when men pursue goals requiring more elaborate means that interests of an *indirect* variety may appear. When a child aspires to play, on the piano, songs that intrigue him, but which are beyond his level of skill, he may develop an interest in the mastery of techniques that would have bored him at an earlier period.

Fundamentally, then, genuine interest, in its direct or indirect (long-range) aspect, occurs when a person has identified himself with a certain course of action and with the objects or skills that are necessary to achieve a desired goal.

Effort is related to interest. Effort, as we recall from "The Psychology of Effort," is evident in a tensional state; a state that arises from an awareness of opposition between an end or ideal desired and the present situation. Effort involves the transformation of the present state in order to realize a goal.

Ideals or ends grow out of the behavior of the person; they function as motives inducing activity or effort. But sometimes the self is in conflict between a choice of ends or ideals.

"The agent has two possible ends before him, one corresponding to one set of his active powers, and another to another set of impulses or habits. Thought, reflection is not focused, accordingly, in any single direction. The self has not yet found itself. . . . It is in process of tentative self-expression, first trying on one self and then another to see how they fit. The attainment of a single purpose or the defining of one final ideal indicates the self has found its unity of expression. . . . The ideal has become a motive. . . .

"Normal effort is precisely this self-realizing tendency of the ideal. . . . The empty or formal ideal is the end which is not suggested by, or does not grow out of, the agent's active powers. . . . whenever the ideal is really a projection or translation of self-expression, it must strive to assert itself. It must persist through obstacles, and endeavor to transform obstacles into means of its own realization." [8]

Persistence in thinking through the steps required to overcome obstacles, securing the behavior and skills needed to achieve goals, however remote and difficult, is the ground in which discipline and will are engendered. Genuine interest is involved when the self is in the process of realizing itself. Learning is marked by spontaneity and personal commitment.

This conception, he said, distinguishes his position from an approach to interest as indulgence of the whims of children. The child's natural interests are, in part, the result of the stage of his development, and in part, the result of his previous habits and environment. They relate to his important personal goals. But they are not to be taken as final or as a standard to define the ends of the teacher. A teacher who views them as such is an enemy of genuine interests.

"The significance of interest is in what *it leads to;* the new experiences it makes possible, the new powers it tends to form. The value of the teacher is precisely that with wider knowledge and experience he may see [children], not only as beginners but also in their . . . possibilities, that is, in their ideals." [9]

The broader human ideals or ends to which children may be directed are contained in subject matters—"in the knowledge of history, science, and the resources of art." [10] The art of teaching involves being sensitive to the child's interests and goals, and being imaginative in knowing how to direct him to the deeper meanings and insights of social ideals.

"This utilizing of interest and habits to make of it something fuller, wider, something more refined might be defined as the

[8] John Dewey, "Interest as Related to [the Training of the] Will," pp. 23–24.
[9] *Ibid.*, p. 30.
[10] *Ibid.*, p. 31.

teacher's whole duty. And the teacher who always utilizes interest will never merely indulge it. Interest in its reality is a moving thing, a thing of growth, of richer experience, and fuller power. Just how to use interest to secure growth in knowledge and efficiency is what defines the master teacher." [11]

He concluded by saying that this essay was not the place to answer the question of how to do it. He was busy at the time of its publication with details of the Elementary School where he would try to demonstrate the answer he had in mind.

It is not a common practice for educational theorists to establish schools in which to test their ideas. In Dewey's case, it meant that the analysis of psychological concepts consistent with the interactionist, organismic theory he was developing had to be translated into more specific ideas for pedagogical purposes.

Since he had argued that a critical educational problem of the time was to "psychologize subject matter" in a manner consistent with his concept of interest, we may follow what happened to this idea as it was worked out for school practice. His later essay, *Interest and Effort in Education*, includes elaborations that reflect the experience Dewey had in the Laboratory School. If the concepts of interest and activity were to be given a critical role toward the end of expanding and enriching mind and experience, clear distinctions had to be made as to when their employment would be *educative*.

As we have seen, his position by this time was based on the proposition that the fundamental condition which gives rise to human learning is the experience of the organism interacting with its world. His psychological and logical theory extended this to characterize intellectual or reflective behavior as special, more refined behavior within the act. Human beings have needs, ends, ideals, which they are seeking to realize; obstacles have to be overcome in order to reach the ends. The emergence of conceptual behavior in processes of thinking provides a better means for the individual to reconstruct, extend, and enrich experience. This was the alternative to the dualistic view of mental life as the special property of a separate, abstract mind. Thinking is described as growing out of concrete, specific experience itself;

[11] *Ibid.*

its abstractions become tools for ordering things and coping with the world. Abstract ideas also change the world, and hence new problems are presented with which thinking then has to come to terms. To equip human beings with the intellectual tools and meanings that have emerged in civilized experience *so that these tools and meanings will be genuinely incorporated into the self and behavior* of each individual was the great task of education.

It was from this frame of reference that Dewey sought to make his discriminations about the use of interest and activity, to define when they were justified educationally, and to create a scheme for incorporating them into a school program.

In the 1913 revision of his earlier essay on interest, Dewey said that the idea of "self-activity" had become by then a popular educational ideal—so popular that it had deteriorated to a barren cliché with little observable relation to practice. To recover it from this familiar fate, he had defined it more sharply as "all the doings that involve growth of power—especially of power to realize the *meaning* of what is done." [12] The essence of an educative activity or experience is not just *doing* or engaging in any activity. An experience is educative only when it leads to the seeing of new meanings about the world or self, which are then incorporated so as to help one live more effectively.

This rules out actions performed under coercion, for these have no personal significance for the person coerced. It excludes random reactions or mere excitations and mere mechanical or routine performance, for these fail to carry into a broadening of experience. Unfortunately, Dewey said, "self-activity" is often mistaken for freedom from restraint and license to do as one pleases.

The kinds of interest and activity that may be classified as truly educative vary with the age of students, with their native endowments, and with their prior experiences and social opportunities. In spite of the variables that these factors introduce, it is possible to catalog them to some extent. Dewey outlined three levels of interest and activity. The levels correspond roughly to stages in the growth of children; and (as we shall see) to stages in the evolution of civilized experience. They correspond to a

[12] John Dewey, *Interest and Effort in Education* (Boston, Houghton Mifflin Co., 1913), p. 66.

pivotal idea he used for organizing work in the Laboratory School.[13]

1. For the infant and the preschool child the first learnings involve proper use of the organs of sense—the eye, ear, hands, etc.—and physical coordinations. The sensory-motor aspects are involved first, but even at this stage they are not sharply marked off from mental life. The child finds out that there are certain consequences that derive from coordinating eye movements and reaching out with the hands. He can reach, touch, and feel objects which then have come within the range of his experience. The joy that comes to the child when he extends his range of control during the first two years is familiar to every parent.

The tendency to make an abrupt break with the sensory-motor aspects when the child entered school was part of a long tradition, which conceived of education in purely intellectual terms as mind training. Dewey, who argued for the continuity of the intellectual with physical and sensory aspects, regarded this break as incorrect pedagogy.

Other movements in educational history had also recognized this mistake and had introduced materials for self-expression, but they were inadequate because they stemmed from inadequate psychologies. The formal, verbal approach had been challenged by the object lessons of the followers of Pestalozzi. But in the latter the assumption was that the senses were gates to the mind, and that the sheer presentation of sensory objects led to knowledge. Dewey, on the other hand, maintained that sound and touch are not important in their mere reception but as they are coordinated to help secure intelligent control.

Froebel tried reform by introducing play and constructive, manipulative activities. He sensed that bodily activities were related to growth of mind. The methods were spoiled, however, by their relation to a romantic spirituality, which saw various forms of play as symbolic aspects of the unfolding of the Absolute. This led to rigid and artificial techniques in arrangement of materials to accord with supposed principles of symbolism.

2. A second and higher form of activity follows the stage of direct sensory and motor behavior of the infant. As the child

[13] *Ibid.*, pp. 65–88, *et passim.*

grows, the range and uses of materials that he encounters increase. He can extend his control, for example, by the use of tools. A child can use a saw, or a needle and thread to attain ends not within the reach of an infant; such tools require mastery of new skills and coordinations. This, in turn, makes possible new levels of development. *"The discovery and use of extra-organic tools has made possible, both in the history of the race and of the individual, complicated activities of a long duration."* [14] The combination of more remote, delayed goals together with the need to develop skills to utilize more complicated tools and techniques leads to the increased use and development of intelligence. In the life of children, simple play is transformed into more elaborate games and work. In games, rules must be mastered. When a child shifts from "playing boat" to making one, he must bring to bear new intellectual skills needed to regulate a series of acts. Play thus gives way to work, which "covers all forms of expression and construction with tools and materials, all forms of artistic and manual activity so far as they involve the conscious or thoughtful endeavor to achieve an end." [15] Later they include, for example, the sequence of acts required to execute scientific experiments. Creative work is thus distinguished from drudgery in which activities are performed in the absence of personal, intrinsic motivation.

3. The transition to the intellectual brings us to a third level. The intellectual interest in discovering new things, in wrestling with and examining ideas, may become an interest in itself—and will normally take place, Dewey held, if interest in learning is not killed at earlier stages.

"Planning ahead, taking notice of what happens, relating this to what is attempted, are part of all intelligent or purposeful activities. It is the business of education to see that the conditions of expression of the practical interests are such as to encourage the developing of these intellectual phases of an activity, and thereby evoke a gradual transition to the theoretical type." [16]

[14] *Ibid.*, pp. 75–76.
[15] *Ibid.*, p. 81.
[16] *Ibid.*, pp. 82–83.

When work with tools, in gardening and cooking, for instance, is carried out under intelligent direction, the skilled teacher will see opportunities to shift interest from mere practical concerns to experimentation for the sake of discovery. When interest is occupied with inquiry and discovery, the intellectual level has been achieved.

Dewey made this elaborate analysis of interest, effort, and activity to underscore two points for educational theory: (1) To show that the intellectual is not an internal matter of an abstract mind, but grows out of organic and personal doing, acting, and striving, and (2) to attack the idea of subject matter as external, "as something complete in its ready-made and fixed separateness," [17] that is to be learned by simple presentation. In his conception, the facts and truths of geography, history, and science are seen as means and ends for the intelligent development of experience.

He warned that the doctrine of interest offered no easy short cuts for education. Nor should elaborate means be used to secure "interested children" as an end in itself. Interest, like happiness, he said, is best attained when least consciously pursued. The job of educators is to provide the materials, the ideas, and programs that will engage children in exploring and inquiring. If we can discover the urgent needs, habits, and powers and

"if we can supply an environment of materials, appliances and resources—physical, social, and intellectual—to direct their adequate operation, we shall not have to think about interest. It will take care of itself. . . . The problem of educators, teachers, parents, the state, is to provide the environment that induces educative or developing activities, and where these are found the one thing needful in education is secured." [18]

This analysis of activity, interest, and thinking had important bearings for the hypotheses used in the school and for the later progressive educational movement. We shall be referring to these as the story unfolds.

[17] *Ibid.*, p. 94.
[18] *Ibid.*, p. 96.

One point may be underscored here. Behind the essays on interest there were ideas much more basic to the Deweyan philosophy than the topic of interest itself. A fundamental conception of the nature of knowledge and its origin was involved. In the essay, Dewey concentrated on the emergence of successively higher levels of interest, effort, and thought processes in the life of children. The idea of this kind of progression was rooted in his evolutionary-organic theory—that these levels correspond roughly to critical stages in the development of civilized experience in general.

Primitive life was characterized by more direct, impulsive activities with sensory and motor behavior predominant. Pursuit of remote, postponed ends was not highly developed.

The introduction of new materials, such as bronze and iron, and the invention of more elaborate techniques and tools opened new possibilities of experience and required more complex human efforts. These were eventually accompanied by more elaborate institutions and geographical explorations, all of which contributed to the refining of intellectual life. The drive for knowledge eventually produced the sciences, where inquiry and learning facilitated greater control and became ends in themselves.

Again this idea was not unique with Dewey. It was part of the general interest in evolutionary theory on the Chicago campus. George Mead, for example, was teaching a course on "The Philosophy of Evolution." A detailed reflection of the idea can also be found in the influential work of Dewey's sociologist colleague W. I. Thomas, *Source Book for Social Origins*. Thomas said that the study of savage and prehistoric man is one of the most fascinating and important of the social sciences. He considered that, as well as being delightful, such studies had vital, though unrealized, relation to historical, sociological, and pedagogical studies.[19]

Thomas suggested a concept to which all activity could be related—the concept of *control*. Control, he said is the object of all purposeful activity. The whole design of nature is to maintain life. Individual and social activity at its basic level is concerned with securing nourishment and producing offspring—food and

[19] William Isaac Thomas, *Source Book for Social Origins* (Chicago, University of Chicago Press, 1909), p. vii.

reproduction are the primal necessities. *Control* can be applied to stages of organic and social development.

The animal, because of its power of motion, has superior control over plant life. It can go after food rather than merely wait for it. This helps explain the organs of sense and prehension. In man, control is extended by his use of animals, by means of mechanical transportation, and the employment of weapons and tools. Gregarious tendencies lead to social life, which makes man's existence more secure through cooperation. Language, a product of society, introduces a critical difference in increasing control, because through it knowledge, tradition, ideals, etc., are transmitted and increased. Social institutions arise which bring order within societies and protect against enemies from without. Finally,

". . . the human mind is pre-eminently the organ of manipulation of adjustment, of control. It operates through what we call knowledge. This in turn is based on memory and the ability to compare a present situation with similar situations in the past and to revise our judgments and actions in view of the past experience. By this means the world at large is controlled more successfully as time goes on. Knowledge thus becomes the great force in control, and those societies are most successful and prosperous in which the knowledge is most disseminated, most reliable, most intensive. This is the sense in which knowledge is power." [20]

This sociological-historical point of view obviously fitted Dewey's organic psychological-logical theory as glove to hand. Thomas was one of Dewey's consultants for the Laboratory School. The whole rationale of the curriculum was centered around themes in this orientation. Dewey's most arduous effort in education was to effect a unity between the development of the mind of the child and of the human mind at large as it was represented in the subject matter. With the ideas just presented, the principle seemed to have been found.

[20] *Ibid.*, pp. 15–16.

CHAPTER EIGHT

# The Sequence of Child Growth and the Educational Program

The existence of an actual school posed the question of what to do in it. The creation of a psychological-philosophical theory that would contain a unified image of man and that would agree with the findings of evolutionary science had been emerging in Dewey's work in something like the organic sense of which he spoke. His own children were born and were growing up in the years when he was preparing his educational program. He and Mrs. Dewey had developed an intense interest in education. We know that Mrs. Dewey had a quick intelligence and shared her husband's interest in philosophy. In addition, her keen concern with social questions was responsible, in part, for the shift in Dewey's interest from the purely intellectual activities of his early Hegelian period to problems of social significance. It is fair to conjecture that while Dewey and Mead were engaged in the intensely exciting effort to map out new theoretical ground, the question of what the new ideas might mean for a more vital education for children was a matter of lively discussion at home as well as on campus.[1] In any case, by the time the school opened in 1896, Dewey had conceived the outlines of a rationale from which the school's program would take its lead in the eight years of his leadership. As he once stated in a letter to Harper, Dewey saw it as his own responsibility to supervise "the selection of the subject matter for the school and [to insure] the proper correlations; and . . . to set forth the general philosophy or general theory of its

[1] Paul A. Schilpp, ed., *The Philosophy of John Dewey* (New York, The Tudor Publishing Co., 1951), see Jane M. Dewey, "Biography of John Dewey," pp. 24–27.

movement." [2] The school's staff was given a great deal of freedom in working out the details and in testing ideas.[3]

His adherence to the organic-evolutionary theory had led to his break with major philosophic traditions. Similarly, he found major aspects of traditional educational practice unsound because of their inadequate psychological foundations. Educational reformers, sensing the need for revision, had introduced interesting innovations in content and method. Dewey was attracted by many of these, but ruled out piecemeal borrowing. He had to formulate an educational program that would be an expression of his philosophy. In the latter, he was trying to bring concepts from the sciences and the humanities into a new unity. An educational counterpart would require an equally imaginative and ingenious design.

One plan within his general design—to bring together the experience of the individual person and social experience as represented in civilization, in a way that would lead to the enrichment of both—was to construct a course of study that would harmonize with the growth of the child, in terms of his capacities and experiences. The kind of analysis found in the essays on interest and activity provided the conceptual framework for three stages of child growth. Each stage was to be accompanied by a different emphasis in subject matter. Those teaching in the Laboratory School would conceive of the mind as

". . . a growing affair, and hence as essentially changing, presenting distinctive phases of capacity and interests at different periods. These are all one and the same in the sense of continuity of life, but all different in that each has its own distinctive claims and offices. 'First the blade, then the ear, and then the full corn in the ear.' " [4]

Approximate age ranges were assigned to these stages with the warning that they were not to be adhered to in a rigid sense (there were, for example, periods of transition between the stages): Stage

[2] John Dewey, Letters to William Rainey Harper, The President's Papers, University of Chicago (December, 1897).

[3] Schilpp, *op. cit.*, p. 28.

[4] John Dewey, "The Psychology of the Elementary Curriculum," *The Elementary School Record*, Vol. 1, No. 9 (December, 1900), p. 225.

I, ages 4 to 8 or 8½; Stage II, ages 8½ to 10½ or 11; Stage III, ages 11 to 14 or 15. The characteristics of these stages may be found in the literature of the school.

As the school grew, the children were divided into ten groups that corresponded roughly to the ages indicated below. Exceptions in grading for certain students were determined by the judgments of the staff. (The age of children in each group may be remembered by adding three to the number of the group.)

|  | Groups | Age |
|---|---|---|
| First stage | I | 4 |
|  | II | 5 |
|  | III | 6 |
| Transition | IV | 7 |
|  | V | 8 |
| Second stage | VI | 9 |
|  | VII | 10 |
| Transition | VIII | 11 |
|  | IX | 12 |
| Beginning of Secondary | X | 13 |
|  | XI | 14–15 |

## STAGE I

In the first stage, the child has direct personal and social interests; there is a direct relation between impulses, ideas, and action. He has a strong need to express himself in motor and expressive activities, in manipulation, investigation, and oral communication. Although the child is interested in exploring his world with all his sensory equipment, longer-range goals requiring delayed achievement and mastery of technical skills were not held to be characteristic of this stage. Such activities as play, games, occupations, storytelling, and informal conversations were felt to be appropriate for this age group. These gave the child a growing command of methods of inquiry and experimental action at an elementary level.

Dewey described, in the school's first year, several emphases in the program for four- to six-year-olds.[5]

1. The goal was to grade the work according to the ability of individual pupils rather than to place children rigidly according to grade. Children varying in age by two or three years were placed together in situations that would involve older children reading and working with younger ones. As children were not required to spend time reciting to a teacher, it was hoped that the chance to communicate freely with each other about experiences would lead to more stimulating intellectual interchange. It was also assumed that children teaching each other constituted a valuable and natural resource that should be utilized. This technique was employed throughout the school.

2. So that studies would not be considered as isolated factors that were irrelevant to the experience of the child during its early years, they were treated as "factors in child-life." Nature study, manual training, and sewing, for example, were considered to be continuous with activities that the child has outside the school. The more formal studies were to be grouped around kinds of activities familiar to the child and, as far as possible, were to evolve from them. Initiation to number work, for example, grew out of the measuring and weighing needed in these activities or occupations.

## STAGE II

In the second period, from eight or nine to eleven or twelve, the child developed a need to secure clearer, more long-range goals. The new objectives required mastery of more complex skills.

In Dewey's school, several consequences for the educational program resulted from his ideas about children's development in this second stage. In terms of the content of study, the general unity of experience of the first stage began to move toward differentiated studies. Dewey's view was that just as mankind had

[5] John Dewey, "A Pedagogical Experiment," *Kindergarten Magazine*, Vol. 8 (June, 1896), pp. 739-741.

been forced to develop more specialized methods of thought and action in order to achieve desired ends, so the maturing child with deeper interests emerging needed to increase his powers by learning more disciplined and refined skills.

The subject matter was planned to help build such attitudes. One objective was to help children see that as men in history had faced more complex challenges, they had developed more effective social cooperation and social institutions. This principle affected the approach to history and science. Instead of studying history chronologically, children studied units that illustrated intellectual or technical advances that gave men added control over their environment. Features in colonial American history, for example, seemed appropriate for this purpose. Study centered around events in the exploration of Chicago and the Mississippi Valley, and of Virginia, New England, and New York. Children were led to see how people had reacted when confronting new geographical, climatic, and social situations; how the total environment presented both obstacles and new sources of help. The colonists needed moral qualities of patience and courage. They experienced different consequences depending on the levels of ingenuity, insight, and judgment they brought to situations. The pedagogical principle was to organize study around pivotal concepts rather than just "covering ground" or "going over" abstract material. The method maintained continuity with the motor-expressive features of the first period. Instead of the classroom being a bare place with rows of seats facing a teacher, a blackboard, and an American flag, new kinds of materials were introduced—tools, household utensils, foods, etc.— that applied to the modes of living of the explorers and colonists under study. Children could reproduce and get "the feel" of conditions they discussed rather than just talk about historic information. This was supplementd by the innovation of dramatic reenactments. Through this device, children took over the roles of people in history as they confronted problems presented by the teacher or other children. Role playing in problematic situations was one method used to move educational experiences to a level of more active involvement.[6]

[6] George H. Mead's analyses of the educative value of play, and the nature of role playing and thinking in the act are evident in such features.

In science, the same principles prevailed: (1) using the concept of control—or adaptation of means to ends—and (2) beginning the differentiation of subject matter, this time dividing science into its geographical and experimental aspects. Yet work in science was related to historical studies. The American colonists had confronted the challenges of a new natural environment. The children studied the physiographical patterns of mountains, rivers, plains, flora, and fauna of each colonial area. They were taken on field excursions and were given materials to reproduce situations from past history. As regards the experimental aspect of science, children were in a transition stage between the early level, when they explored materials directly, and the later secondary stage when the intellectual interest in discovering facts and verifying principles would emerge. In this middle period, more practical interests still prevailed, so the stress was on applied science. The rather crude methods used by the colonists to meet the basic needs of living were analyzed to illustrate elementary principles of chemistry and physics. The children, by engaging in the processes of bleaching, dyeing, soapmaking and candlemaking, were introduced to the chemical properties of oils, fats, acids, etc. The use and transfer of energy in spinning wheels and looms were studies, as were the mechanical principles involved in locks and scales, for example. Such efforts showed a concern for the problem of correlating intellectual understanding with activities involved in producing basic necessities.

An additional responsibility was assigned to this second stage: systematic teaching of the three R's. Their inclusion follows from the rationale that had been developed. The pursuit of more complex ends, goals, and interests required mastery of higher level skills. This had been true for man in general, and was applied to the child's learning of the three R's. They were accorded great respect.

"These subjects are social in a double sense. They represent the tools which society has evolved in the past as the instruments of its intellectual pursuits. They represent the keys which will

---

See, for example, George H. Mead, "The Relation of Play to Education," *University Record*, Vol. 1, No. 8 (May, 1896), pp. 141-145.

unlock to the child the wealth of social capital which lies beyond the possible range of his limited individual experience." [7]

Dewey criticized the teaching of the three R's in traditional education because it was done so inefficiently, with wasted time and little success. He argued that from 60 to 80 per cent of the time in elementary schools was devoted to drill, with results that were widely deplored. This meant that much of the content of elementary education was trivial. Time was given to meaningless and ineffective drill that should have been used to introduce more substantial intellectual content, as required by the expansion of knowledge.

Having defined the problem of the three R's in these terms, he offered some hypotheses for remedying it. So that waste might be avoided, two conditions must be provided:

"(1) The need that the child shall have in his own personal and vital experience a varied background of contact and acquaintance with realities, social and physical. This is necessary to prevent symbols from becoming a purely second-hand and conventional substitute for reality. (2) The need that the more ordinary, direct and personal experience of the child shall furnish problems, motives, and interests that necessitate recourse to books for their solution, satisfaction, and pursuit. Otherwise, the child approaches the book without intellectual hunger, without alertness, without a questioning attitude. . . ." [8]

In terms of program, the school was to introduce the use of direct observation, through activities requiring construction and experimentation instead of the traditional recitation. The objective was to present these in such a manner and sequence that the child would feel the need to gain command of the traditional tools. He could not operate effectively without being able to read, write, figure, and use his hands with better skill. This, it was hoped, would make the use of the three R's more intellectual than mechanical, and the amount of time spent in drill could be reduced. Dewey did recommend, however, that periodic concentra-

[7] John Dewey, *The School and Society*, revised ed. (Chicago, University of Chicago Press, 1923), p. 104.
[8] *Ibid.*, pp. 104–105.

tion in studying the skills should be alternated with substantial study. This could happen within a given year or semester; also, greater attention to skills would be given in certain stages of the child's development, such as in this second period. This would be an alternative to taking logically organized knowledge and slicing it in equal pieces throughout the entire elementary and secondary program, with long periods of isolated drill offered parallel to it.

## STAGE III

The third period of the elementary school was the threshold to secondary education. By this time, the child would have had a range of experience with materials and activities that opened his eyes to the possibilities and joys of learning about his world. He would have attained some sense of the origin of learning and its role in human affairs. He would understand that school study dealt with matters of significance, with relation to things he could see in his home and neighborhood and also to the larger events beyond. He would have made a good beginning at mastering the tools of thought and methods of inquiry and activity that would enable him to begin more specialized study for technical and intellectual ends.

At the secondary level, his interest would take on the adult form, and he would be ready for systematic work in fields such as geography, chemistry, physics, history, mathematics, literature. It was hoped that youth would then see the indispensable value that classified, organized knowledge has in mature investigations; interest would be in inquiry itself, and the motivation to acquire advanced intellectual means would have been established.

Later, we shall examine, in more detail, Dewey's ideas about secondary education. At this point it may be noted simply that the school, in the fall of 1903, had just taken on a secondary program that might have been integrated with elementary work. Up to that time, energy and attention had been concentrated on the lower levels, and only a few students in the twelve to fifteen age bracket were enrolled. In records on the school, remarks about the program for older children are characteristically brief and tentative. Several sentences in *School and Society* (1900) are typical:

"While the school has a number of children who are in this period (12–15), the school has not, of course, been in existence long enough so that any typical inferences can be safely drawn. There certainly seems to be reason to hope, however, that with the consciousness of difficulties, needs, and resources gained in the experience of the last five years, children can be brought to and through this period without sacrifice of thoroughness, mental discipline, or command of technical tools of learning, and with a positive enlargement of life, and a wider, freer, and more open outlook upon it." [9]

We have here the theoretical germ for work in secondary education. We may only guess as to how Dewey would have spoken if he had worked in the field another ten years.

Problems of the lower schools occupied Dewey's attention, but his goal was a rationale that would provide a unity of conception from the kindergarten through the university. He did make reference to higher education as the stage of advanced specialization and generalization; *specialization* to pursue study or training for a life work or profession; *generalization*, in the sense of seeking to clarify fundamental principles which underly all the various studies and which hold them together.[10]

The concept of developmental stages was very much in the air at the time. For example, G. Stanley Hall, in a 1901 address to the National Council of Education, spoke on the topic "The Ideal School Based on Child Study." He stated that his studies led him to the conviction that the stage from eight or nine to puberty is the period especially suited for "drill, habituation, and mechanism"—the period when teachers should seek to establish the fundamentals of reading, writing, and arithmetic. "Accuracy, which, when out of season is fraught with so many dangers for mind and body, is now in order." [11] This conviction was based on his belief that, in this stage, there is a decreased rate of physical growth, but a striking increase in vitality, activity, and power to

[9] *Ibid.*, p. 108.
[10] John Dewey, *Lectures for the First Course in Pedagogy*, No. 5, p. 7.
[11] G. Stanley Hall, "The Ideal School" in National Education Association *Proceedings and Addresses* (Washington, D.C., 1901) pp. 474–488. See also, for Hall's contributions to educational theory, Vivian T. Thayer, *Formative Ideas in American Education* (New York, Dodd, Mead and Co., 1965), Ch. 9.

resist disease—a stage, Hall believed, that corresponded to the period of race history above the simian but before the historic period. Dewey was working with a similar assumption about the kind of educational readiness that was characteristic of children in this age group. He did not adopt Hall's theory that natural instincts determined the characteristics of each stage and that these instincts dovetailed neatly with stages in social experience.

Dewey and his staff did not give a systematic account of the rationale for their concept of stages of development. Rather than borrowing *in toto* a frame of reference from other contemporary theorists, such as Hall or the Herbartians, they preferred to formulate generalizations on the basis of their own experiences with children in the Laboratory School. Thus one finds phrases such as "The practical experience of the School so far had demonstrated that there were certain stages in child growth," or "As a result of such a critical interpretation of the practices of the School from the point of view of both the teacher and the learner, a clearly defined principle of mental growth emerged which was of primary importance in understanding the needs of the growing child and in planning a program which would answer to these needs." [12]

## LEVELS OF DEVELOPMENT AND CULTURE-EPOCH THEORY

Darwinism had sparked a revival in the culture-epoch notion. G. Stanley Hall popularized the idea with his thesis of the "general psychonomic law," which states that ontogeny recapitulates phylogeny: that the stages of development of the individual roughly corresponded to stages through which the race had evolved from savagery to civilization. Hall's extensive psychological studies of child development were related to his pedagogical theory. [13]

The Herbartians, with their interest in child development and

[12] Katherine C. Mayhew and Anna C. Edwards, *The Dewey School* (New York, Appleton-Century-Crofts, 1936), pp. 52–53. See also Dewey's statement on the psychological order of development in "The University Elementary School, General Outline of Scheme of Work," *University Record* (December 30, 1898).

[13] For an account of Hall's position and his influence on the burgeoning child-study movement, see Lawrence Cremin, *The Transformation of the School* (New York, Alfred A. Knopf, 1961), pp. 101–105.

their search for unifying principles in education, had come up with new interpretations of the culture-epoch theory.[14] At first glance, Dewey's concept of the parallel ways in which knowledge and stages of thinking develop both in the child and in race experience appears to exemplify the idea. A closer look reveals that this is another instance where Dewey was stimulated by the Herbartians but recast their proposals in terms of his own theory. The *First Yearbook* of the Herbart Society (1895) [15] contained a number of articles on the culture-epoch topic, including a comprehensive view of a variety of interpretations by Professor C. C. Van Liew. This is, of course, the period in which Dewey was clarifying details for his own school. He was stimulated to write a reply—"Interpretation of the Culture-Epoch Theory" [16]—in which he focused on what consequences were expected to follow for educational work. Van Liew's article had maintained that: (1) a principle is needed to give correspondence between the child and subject matter, (2) the culture-epoch theory supplies such a principle, and (3) therefore, the cultural products of each epoch will contain material that will appeal most to the child passing through the corresponding stage in his own development.

Dewey pointed out that this theory assumed an exact parallelism between race history and child development, but that no evidence for such an *exact* parallel existed. He argued that this meant that attempts first to study epochs in the history of the race and then to transfer to the child what is found is unjustifiable. Educators, he said, must begin by discovering the psychological stages in children. They must first investigate the child. Their knowledge of epochs in man's history may then be used to raise certain questions for pedagogical purposes.

[14] See, for example, chapters in the *First Yearbook* of the Herbart Society, Charles A. McMurry, ed., *Publications of the National Herbart Society* (*1895–1900*) (Chicago, University of Chicago Press, 1908), especially C. C. Van Liew, "The Educational Theory of the Culture Epochs," Vol. 1 (1895), pp. 85 ff.

[15] *Ibid.*

[16] John Dewey, "Interpretation of the Culture-Epoch Theory," *Second Yearbook*, Charles McMurry, ed., *op. cit.*, pp. 89–95, first published in the *Public School Journal*, Vol. 15 (January, 1896), pp. 233–236. The former version is used here.

"Since this epoch was passed through by the race, it is possible we shall find its correlate in the child himself. All the racial side can do is to suggest questions. . . . Let us then be on the lookout for it. Do we find it? But the criterion must come back in all cases to the child himself." [17]

Such an approach will also remind us that stages that once dominated man's life, such as hunting or nomadic phases, have given way to higher, more complex levels. To devote a year of schooling to hunting or pastoral activities in an urban, industrial age is ridiculous.

He criticized, too, the suggestions to use literature as the basis for organizing studies. Ziller's school in Leipzig, for instance, had been a notable proponent of such a theory of concentration. Each of the eight years of the Volksschule was arranged around a literary center: (1) epic, folklore stories, (2) *Robinson Crusoe*, (3) history of the patriarchs, (4) times of the judges, (5) times of the kings in Israel, (6) the life of Jesus, (7) history of the Apostles, and (8) history of the Reformation and catechism. Dewey said this made literature an artificial entity, divorced from the total social context. It became part of a mystique, designed to build moral character. He saw value in literature, story, and myth, to the degree that children are led to see the natural facts and social conditions reflected in them, but he held that misuse was the result when literary works were considered to provide a kind of direct spiritual baptism into ancient moral values.

In Dewey's analysis and interpretation of the culture-epoch idea, we encounter again his characteristic way of defining the problem of relating the child and the curriculum. He *was* in "revolt against formalism" [18] in his general philosophy and in his educational theory. The problem was how to keep knowledge alive in individual learners. He wrestled endlessly to work out ideas in education that would be consistent with the analysis he had made of the evolution of levels of activity, interest, and thought. The job of educators was to introduce children to the insights, meanings, and methods of thought represented in the

[17] *Ibid.*, p. 91.
[18] See Morton White, *Social Thought in America: The Revolt against Formalism* (Boston, The Beacon Press, 1957).

content and discipline of the subject matter. But his concept of the evolution of mind and experience ruled out the approach of starting with the end product of adult scholars, slicing it up, and presenting it to immature minds. This would be to violate the continuity of experience of the child; it would divorce knowledge itself from the processes that led to it. In the education of human beings, history, science, and literature become subject matters that make a difference in experience only as they

". . . become a part of what an individual reports, expresses, lives. . . . [The] subject is a mode of personal experience not simply an ordered collection of facts and principles, the curriculum as a whole, and every study in detail, has a psychological side whose neglect and denial lead to confusion in pedagogic theory; and in educational practice to the dead following of historic precedent and routine, or else to the substitution of the abstract and the formal for the vital and personal." [19]

This meant that he gave a qualified assent to Dr. W. T. Harris' definition of a school subject as

". . . the gathering up and arranging of the facts and principles relating to some typical aspect of social life, or which affords a fundamental need in maintaining that social life; that the standard for adapting and placing a study is the worth which it has in adapting the pupil to the needs of the civilization into which he is born." [20]

This, he held, is a useful definition of the logical aspect of subject matter, but it ignores the psychological.

"From the psychological standpoint we are concerned with the study as a mode or form of living individual experience. Geography is not only a set of facts and principles which may be classified and discussed by themselves, *it is also a way in which some actual individual feels and thinks the world*. It must be the latter before it can be the former. . . . Only when the individual has passed through a certain amount of experience, which he vitally realizes on his own account, is he prepared to take the

[19] Dewey, "The Psychological Aspect of the School Curriculum," pp. 368–369.
[20] *Ibid.*, p. 359.

objective and logical point of view, capable of standing off and analyzing the facts and principles involved.

"Now the primary concern in education is beyond question with the subject as a special mode of personal experience, rather than with the subject as a body of wrought out facts and scientifically related principles." [21]

The import of this for educators, he said, is that the first questions in approaching a study are: What is the subject as a form of living, immediate experience? What is the interest in or end of that experience? How does it function to give other experiences richness of meaning? These questions must be asked with reference both to all children and to each specific child—the individual of a certain age, ability, and background.

The genuine course of procedure may be stated as follows:

"We have first to fix attention upon the child to find out what kind of experience is appropriate to him at the particular period selected; to discover, if possible, what it is that constitutes the special feature of the child's experience at this time; and why it is that his experience takes this form rather than another. This means that we observe in detail what experiences have most meaning and value to him, and what attitude he assumes toward them. We search for the point, or focus, of interest in these experiences. We ask where they get their hold upon him and how they make their appeal to him. We endeavor by observation and reflection to see what tastes and powers of the child are active in securing these experiences. We ask what habits are being formed; what ends and aims are being proposed. We inquire what the stimuli are and what responses the child is making. We ask what impulses are struggling for expression; in what characteristic ways they find an outlet; and what results inure the child through their manifestation. . . . Once more, these phenomena of interest are not final. They do not say to the teacher: We are your final end, and all your energies are to be devoted to cultivating us just as we are. None the less, they are indices and instruments; they are the only clews which the instructor can possibly have to what experiences are such really, and not simply in name. They reveal the general standpoint from which any subject must be presented

[21] *Ibid.*, p. 361. (My italics.)

in order to lay hold on the child. The problem of the teacher is to read the superficial manifestations over into their underlying sources. Even 'bad' interests, like that of destruction, are the signs of some inner power which must be discovered and utilized.

"In the second place, in saying that these psychical phenomena afford opportunities, give clews, and furnish leverages, we are virtually saying that they set problems. They need to be interpreted. They have the value of signs, and, like all signs, must be interpreted into the realities for which they stand. Now it is the province of the subject-matter on its logical and objective side to help us in this work of translation. We see the meaning of the beginning through reading it in terms of its outcome; of the crude in terms of the mature." [22]

Dewey accused other theorists of being confused about the real task of educators. Their confusion was due to their failure to see clearly the psychological side—the problem of "psychologizing" subject matter in order to introduce it into the student's experience. It is fair, however, to ask whether Dewey's effort to resolve the psychological-logical dualism in education led to the reduction or to the increase of confusion. We shall turn shortly to an examination of the specific plan he developed in his school to deal with the problem. Another question, however, is, What was the effect on progressive educators who followed his lead?

On the one hand, he stressed, over and over again, the pedagogical importance of honoring the interests, experience, and needs of children—more specifically, the concrete interests of *each* child. On the other hand, he warned against treating these interests as ends in themselves and indulging them. The direction of school work was to lead toward the systematic study of differentiated subject matter at the secondary level and beyond. He also stressed that in the early years of schooling the expressive-motor activities of the child were keys to developing sound habits of investigation and learning. The movement toward intellectual procedures should come later. In speculating on the consequences for the progressive movement, we must consider an historical fact about the Dewey school. Most of the energy, during the eight years of its existence, was channeled into elaborating the

[22] *Ibid.*, pp. 364-366.

theory and program for the early levels—the stages when the stress was to be (1) on connecting school with immediate interests and activities in the child's home and neighborhood, and (2) on beginning with direct, overt motor behavior. The cardinal sin charged against traditional education was the method of reciting abstract verbal material. The bad classroom was one where passive, rote learning went on under the coercion of an authoritarian taskmaster. Dewey himself was arguing that mind as represented in subject matter was to share equal honors with the mind of the child. The thrust of the "new education," however, tended to cast logically organized subject matter in the role of villain. Dewey's insistence on the need to start with the child's interests tended to get the lion's share of attention, even though he quickly followed with the admonition that this should lead into transitions to the intellectual emphases he advocated for secondary education. Historically, the direct, active features of the lower grades tended to be identified as the distinguishing marks of progressive education.

*Part* II

# CURRICULUM AND METHODOLOGY IN THE LABORATORY SCHOOL

# CHAPTER NINE

# *The Occupations:*
# *In Theory and Practice*

Some thirty years after Dewey left the school, he reflected again on its theory and practice in "The Theory of the Chicago Experiment." [1] He said that conceptions for work in the school originated in his philosophical and psychological work rather than in educational experience or precedent. This meant that answers to practical questions—What should be taught? How? In what order?—had to be answered in terms of the general theory. He referred to his original 1895 *Plan of Organization* to remind us how it defined *the* problem of education:

". . . the harmonizing of individual traits with social ends and values. Education is a difficult process . . . precisely because it is so extremely difficult to achieve an effective coordination of the factors which proceed from the make-up, the psychological constitution of human being with the demands and opportunities of the social environment." [2]

The *first* sentence of the *Plan* says simply, "The ultimate problem of all education is to coordinate the psychological and social factors." [3]

This definition of the problem was, he insisted, a distinctive feature of his school and marked it off from many other reform

[1] Mayhew and Edwards, *The Dewey School* (New York, Appleton-Century-Crofts, 1936), Appendix II, pp. 463–477 (written especially for this volume by Dewey).

[2] *Ibid.*, p. 465.

[3] John Dewey, *Plan of Organization of the University Primary School* (unpublished, 1895(?) Copy in the William Rainey Harper Library, University of Chicago), p. 1.

efforts. He said that the emphasis of progressive schools tended to center on the ideal of the harmonious development of all the powers of the individual—emotional, intellectual, and moral. Progressive schools had underestimated the importance of society or civilization: "the emphasis today is so largely upon the instincts and aptitudes of individuals as they may be discovered by purely psychological analysis, that coordination with social purposes is largely ignored." [4] Many public schools, he stated, concentrate on preparing students for individual economic success as if this were the only significant aspect of social life. Still others teach the doctrine of "social adjustment" as if "social" signified merely fitting the individual into some preordained niche of the particular social arrangements that happen to exist at the time.[5] In another comment he added:

"The controlling aim of the school was not the aim of present *progressive education*. It was to discover and apply the principles that govern all human development that is truly educative, to utilize the methods by which mankind has collectively and progressively advanced in skill, understanding, and associated life." [6]

In his reflections of the 1930's, he made special note of the social phase of education in the school. He pointed out that it was mentioned first in *The Plan*.

"This fact is contrary to an impression about the school which has prevailed since it was founded and which many visitors carried away with them at the time. It is the idea which has played a large part in progressive schools: namely, that they exist in order to give complete liberty to individuals, and that they are and must be 'child-centered' in a way which ignores, or at least makes little of, social relationships and responsibilities. In intent, whatever the failures in accomplishment, the school was 'community centered.' It was held that the *process* of mental development is essentially a social process, a process of participation; traditional psychology was criticized on the ground that it treated the growth of mind as one which occurs in individuals in contact with a merely physical environment of things. And, as has been

[4] Mayhew and Edwards, *op. cit.*, p. 465.
[5] *Ibid.*, p. 466.
[6] *Ibid.*, p. 6.

stated, the *aim* was ability of individuals to live in cooperative integration with others." [7]

He described two factors that led to the association of his school with exaggerated individualism. One was that visitors were accustomed to thinking of classrooms as highly controlled places where lessons were recited. In contrast, the freedom of movement and range of activities they found in the Dewey school *appeared as uncontrolled* liberty.[8] (An observer reports seeing the door of the school open suddenly one day to bring forth a child and a teacher in hot pursuit of a white rabbit.) [9] More important, he said, was the fact that he and his staff were breaking new ground. They were trying to discover what some of the natural interests, needs, and capabilities of individual children were, in order to try the hypothesis of guiding them toward social and academic ends. The "individualistic" was overweighted in order to obtain data upon which to act.

It may be noted that the word "social" was one of Dewey's terms, like "experience" or "activity," that was a heavily loaded concept. It had more than a single meaning in his own writings; the meanings received their special character from his philosophical theory. One usage was that man is a social being who attains mind and self only when nourished in social experience.[10]

[7] *Ibid.*, p. 467.

[8] For a comparison that vividly contrasts the two, see Joseph Mayer Rice, *The Public-School System of the United States* (New York, The Century Co., 1893) with his descriptions of the mechanical, rote learning of classrooms in New York and Chicago of the 1890's, and Mrs. Laura L. Runyon's account of her visit to the Dewey school; Laura L. Runyon, "A Day with the New Education," *The Chautauquan*, Vol. 30, No. 6 (March, 1900), pp. 589–592. She visited the school after she became appalled at the quality of teaching in the public schools. George Mead had told her husband that the Dewey school was "one of the greatest movements of this century." Her visits convinced her of its merits. She eventually joined the staff as an instructor in the history area, and became editor of *The Teachers' Reports*, which constitute the primary sources on the work of the school.

[9] Interview with Dr. (Mrs.) W. W. Charters.

[10] Dewey developed the idea that the "minded quality" of human life, which embraces man's capacity to grasp the meaning or connectedness of things in his world, is itself made possible by the association of phenomena to each other in the universe. See the chapter on "the social" in *Philosophy and Civilization* (New York: Minton, Balch and Co., 1930), titled "The Inclusive Philosophic Idea." He began with the premise that "associated or

But "social experience" has a number of other dimensions, too. One is the direct, interpersonal relations one has in a group. Another involves a person's relations with his contemporary culture as in his local community and as affected by social happenings in other places. There is also the individual's contact with civilization's immense storehouse of accumulated knowledge and with the institutions that transmit and advance it. "Social" also has a moral connotation. Dewey saw the individual as a member of a community that had a past, a present, and a future. The moral dimension involved the responsibility of absorbing into selfhood the values and skills made available by civilization, thereby increasing the growth of self and others.

A common interpretation is that Dewey meant social only in the sense of "social adjustment" to the group, or to contemporary social realities. This is false. It must be remembered that one of his uses of "social" referred to the products and processes of human inquiry as represented in scholarship, science, and school subject matter. In order to distinguish this use of the term, we shall refer to it as "civilizational." Since Dewey stressed that he put the social-civilizational feature first, its educational bearing deserves attention.

The school was designed to be a commnuity because an important feature was the coordination between individuals and society that could result. Minds and selves are formed by free interaction with others—through communication, cooperation, inquiry, and thinking. This was a radical departure from the image of the schoolroom as a place where lessons are repeated. Furthermore, social life of the adult world was too complex for a child to grasp with understanding, and the amount of knowledge was

conjoint behavior is a universal characteristic of all existences. Knowledge is in terms of related objects, and . . . relation as the nerve of science correlates with association among things. . . . [The] qualities of things associated are displayed only in association since in interactions alone are potentialities released and actualized" (p. 77). He then went on to treat human interaction or association as the "richest, fullest and most delicately subtle of any mode actually experienced" (p. 80) and described the whole fabric of civilized knowledge as a natural emergent, which grew out of man's special form of interaction with the physical, organic, and mental phenomena of the world. This hypothesis of basic continuity warranted a denial, in Dewey's view, of definitive separation of the physical and social sciences, as they are all concerned with creating knowledge about phenomena of the natural world, of which man is a part.

overwhelming. To help the child there should be continuity be- ⟵
tween the school's activities and basic aspects of the out-of-school
world; study should be organized in terms of a framework of
simplified principles and concepts that would introduce order
into a welter of data. The school should also represent, in the
pattern of its life, the values and qualities of human relations that
promoted growth; the *ways* of learning and living should demonstrate habits of cooperation, free communication, and reflective
thinking—the values of the democratic ideal. The theory held that
values were learned better when they were lived than when they
were merely talked about. Dewey wrote on this point in the *University Record* in May, 1897.

"As regards the Spirit of the School, the chief object is to secure a free and informal community life in which each child will
feel that he has a share and his own work to do. This is made the
chief motive towards what are ordinarily termed order and discipline. It is believed that the only *genuine* order and discipline are
those which proceed from the child's own respect for the work
which he has to do and his consciousness of the rights of others
who are, with himself, taking part in this work. As already suggested, the emphasis in the school upon various forms of practical
and constructive activity gives ample opportunity for appealing
to the child's social sense and to his regard for thorough and
honest work." [11]

But the meaning of "social" as represented in scholarship also
was essential. Dewey pointed out that, after conceiving of his
school as a form of "community-life," he had to work out a program of subject matter. His theory of interest committed him to
seek hypotheses for the first part of his school's program that
would build school work on the experience and activities of the
preschool child. The theory also insisted on the necessity of directing these immediate interests to significant educative ends.
Basic skills and the knowledge contained in the subject matters
had to be made vital parts of the school program. As it was an
experimental school, two of the most obvious courses were rejected: (1) to follow the traditional organization of subject matter, and (2) to permit children to engage in a free selection of

[11] Mayhew and Edwards, *op. cit.*, p. 32.

activities that had only immediate appeal. In reviewing educational events of the thirty years after he had left the school, Dewey expressed satisfaction at seeing considerable enrichment in school studies. However, "enrichment" often followed the two paths he had rejected. One response to the increase in knowledge was merely to move down into the elementary school material that had formerly been taught at upper levels. When this material was introduced in isolated segments, the results were questionable. The other tendency had been to introduce "under the name of projects disconnected jobs of short-time span in which there is emotional stimulation rather than development into new fields and principles, and into matured organization." [12]

He then stated the approach to the civilizational–subject matter aspect that was represented in his school.

"It was an essential part of the conception of proper subject-matter that studies must be assimilated not as mere items of information, but as organic parts of present needs and aims, which in turn are *social*. Translated into concrete material, this principle meant in effect that from the standpoint of the adult the axis of the course of the study was the development of civilization; while from the standpoint of those taught, it was a movement of life and thought dramatically and imaginatively reenacted by themselves. The phrase 'development of civilization' suggests something both too ambitious and too unified to denote just the materials actually used. Since some forms of social life have made permanent contributions to an enduring culture, such typical modes were selected, beginning with the simple and going to the complex, with especial attention to the obstacles which had to be met and the agencies which were effective, including in the latter new inventions and physical resources and also new institutional adaptations." [13]

This leads us to consider the basic structure of the curriculum, which consisted of the "occupations" and three intellectual strands related to them—(1) historical or social studies, (2) science, and (3) communication and expression.

[12] *Ibid.*, p. 470.
[13] *Ibid.*

## THE OCCUPATIONS

The occupations represented the most dramatic departure from traditional programs, and became perhaps the most highly publicized feature of the school. Full accounts of the occupations are available in the literature about the school.[14] We shall limit ourselves to observations that attempt to show their relation to the over-all plan.

The hypothesis of the occupations was an ingenious one, which seemed to contain possibilities for correlating a number of ideas stemming from the general philosophical-psychological theory. The epistemological thesis was that human intellectual life developed in relation to needs and opportunities for action. The curriculum problem was to create a program that would include initial school experiences appropriate for children beginning their school work, and that would also serve as a basis for developing a unified progression of studies at more advanced levels. The occupations seemed to supply the answer. Since they held such an important place in the plans for the school, we shall examine them, first, in terms of their theoretical origins, and second, with respect to their pedagogical applications.

### The Theory of the Occupations

The use of occupations—such activities as gardening, cooking, textile work, and carpentry—may seem to be a strange or esoteric foundation on which to build an educational program. Critics may even point to them as "proof" of the latent anti-intellectualism in Dewey's educational theory. No serious student of Dewey's work at Chicago can avoid confronting them.

They become intelligible only when we see them in relation to Dewey's efforts to take a genetic approach to the study of psychic life and thought processes, and to incorporate anthropological insights into educational theory. In "Interpretation of the Savage

[14] See for example, Mayhew and Edwards, *op. cit.*, Ch. 4, "Household Occupations," and Ch. 5, "Social Occupations Serving the Household." Also, John Dewey, "Monograph Number 4—Textiles," and "Monograph Number 7—Manual Training," *The Elementary School Record*, Vol. 1 (April, 1900 and October, 1900).

Mind" (1902),[15] we find an elucidation of how the concept of "occupations" was an intrinsic part of his general orientation. One can understand his conviction that the idea contained serious possibilities as a liberalizing as well as a unifying educational feature.

In the article, Dewey argued that a reconstituted genetic approach to psychology is necessary to understand the evolution of mind. The theme is familiar; but, in this case, he illustrated it with anthropological material and related it to the concept of occupations. The opening paragraph states:

"The psychical attitudes and traits of the savage are more than stages through which mind has passed, leaving them behind. They are outgrowths which have entered decisively into further evolution, and as such form an integral part of present mental organization. Such positive significance is commonly attributed, in theory at least, to animal mind; but the mental structure of the savage, which presumably has an even greater relevancy for genetic psychology, is strangely neglected." [16]

The failure was due, he said, to a faulty employment of comparative method. In Herbert Spencer's *Sociology*, for example, generalizations are made about *the* "primitive mind" that are based on a miscellaneous hodge-podge of primitive peoples including Bedouins, Papuans, Andamanese, Hottentots, Malays, and Bechuanas. These have been torn away from their special cultural and natural environments, and have been handled as a single phenomenon by virtue of their being "primitive." As such, they are treated negatively and traits such as mirthfulness, improvidence, chaotic temperament, and lack of curiosity and ingenuity are ascribed to them. The method of collecting and listing incoherent traits fails to provide a meaningful conception of mind. Dewey insisted that this sterile method had to be abandoned so that different qualities of mind may be seen as functioning modes

[15] John Dewey, "Interpretation of the Savage Mind," *Psychological Review*, Vol. 9 (May, 1902), pp. 217–230, reprinted in Dewey's *Philosophy and Civilization* (New York, Minton, Balch and Co., 1931), pp. 173–187. (The former version is used here.)

[16] *Ibid.*, p. 217.

of adaptation, varying with different cultural patterns. Dewey presented his own method:

"The biological point of view commits us to the conviction that mind, whatever else it may be, is at least an organ of service for the control of environment in relation to the ends of the life process.

"If we search in any social group for the special functions to which mind is thus relative, occupations at once suggest themselves. Occupations determine the fundamental modes of activity, and hence control the formation and use of habits. These habits, in turn, are something more than practical and overt. 'Apperceptive masses' and associational traits of necessity conform to the dominant activities. The occupations determine the chief modes of satisfaction, the standards of success and failure. Hence they furnish the working classifications and definitions of value; they control the desire processes. . . . The directions given to mental life thereby extend to emotional and intellectual characteristics. So fundamental and pervasive is the group of occupational activities that it affords the scheme or pattern of the structural organization of mental traits. Occupations integrate special elements into a functioning whole." [17]

He argued that one can identify patterns of mind that correspond to cultural occupations such as hunting, farming, trading, and manufacturing. Analyzing the hunting vocation of Australian aborigines as a case in point, he demonstrated, at length, that mental patterns developed in the basic occupation or activity of hunting are carried over into the whole gamut of cultural customs, feelings, and products; approaches to courtship, war, art, and religion are psychologically assimilated to the pattern developed in the hunting vocation. This method could therefore be used for interpreting social institutions and cultural resources. It was, in short, a psychological method for sociology. Dewey said that if, by contrast, one looks at an agriculturally centered culture, one finds a markedly different pattern of mind; direct psychophysical activities have given way to technical modes,

[17] *Ibid.*, pp. 219–220.

social divisions of labor, and more complex and conscious mental habits.

Enough has been said to establish that Dewey was responding to the anthropological developments of his time and was incorporating them into his philosophical-psychological point of view. The occupations therefore played a central role rather than a trivial one in his program. In the concluding sentences of "The Savage Mind," he said that

". . . the adjustment of habits to ends, through the medium of a problematic, doubtful, precarious situation, is the structural form upon which present intelligence and emotion are built. It remains the ground pattern. The further problem of genetic psychology is then to show how the purely immediate personal adjustment of habit to direct satisfaction, in the savage, became transformed through the introduction of impersonal, generalized objective instrumentalities and ends; how it ceased to be immediate and became loaded and surcharged with a content which forced personal want, initiative, effort and satisfaction further and further apart, putting all kinds of social divisions of labor, intermediate agencies, and objective contents between them. This is the problem of the formation of mental patterns appropriate to agricultural, military, professional and technological and trade pursuits, and the reconstruction and overlaying of the original hunting scheme.

"But by these various agencies, we have not so much destroyed or left behind the hunting structural arrangement of mind, as we have set free its constitutive psycho-physic factors so as to make them available and interesting in all kinds of objective and idealized pursuits—the hunt for truth, beauty, virtue, wealth, social well-being, and even of heaven and of God." [18]

*Pedagogical Role of Occupations*

As his school was to be a laboratory in educational psychology, committed to the study of the development of mind both in the child and in race experience, it is not surprising that he turned to the concept of "occupations" for the pedagogical purpose of integrating his theory with school practice. But from the begin-

[18] *Ibid.*, pp. 229–230.

ning he had trouble winning understanding and acceptance of the idea. He repeatedly emphasized that he had no interest in the occupations as busy work, nor was he interested in training children to be chefs, seamstresses, or carpenters.

We shall consider the case made for placing the occupations in the curriculum.

1. They seemed to offer the opportunity to relate the learning activities of the school to the out-of-school experiences of the child. They included activities that the child was familiar with in the home. They also represented "the fundamental processes and instruments by which society has made itself what it is in the subordination of nature to human ends." [19] Dewey wanted to capitalize on the interests of children without having to ask, "What are you interested in doing today?" As we saw earlier, an *educative interest* was one that could be guided into significant learning. His hope that the occupations would be interests of this quality is reflected in a description of them:

"The activities selected for school life . . . should be basic, that is those that provide for fundamental needs such as food, clothing, or shelter. Such activities are genuine and timeless. Their reality excites the interest of the child and enlists his effort, for they are what his elders do, have done, and must continue to do." [20]

Thus the assumption was that interests that dealt with universal human needs such as food, shelter, and clothing could be identified. Because such interests were also basic in the life of a child, they would engage his efforts.

2. The occupations conformed with other aspects of the psychological theory. Dewey held that the first level of child development was predominantly a stage of motor-expressive activities. The occupations provided avenues for utilizing four natural instincts, or impulses, of children: the *constructive*, which begins with simple physical coordinations and moves into the use of tools and technical skills; the *investigative* and *experimental;* the *social*, which urges the young child to share and communicate

---

[19] John Dewey, *Lectures for the First Course in Pedagogy*, No. 7.
[20] Mayhew and Edwards, *op. cit.*, p. 256.

his experiences; and the *expressive*, which is related to the others, but requires adequate materials for outlets.[21]

"The fundamental point in the psychology of an occupation is that it maintains a balance between the intellectual and practical phases of experience. As an occupation it is active or motor; it finds expression through the physical organs, the eyes, hands, etc. But it also involves continual observation of materials, and continued planning and reflection in order that the practical or executive side may be successfully carried on. . . . It differs from a trade because its end is . . . in the growth that comes from the continual interplay of ideas and their embodiment in action, not in external utility." [22]

[21] See, for example, Ch. 2, "The School and the Life of the School," in *The School and Society.* In the late 1890's Dewey was using instinct and impulse as rough equivalents. His training under G. S. Hall may have influenced his concept of instinct, but he remained unsatisfied with it, as instincts were viewed as rigid, inherent determinants of behavior. Dewey sought to define a position that would avoid two extremes: the idea of behavior as being prescribed either by instincts, or by environment. In *Human Nature and Conduct* (New York: Henry Holt and Co., 1922, p. 107) he described the "radical reformer" as one who underestimates the influence of habits and of institutions in shaping raw human nature, and the conservative as one who attributes too much to instincts. By 1922 Dewey had introduced the concept of "flexible habit" as an alternative. In *Human Nature and Conduct* he described the child as beginning life with vague, random, undefined impulses that are quickly shaped by the customs of his family and culture. These habits, which are acquired, are essential for him to deal with the environment, but the environment does not remain constant, and habits, to be effective must not be too rigid so that the child can adapt to changes. The job of the schools, therefore, was to help children develop habits "which are more intelligent, more sensitively percipient, more informed with foresight, more aware of what they are about, more direct and more sincere, more flexibly responsive than those now current." (*Human Nature and Conduct*, p. 128.) For an analysis of this transition in Dewey's thought, see Vivian T. Thayer, *Formative Ideas In American Education* (New York, Dodd, Mead, and Co., 1965), pp. 258–266.

[22] John Dewey, *The School and Society*, revised ed. (Chicago, University of Chicago Press, 1923), pp. 131–132.

Dewey was in touch with the Manual Training movement, which had come very much alive in the 1880's. The spur had been provided by the exhibit of Victor Della Vos, Director of the Moscow Imperial Technical School, at the Philadelphia Exposition of 1876. This had started a crusade

3. The occupations could also affect the child's attitudes to the learning activities of the school. The child entering school was to find it a place in which activities of social life were carried on. The idea was to guide the child's interest in his family, in his natural environment, and in himself so that he would gain scientifically sound ideas of the basic functions of people in the home and neighborhood; of plant, animal, and human life, and their interdependence on each other. The children would realize that the classroom was not isolated from life; that the skills, knowledge, and ways of thinking learned there were of the same nature as those employed in his home and community, and in societies of other times and places. With this kind of initial experience, the child could be led to richer intellectual fare.

4. The occupations were educationally justifiable only if they became a means for securing a deeper liberal educational experience.

"In educational terms, this means that these occupations shall not be mere practical devices . . . but active centers of scientific insight into natural materials and processes, points of departure whence children shall be led out into a realization of the historic development of man.

"The occupation supplies the child with a genuine motive; it gives him experience at first hand; it brings him into contact with realities. It does all this but in addition it is *liberalized throughout by translation into its historic and social values and scientific equivalencies*. With the growth of the child's mind in power and

by American educators like John D. Runkle of M. I. T. and Calvin W. Woodward of Washington University. Dewey was receptive to approaches that would involve the "constructive" impulses but he did not accept either the emphasis on teaching manual skills through a specified, graded series of exercises with various tools, or the mystic faith of some adherents that reform of mind and character would follow from manual training. Dewey's stress was on the social benefits that could result, on the group skills that could be learned, and on the opportunity to use experience in the occupations as motivation for obtaining insight into the structure and evolution of civilized societies. For a general description of the movement, see Lawrence A. Cremin, *The Transformation of the School*, Ch. 2. For a description of the missionary quality that characterized one of the Chicago leaders, see Charles H. Ham, *Mind and Hand* (New York: American Book Co., 1899, 3rd ed.).

knowledge it ceases to be a pleasant occupation merely and becomes more and more a medium, an instrument, an organ of understanding—and is thereby transformed." [23]

The occupations qualified as a fruitful hypothesis for beginning the school experience of the child. As a *continuing* part of the program, they provided a means of keeping the theoretical and the concrete in interaction. But Dewey's concept of the levels of thought and experience demanded a progression toward another emphasis. As he put it:

"The pressing problem with respect to 'subject matter' was to find those things in the direct present experience of the young which were the roots out of which would grow more elaborate, technical, and organized knowledge in later years. . . .

"The solution of the problem is extremely difficult; we did not reach it; it has not been reached and in its fulness will never be reached. But at all events we tried to see the problems and the difficulties which it presented." [24]

The shift toward intellectual, specialized studies was to become more marked as the secondary level was approached. The kind of feature represented in the occupations was never to disappear completely, but the more direct activities would give way to methods more characteristic of laboratory experimentation and field investigations.

In the curriculum design, the occupations were to be accompanied by three intellectual themes or strands: history, science, and communication and expression. We are now ready to examine the approach followed in these areas.

[23] *Ibid.*, pp. 17, 20. (My italics.)
[24] Mayhew and Edwards, *op. cit.*, pp. 468–469.

# CHAPTER TEN

# History as "Indirect Sociology"

Dewey recognized that the pedagogical path he had plotted was difficult and untried. To achieve his objective—to shape an educational program providing truly rich experiences in liberal and scientific studies—he forged a general design. The details were to be developed and modified in the light of actual efforts. His inner confidence was based on the conviction that his theory of knowledge and learning was rooted in the reality of the human situation. There is no warrant for charges that the school was an experiment in *laissez-faire* education.

The intellectual content of the curriculum was to be consistent with the psychology of experience and its development. In practice, the development of the curriculum fell into two phases.[1] In the first (1896–1898), specific ideas for school purposes, based on the theory, had to be clarified. The 1895 *Plan of Organization of the University Primary School* provided a sketch of the vision. As enrollment grew, a sequence of studies was created. The first two years contained a good deal of groping and a number of false starts. Efforts were complicated by ever-present financial difficulties and a search for adequate housing. Because of increasing numbers, the school had to be moved from its original quarters in a residence at 5718 Kimbark Avenue to the South Park Club House in 1897, and then, in 1898, to an old residence at 5412 Ellis Avenue, which brought it within the University complex. A staff capable of sharing the dream and possessing initiative and creativity to forward it had to be organized. The second period (1898–1903) was a time for consolidating and revising the

[1] Katherine C. Mayhew and Anna C. Edwards, *The Dewey School* (New York, Appleton-Century-Crofts, 1936), Ch. 3, "Experimental Practices Developing the Curriculum."

program on the basis of courses and methods that had proved promising. Transitions to emphases appropriate for older groups were begun.

The basic theory held that the several fields of knowledge represented the products and processes of man's "minded activities." The common origin of these activities lay in social life, in the joint efforts of men to order and control their experiences in a natural and social environment.

". . . the unity of the curriculum is found in the unity of social life which that curriculum represents. Each study stands for one differentiated phase of social life, and the problem of correlation is to make the studies act and react upon each other in the same way in the school that the processes for which they stand do in actual social life." [2]

Dewey rejected the notion that bodies of knowledge were self-contained entities. An approach to knowledge that would avoid the pitfalls of isolated abstraction had to be rooted in the concept of the social origin of learning. As we have seen, Dewey held that the occupations, in which men worked out answers to fundamental needs, were necessary for the advancement of skills and knowledge. The child had this dimension of human experience represented in himself; first, in his personal strivings to handle his world through sensory-motor strivings, and second, through more complex intellectual behavior. He experienced the occupations in a partial but first-hand way in his home and community. They were to form a bridge to vital and advanced levels of learning in the studies that were the special province of the school. These connections having been established and maintained, learning could go forward into the farthest reaches of intellectual life: history, the physical and social sciences, language, literature, and mathematics.

We shall forego an attempt to give an exhaustive account of the details of the curriculum. The aim will be to describe enough to indicate the basic intention. As Dewey insisted that content and method had to be coordinated, we shall include examples of methodology with descriptions of subject matter.

[2] Dewey, *Lectures for the First Course in Pedagogy*, No. 4, p. 7.

The 1895 *Plan of Organization* recommended that beginning school experiences include three typical activities: cooking, carpentry, and sewing or textiles, since they afford "adequate opportunity, on the psychological side for constructive work, while socially they represent the fundamental activities of the race." [3] The method, he said, is to analyze these activities and present a knowledge of the materials and processes contained in them. In contrast to "object lesson" approaches, materials such as water and soil, vegetable and animal life should be studied as aspects of nature that are interacting with man's activities. Arithmetical, chemical, and physical processes would be studied, not as sections of a textbook, but as the forms in which materials are controlled. A basic attitude toward *science* would thus be established.

The *social* ramifications of these activities would involve tracing the historical changes in the processes invented for handling materials to meet man's basic needs. One of the major themes in the approach to history would be the changes in the nature of work. Geographical questions would naturally arise, as the physical environment is a major factor in determining the character of man's work.

The child's constructive activities in working with materials and in seeing sets of relations in human affairs also called for modes of *expression* or *communication*. Drawing, coloring, modeling, and verbal and written expressions would be required. Literature would be seen as one form of communication or artistic expression that grew out of vital, complex activity.

Through all this, the young child was to gain a clear sense of man as a social being. This would be reinforced by his participation in a school that would itself be an active, cooperative, inquiring human community. It might not be completely farfetched to make an analogy between one of the occupations—weaving—and the educational venture he envisaged. His objective was to create rich educational tapestries. The direct, relatively undifferentiated experiences in the occupations are analogous to the rough, matted wool. From this base, strands representing important intellectual themes (history, science, and communication and expression) would be developed. These, in turn, would

[3] John Dewey, *Plan of Organization of the University Primary School* (unpublished, University of Chicago, 1895(?)), p. 10.

lead to the intricate and elaborate textures of the specialized subject matter. The student was to be an active participant in the
processes that would lead to the reconstruction of experience.
We shall treat history here, science in Chapter Eleven, and communication and expression in Chapter Twelve.

## HISTORICAL SEQUENCE

A basic style of analysis in all of Dewey's thought was the
genetic method. This involved the effort to gain insight into a
complex process or problem of the present by tracing its history
through the successive stages of its growth. It is not surprising,
then, to find that the study of history occupied a prominent
place in the Dewey school.

Dewey was a critic, of course, of the common tendency to
make history a study of a mound of facts with an emphasis on
kings and battles. In Dewey's view, the fundamental thing about
man's history, below the diversity and welter of data, was man's
growing ability to control nature and transform it into an instrument for realizing human ends.

Historical ways of thinking were introduced in the first stage
to promote insights into underlying facts that cause societies to
take on their characteristic forms. The subprimary children were
involved in the occupations of their contemporary world. They
engaged in role playing when re-enacting the fundamental occupations of the home; perspectives were then broadened to include an understanding of the interaction between the family
and the community; thus, playing "store," "mailman," and
"milkman," as well as "house," became relevant activities in the
school during the first and second years. The children were engaged in pursuits like building playhouses and in taking a variety
of adult roles in games.[4] In these activities relevant questions
would be raised which would lead to amplification and refinement in the later school years: Where does it come from? Where
does it go? How does it work?

[4] Mayhew and Edwards, *op. cit.*, pp. 45–46, 60. George H. Mead's insights into the educative value of play and roletaking are reflected here.
See George H. Mead, "The Relation of Play to Education," *op. cit.*, pp.
141–146.

Children in Group III (age six) turned to other aspects of social occupations. Food, fibers, wood, and metal as the stuff of cooking, sewing, and carpentry (construction) were studied, from their state as raw material to that of finished product. Farming, weaving, mining, and lumbering were analyzed in terms of the roles each played in preparing materials for use. Considerable time was devoted, for instance, to the study of cotton. Physiographic conditions for planting, requirements for growth, etc. were all related. The mode of attack was "play"—if we  ⟵ define "play" as active, constructive involvement with materials and without a long-range objective. Dewey argued that, at this age, although much energy is expended and the child is intent upon the project at hand, there is no *conscious* effort or attention.[5]

" . . . the child's concepts are built up chiefly through his activities, rather than through his language. He must therefore play farmer, ranchman, miner, etc., and in his small way perform the occupations he could comprehend—not with imaginary materials, but real ones, though his farm be but a 4 x 6 foot sandbox, his dairy but a glass bottle in which the cream is shaken or churned, and his mine the same sandbox at another time, modeled to represent the mountains from which the ore is extracted." [6]

He called this the principle of *indirect* learning: when "attention is not upon the *idea of learning*, but upon the accomplishing of a real and intrinsic purpose." [7]

Historical study was first undertaken by the seven-year-olds. The evolutionary development of civilization was the theme around which work in history was organized. The study began as an investigation of the occupational activities from their simple origins to their present complex state. Dewey argued that a child's interest in the historical evolution of the occupations and social life would proceed naturally from a personal involvement with them in the present.

[5] John Dewey, "Reflective Attention," *The Elementary School Record*, Vol. i, No. 4 (May, 1900), p. iii.

[6] Laura Louise Runyon, *The Teaching of Elementary History in the Dewey School* (unpublished M.A. Dissertation in History and Education, University of Chicago, 1906), p. 22.

[7] Dewey, *Plan of Organization of the University Primary School*, p. 8.

"Further, the method is to follow out these activities into their social ramifications. Present social life, on the one hand, is too complex for realization by the child, while past life, taken as past, is remote and psychologically inert. But through his interest in his own activity of cooking and primitive building, the child is interested in the different forms this activity has assumed at different times. He can be led to analyze the existing complex social structure by following up the growth of the homes, foods, etc. of men, from the pre-historic cave dweller through the stone and metal ages up to civilization, etc." [8]

The pivotal question, "How did it all come about?" was the springboard for taking the children of Group IV back in time to the life of the primitive man.

The child was to imagine himself facing a hostile environment stripped of all civilized conveniences. He was to gain a sense of the need to survey materials and to give shape to them to ward off dangers and secure the necessities of life. No effort was made to establish a one-to-one correspondence between a primitive era and a supposed primitive stage in child development as recommended by some culture-epoch approaches. The emphasis in the Dewey school was shifted to a consideration of innovations and inventions developed in prehistoric times.

Because the child's skills with the written word were too limited, he did not read and write about the life of primitive man's development to the Iron Age; instead, the approach combined thinking and doing. The students wrestled with hypothetical situations like the following: "What would happen if a primitive tribe encountered, in their wanderings, a rushing stream?" "Build a bridge." "How would they go about it?" "Let's pretend. . . ," etc. And the children would fashion a miniature bridge in the sandbox, using the kinds of crude materials and implements that would have been available to prehistoric man.

Mayhew and Edwards, from their experience in the Dewey school, describe this fourth year as a transitional one—an age when "the lure of the how and why begins to leaven the questioning mind." [9] Through investigation, discovery, invention,

[8] *Ibid.*, p. 10.
[9] Mayhew and Edwards, *op. cit.*, p. 97.

and re-invention, the child was to find the "secret of advance which has resulted for the race in an upward spiral of progressive action." [10]

The approach to history in the school was primarily industrial and economic (in terms of the way people make a living), and social (in terms of the effect of occupations on social life). According to Dewey:

"Whatever history may be for the scientific historian, for the educator it must be an indirect sociology—a study which lays bare its process of becoming and its mode of organization." [11]

A concern with political history was deferred until the later years.

It must be noted that for the younger children the different subjects were not marked off sharply. The teachers who were hired were specialists, and children did move from class to class in history, art, science, manual training, and other subjects. But a serious effort was made to coordinate studies through faculty discussion and planning. It was an early form of team-teaching.

In history, when the focus was upon man's confrontation with the physical-natural world, the affinity with science was very close. Dewey saw the relationship thus:

"When history is completely organized, therefore, the fundamental branch of history around which the others will group themselves, and by which they check themselves, will be what we may call industrial history, meaning by that the record of the growth of agencies and instrumentalities for administering natural forces in subservience to human wants and ideals. If this is true, history has the most intimate connection on the one side with man's constructive activities, and on the other side with the development of natural science, and cannot be arbitrarily severed from these things educationally without great loss of its meaning." [12]

The fourth and fifth years, for seven- and eight-year-olds, were pivotal ones, and were most thoroughly and systematically

[10] *Ibid.*
[11] John Dewey, "The Aim of History in Elementary Education," *The Elementary School Record*, Vol. 1, No. 8 (November, 1900), p. 199.
[12] Dewey, *Lectures for the First Course in Pedagogy*, No. 7.

developed. Group IV, as already discussed, concentrated on the laying of sociohistorical foundations. Group V (eight-year-olds) shifted study of the restricted primitive setting to that of a world that had been expanded by migration, exploration, and discovery. The psychological theory held that this was the period in which to shift from direct to "derived modes of activity." By the age of eight, the child had a psychological need to acquire skills in reading, writing, and number tools in order to progress. The acquisition of tools and techniques became imperative when remote ends replaced immediate gratifications as motivations to work.

"Generally, the Phoenicians were chosen as the focal point for work in history in the fifth year. The Phoenician, as a trader rather than a farmer or a hunter, was a new kind of man confronted with new types of problems. Tools and weapons had to be supplemented by knowledge of the alphabet and a number system in order to carry out the commercial occupations which prevailed in their area of the Mediterranean. [Miss Runyon noted that it was at this age that the child for the first time received formal work in reading, writing, and numbers.] It was particularly desired, however, that the child, who took up seriously in this year, the use of symbols in reading, writing, and number, should realize the conditions in which these conveniences originated." [13]

Miss Runyon reported a lesson in which the students were struggling with the problem of establishing a standard of measurement by which lengths and distances would be judged among the merchants of the market place:

"Parts of the body as means of measurement were suggested. The distance from the end of the thumb to the first joint was used as a unit of measure, the span of the hand; the full length of the forearm and the pace were also suggested. The translation from a somewhat irregular unit to an adopted unit could usually be obtained from the class. For example, the distance from the middle finger to the elbow was used as a unit for measuring cloth and called a cubit. After this had been used in many measure-

[13] Runyon, *op. cit.*, p. 30.

ments, the teacher one day told a story of a Phoenician who went to trade in cloth, and, noticing that the men in the market place were of different heights, selected the man with the longest arm from whom to purchase cloth. The other merchants noted this, and called a meeting to decide what should be done. At this point, the class was called upon for suggestions. One child thought the shortest man's arm might be taken as a standard, and others stop short of the elbow in their measurement; others that the tallest man's arm be used, and the little man measure above the elbow. When, however, someone suggested that a middle-sized man be selected and the rest get sticks just the length of his cubit, all agreed this would be better." [14]

Later in the fifth year, horizons were expanded by studies of great explorers. The accomplishments of Prince Henry the Navigator, Magellan, Marco Polo, and Columbus were followed in great detail. The study of explorations and navigation led to questions about the oceans, meteorology, astronomy, the use of the compass, and astrology. Typical activities included map work and the charting of courses followed by explorers.

By the age of eight, the child had enlarged his perspective from the occupations in his own home to a larger view which included the beginning of the history of civilized human experience.

In the sixth year (Group VI, age nine) attention was turned to the history of the United States. An introductory unit to the study of American History—one that would provide a natural transition from the study of the explorations—was sought. The history of Chicago was settled upon, beginning with the penetration into the Great Lakes region by the early French explorers.

"This gives an opportunity to enlarge the concepts formed in the study of the Phoenicians and the early explorers. In imagination the child sees the frontier life develop into a thriving village, with needs of local government, system of taxation, improvements, etc. Through this discussion he is guided to comprehend simple forms of civic politics, so that the paved and sewered streets, the policeman and the postman, the alderman

[14] *Ibid.*, p. 33.

and the mayor, with all of whom he has been somewhat familiar, have now more definite parts in the social world." [15]

For Groups VI through X, history dealt with the American story: the exploration and conquest of the continent, the establishment of the colonies, and the founding of the republic.

More specialized study of history was gradually introduced. The children read historical accounts and prepared written and oral reports. However, they still continued their work in the occupations. Much time, for example, was devoted to the strategic geographical location of Chicago and the consequences of this factor in the lives of the inhabitants. One year the village of Chicago and its environs were constructed in sand. Students saw the role it played in the fur trade; then, with the coming of stage coaches and railroads, they saw how it became a center for trade in wheat, cattle, and other food staples.

During the study of colonial history, children in the textile studio had firsthand experiences with the spinning wheel and the loom. Several of the children reconstructed typical industries. The home life of the colonists was studied in some detail, and one group planned and carried out the furnishing of a colonial room. Plans were drawn for building a fireplace, which was then built with some difficulty. Furniture and articles for cooking were made in the shops. The intention was to show how occupations and industries grew out of real needs, how individuals and communities became experts in making or growing certain things, and how trade between the colonies began.

We turn now to some of the methods employed in the teaching of history. Textbooks were rarely used, but biographies were studied extensively, such as the story of Captain John Smith in the Virginia Colony. Biographies were also used to introduce discussion of the ethical qualities of men who faced difficulties and marshaled strengths to overcome them. Dewey, however, qualified the use of the biographical method in the teaching of history:

"Now while it is a valuable thing to teach history in connection with the biography of great persons, and to arouse in the pupil an appreciation for great characters, this after all, leaves us

[15] *Ibid.*, p. 49.

with too individualistic a conception of history. We need also to know how the social forces were at work and expressing themselves through these individuals." [16]

Frequent use was made of methods more recently popularized under the label "method of discovery." In studying the campaigns of the Revolutionary War, for example, students worked from a relief map and made predictions of the strategy the British would follow after the seige of Boston. Aware that the British Army was in Canada, they decided that a likely plan would be for the British to effect a juncture near Albany by moving via waterways in New York from the north and south.

Of Group IX, before their reading about Virginia's House of Burgesses, Miss Hoblitt reports:

"In discussing the first House of Burgesses the children were asked to suggest laws which would probably be enacted, and from their remembrance of the early mistakes and difficulties of the colony, were able to propose laws against idleness, trade with the Indians, laws regulating agriculture, etc. They decided in advance that King James would not be likely to tolerate for long Virginia's growing independence. As to the significance of his seizure of the charter there was a division of opinion, some thinking that Virginia would thrive better under the king's protection because he had so much to think of and would not interfere with them, and others remaining loyal to the London Company." [17]

According to Dewey's theory, the child by the age of nine (and through the remaining school years) had attained "the level of reflective attention," which made it possible for him to cope with the material and the methods of the later years. "With growing power, the child can conceive of the end as something to be found out, discovered; and can control his acts and images so as to help in the inquiry and solution." [18]

[16] *Ibid.*, p. 9 quoting from Dewey, "Lectures on the Philosophy of Education."

[17] Margaret Hoblitt, "History: Group IX," *Teachers Reports of the University Elementary School* (unpublished, January, 1900), p. 65, in the archives of the University of Chicago Laboratory School. Extensive scrapbooks from the *Reports*, organized according to subjects, may also be found in the library at Teachers College, Columbia University.

[18] Dewey, "Reflective Attention," p. 111.

"In history work there is a change from the story and biography form, from discussion of questions that arise, to the formulation of questions. Points about which differences of opinion exist, matters upon which experience, reflection, etc. can be brought to bear, are always coming up in history. But to use the discussion to develop this matter of doubt and difference into a definite problem, to bring the child to feel just what the difficulty is; and then throw him upon his own resources in looking up material bearing upon the point, and upon his judgment in bringing it to bear, or getting a solution, is a marked intellectual advance." [19]

By the time the student was ready to enter the final Group XI, he had followed the Americans through the period of colonization (especially Virginia, Plymouth, and New York colonies); the American Revolution; the framing of the Constitution; and westward expansion. In addition, as a member of Group VIII (age eleven), he had spent a better part of a year studying the European backgrounds of the colonists. Here the emphasis was on the social and cultural patterns that were in the experience of those people who had left Europe for the New World. (English village life was studied in depth.)

The actual program for the older children in Group XI (ages fourteen to fifteen) was in operation for only two years. The records are most sketchy for this level, and the impression conveyed is that the staff never got beyond a very tentative program. Some of the basic intentions, however, were apparent. A new kind of specialized study was to be introduced. The six preceding years had emphasized social and industrial history. It was felt that material about political institutions could be introduced more appropriately in the program of older children. One idea was that political institutions could best be illustrated by study of the early Roman State, especially its organization and governmental machinery. Governmental forms were to be studied as institutions for the regulation of industrial and social life, with special attention directed to the need to change in response to new situations. The general plan seemed to embrace the idea that after the sociological emphasis in history had prepared students

[19] *Ibid.*, pp. 111–112.

to differentiate peculiar types of social life, they would be ready to study civilizations other than the American, and would appreciate the special contributions of each to world history. The plan, therefore, was to shift from a psychological to a chronological emphasis; to begin with the ancient Mediterranean World and come down through the European story to the peculiar and differentiating factors in American history.

We end this chapter with a quotation that underscores the pedagogical significance Dewey attached to equipping students with the skills of historical analysis:

"The historical method is invading education, and is likely to be one of the most fundamental forces in directing its immediate future. In some sense, every advance in civilization makes the problem of education more and more difficult. It widens the distance between the immaturity of the child (which remains, so far as we know, practically unchanged upon the physical or heredity side) and the comprehensive, complex, remote, and subtle conditions which he needs to master. The newcomers into civilization find themselves face to face with technical, mechanical, and intellectual devices and resources in the development of which they had had no share or lot; and which are so far beyond them that they have no instinctive or natural means of understanding them. The problem of education—the problem of establishing vital connections between the immature child and the cultural and technical achievements of adult life—thus continually increases in difficulty. It is coming to be recognized that the historical method, more than any one thing, is the key which unlocks difficulties. By knowing the social and intellectual conditions under which arose a given industrial device, plan of government, or type of scientific interest and theory, and by presenting that to the child in connection with its social and human context, we put him in the simplest and freest attitude toward it." [20]

[20] John Dewey, Review of Katherine Elizabeth Dopp, *The Place of Industries in Elementary Education* in *Elementary School Teacher*, Vol. 3 (June, 1903), p. 727.

# CHAPTER ELEVEN

# *Science*

In Dewey's analyses of the nature and evolution of psychic processes, the capacity for reflective thinking was designated as the culminating feature of evolutionary development. His rationale held that human progress was dependent on strengthening the skills of reflective thinking. Dewey saw, in the procedures and values of science, a model of man thinking at his best. It is natural, then, to find science occupying an important place in his recommendations for the curriculum. In the Dewey school, science was both content and method, the *what* and the *how;* a study of the products and processes of the mind at work.

The amount of detail about the science program in the literature of the school is extensive but badly organized. A comprehensive description of the science curriculum and of the principles of teaching it would require a lengthy paper in itself, and a briefer account is bound to be partial and subject to distortion. We shall, however, discuss some of the major intentions. In order to give a feeling of the spirit, we shall make liberal use of quotations and examples of methodology.[1]

How did the science program appear in operation? The progression of experiences in science coincided with the general principles discussed in Chapter Ten. The unifying theme was to see scientific advances as events in the growth of man's insight into the nature of his world and his capacity to control it. The teacher was expected to keep two purposes constantly in view:

[1] We draw extensively from the account of the science program given by Katherine Camp Mayhew in Katherine C. Mayhew and Anna C. Edwards, *The Dewey School* (New York, Appleton-Century-Crofts, 1936), Ch. 15 *et passim.* She was head of the Science Department and Vice-Principal in charge of curriculum. An inspection of primary sources in *The Teachers' Reports* shows that her description is based on the record in addition to recollection of her experiences.

"(1) to provide the child with opportunity to develop and use, thereby learning, great scientific truths, and (2) to preserve through use, the child's instructive spirit of inquiry, to build in his mind a concept of scientific method as a practical tool and thereby guide him into the experimental, the scientific habit of mind." [2]

In order that these purposes might be realized, an ordered sequence, coinciding with the levels of the child's development, was deemed essential. The attitudes about science developed in the preprimary and early elementary levels were felt to be crucial for later studies.

The original impetus for work in science was to come through the concern with the home and social occupations, and later with the specific occupations of cooking, sewing, and carpentry. At the preprimary level, it was assumed that the young child "comes to the school to *do*." The teacher's job was to work so that even children from four to six years old would gain a sense that activities of many kinds required processes of active investigation: imagining possible results of this or that idea, projecting guesses and testing them to find the results. Gradually, each individual would be led to see how he needed the results of scientific knowledge to secure certain ends. Then he would be taught how he could acquire knowledge for use in his constructive activities or inquiries.

A concomitant attitude to be developed was the sense that science is a social activity. Dewey wanted to avoid giving children the impression that science is a separate, abstract thing. His epistemology held that knowledge grows out of man's efforts to meet the range of his needs. In the curriculum design, the nature of man's occupations or work was held to provide a useful device for establishing this insight. During his early years at school, the student was made aware that science was relevant to history.

"The text of the story was always the way different groups of people had dealt with, used, and subdued their environment, how they had won from it the means for further subduing and more adequately ministering to their rapidly increasing needs. In

[2] Katherine C. Mayhew and Anna C. Edwards, *The Dewey School* (New York, Appleton-Century-Crofts, 1936), p. 283.

following the details of this oft repeated story, these children saw that as man's needs increased in number and kind, so did his appreciation of the value of satisfied senses, of convenience, of comfort, of beauty deepen. Each child saw and often enacted the part that activity played in all this moving and dynamic drama. Ideas became deeds and brought about results that changed current ways of living and gave incentive to a further quest . . . (the arrow, the sail, etc.). . . . Into the small rivulets of each child's experience, therefore, flowed these tricklings from the great stream of human endeavor; the doings of man, his inventions, his discoveries, his accomplishments in the physical world, his method of thinking, and the growing fabric of his social relationship." [3]

Describing the work undertaken in science by Group III (six-year-olds), Dewey summed up the rationale for the early years.

"The study of natural objects, processes, and relations is placed in a human setting. During the year, a considerably detailed observation of seeds and their growth, of plants, woods, stones, animals, as to some phases of structure and habit, of geographical conditions of landscape, climate, arrangement of land and water, is undertaken. The pedagogical problem is to direct the child's power of observation, to nurture his sympathetic interest in characteristic traits of the world in which he lives, to afford interpreting material for later more special studies, and yet to supply a carrying medium for the variety of facts and ideas through the dominant spontaneous emotions and thoughts of the child. Hence their associations with human life. Absolutely no separation is made between the 'social' side of the work, its concern with people's activities and their mutual dependencies, and the 'science,' regard for physical facts and forces —because the conscious distinction between man and nature is the result of later reflection and abstraction, and to force it upon the child here is not only to fail to engage his whole mental energy, but to confuse and distract him. The environment is always that in which life is situated and through which it is circumstanced; and to isolate it, to make it with little children an object of observation and remark by itself, is to treat human na-

[3] *Ibid.*, pp. 221–222.

ture inconsiderately. At last, the original open and free attitude of the mind to nature is destroyed; nature has been reduced to a mass of meaningless details." [4]

By the fourth year (seven-year-olds), science, geography, and history formed an inseparable curricular unity. In the study of primitive people the central theme was the adaptation of man and his occupations to physiographical conditions: man operates in and comes to terms with a natural world, which requires understanding in order to be subdued and controlled. The students grappled with such problems as: "Which areas would be particularly suited to agrarian life, maritime life, pastoral, or hunting life?" Out of this general concern grew the related study of plants, animals, minerals, metals, and the typical mechanical and chemical processes utilized in primitive life such as smelting, dyeing, and fashioning pottery, all of which the students re-enacted experimentally. Much of the early work in science was devoted to biological and geological subject matter, as plants, animals, and rocks were readily observable and lent themselves to simple experiments.

Instead of the method of the recitation, they used a variety of approaches that coincided with the attitudes of scientific inquiry. For the study of biological aspects of the environment, excursions and planned observations were conducted. Children learned to make tentative generalizations and to check them against observed data. They were taught to view living things in terms of function and of adaptation to environment. Noting the adaptive patterns of the plants in wooded areas and along streams, they compared the characteristics of these plants with those of plant life in the cultivated school gardens. In an introduction to the earth sciences, the children were taken on rock-collecting expeditions. The rocks were categorized and discussed in terms of their various uses in human affairs—e.g., some for making cements or plasters and others for paints.

Examples of inductive methods, consistently employed, are described in the *Teachers' Reports*. Miss Camp, the science teacher for the eight-year-olds, made the following entry:

[4] John Dewey, "General Principles of Work, Educationally Considered," *The Elementary School Record*, Vol. 1, No. 1 (February, 1900), p. 13.

"They have brought together what they know of the formation of the earth. This week they have worked out what soil is. They named the things that they would find in tracing it back to its source in the rocks, giving their ideas of the way in which it was formed. They mentioned sandstone first as an ingredient of soil. It took a good deal of questioning to get them to formulate what the black earth or loam was as plant mould. I tried to get them to give me an idea of organic matter as what was left of plants and animals after life was extinct, but they have not yet given me anything about animals forming part of the soil. The first time in going over this one of the children told me that there would be 'lime' in the soil from the breaking up of the limestone. On making a list the second day no child suggested lime or any other part of a rock as being dissolved in water in the soil. I showed them all sorts of shells and corals and limestone with shells in it, but as yet they have not drawn the conclusion as to how these shells were made or even the step that the rock full of shells was made from shells similar to those they have been observing." [5]

Although the relation between teacher and students was one of free interchange, which encouraged the raising of questions and suggestions for follow-up activities, the basic disciplines of experimental work were insisted on. The children were taught that they could put certain questions to nature, but the results depended on the clarity of the questions.

"After the children have started their experiment, they begin their record, stating as minutely as their ability to write and compose will allow all that they did, sometimes illustrating with drawings. What takes place is recorded, and they discuss the meaning of the result. It is rarely that some member of the group does not arrive at the correct conclusion; if this is challenged, a check experiment is started. In order to maintain alertness it is desirable to encourage this, and not have the children think the matter is all settled, or merely appeal to the teacher's opinion. The conclusions are then added to the record.

[5] Katherine B. Camp, "Science: Group V," *Teachers' Reports of the University Elementary School.* Unpublished (February, 1900), pp. 112–113. In the archives of the University of Chicago Laboratory School.

"The writing of records, so essential to scientific work, also serves the purpose of lessons in writing and composition. Individuality of expression is encouraged, but the three points of a good science record—what was done, what happened, and the conclusions—are insisted upon. One of these brief records is as follows:

"We put a geranium plant under a bell jar with a glass of lime water, and the lime water was clear. We put the bell jar in the dark overnight, and in the morning the lime water was white on top; it showed that the plant breathed out carbon dioxide." [6]

In cooking classes, the children were confronted with scientific questions about the effects of heat on various substances, the nature of the growth patterns, and the composition of food stuffs. In sewing, the processing of flax, cotton, and wool was studied from raw material to finished product. The teacher of manual training raised questions about the properties of wood and metals, and the principles involved in simple tools and machines. By meeting problems and raising questions in these activities, the teachers felt that the children were re-enacting experiences of the human race. Because the studies provided practical insights into conditions that required extension of learning, children could sense how knowledge was essential to the whole of human life. In addition, they would gain insights into the evolution of the arts.

At the beginning of the first stage, the emphasis was on direct use and manipulation of materials. Toward the end of that period, interests requiring more prolonged study emerged. A unit on the physical history of the world was undertaken which included an introduction to the idea of geological epochs, the nature of the atmosphere, climate, and plant and animal zones. The intention was to give children an idea of the earth as man's home.

An entry in the records of one of the science teachers showed that the children developed an image of the earth as:

". . . a rock ball, on which the continents are slight elevations covered with a thick soil produced by the crumbling of

[6] Katherine Andrews, "Experiments in Plant Physiology," *The Elementary School Record*, Vol. 1, No. 4 (May, 1900), p. 108.

the rock. They pictured this ball surrounded by great bodies of water in which warm and cold currents circulate and modify the climate of the shores. It is covered with an atmosphere, a medium of exchange, by means of which the most important conditions of life—water, light, and heat—are distributed. They thought of it as covered with plant and animal life, its kind and abundance being determined by physical environment. For the most part, they had a fairly definite idea of the chief causes affecting climate and the zonal distribution of plants and animals, and of man's continuous control and adaptations of conditions about him." [7]

There is evidence of the collaboration of Dewey's colleagues in conceptualizing an approach to elementary work in science. One report describes the participation of Professors Chamberlin and Coulter in a conference on nature study sponsored by the Department of Pedagogy. Conferences like these were arranged so that "the University, the Public Schools and other educational agencies will meet on common ground for the purpose of furthering the different educational movements." [8] Papers were presented by principals of two of Chicago's public schools in addition to those presented by Professors Chamberlin and Coulter. Chamberlin's paper dealt with the adaptation of nature study to the early mental processes of the child. He took the position, among other things, that "the natural development of the mental processes of the race arose from contact with nature, and from this origin man's thought took its flight. In the development of the child, the same basis for development is found." The child, even before the mastery of language,

"is an original investigator . . . and it is an educational heresy to postpone the habit of investigating in schools until maturity. . . . The little child tastes, feels, smells, and sees, and synthesizes his results. He notes differences in form, position, color, and motion, and thus he begins to classify. All this is antecedent to information, and it is only when he has this foundation that

[7] Mayhew and Edwards, *op. cit.*, p. 286.

[8] "Conference on Nature Study," *The University Record*, Vol. 1, No. 41 (January 8), 1897, unpaged reprint found in Teachers College Library, Columbia University.

language is acquired. This is his next great step of discovery. With language he is no longer obliged to creep along by his own observation, since the acquired knowledge of the world is now opened to him." [9]

Dr. Coulter, Chairman of the Department of Biology, presented another paper on the relation of botany to elementary education.

"Dr. Coulter touched first upon some mistakes that had been made in bringing young children into contact with life phenomena. The dissection that calls attention mainly to the parts of plants is one of these. The analytic process is neither natural nor inspiring to young children, and creates no genuine interest in plant life. Attempting too much has been another error. A few simple things of natural interest will be of more value than a complete system that lacks vital relations to the child's life. The cultivation of observation merely for the sake of observation is another. Thus plants should be considered as things at work, not simply things with parts: as things moving, breathing, pulsating with life. A number of suggestions were given as to what might be observed with profit. The position plants take with reference to the light shows that they are not dead affairs, but living forces. That color holds some relation to light which enables the plant to perform its work better, instead of being ornamental only, can be studied by observation. The rain adaptations of plants, the relations between the root and leaf systems: the adaptations to droughts by the reduction of the exposed leaf surface, like a vessel taking in its sails, all these are vital and important as well as interesting to young and old. The right positions of plants, their behavior toward each other, suggest other lines of observation appropriate to young pupils." [10]

In the second period of elementary education, a move was made toward dividing the study of science into two broad areas: physiography (related to the study of history) and experimental science (biological and physical). Physical geography, for eleven-year-olds, dealt with the general physical characteristics of the

[9] *Ibid.*
[10] *Ibid.*

United States. Included was a course, developed with advice from Rollin D. Salisbury, Professor of Geography,[11] on the physiography of Chicago and the glacial origins of the Great Lakes. More formal methods were employed—discussion, written papers, assigned readings, and construction of relief maps. This shift in method was explained on the grounds that children, at this stage, developed an interest in the value of classified knowledge for use in more mature investigations.

In the third stage, the trend toward more specialized study continued. Group X (age thirteen) took the first general course in biology. This centered on the evolution of animal life, beginning with simple forms and ending with the physiology of man. Earlier, the physiology of the body was introduced through analysis of gymnastic exercises. Students took up the general subject of walking, for example, as involving a series of joints.

"They found the nature of the hip joint and of the knee joint as a hinge in one direction and of the ankle as possessing more pivotal motion and the toes as they move as a whole. Several of the children insisted that there was a joint between the toes and the ankles, but found by examining the feet that there was no movement there. One child asked why there were no large muscles on top of the shinbone and satisfied herself as to the reason by finding there were no movements of the lower leg forward and upward from the knee beyond a perpendicular line. The other exercise taken up was the arm movements. Starting from the shoulder and upper arm muscles they worked out the mechanism of the forearm. They located the biceps muscles by feeling of them and found that they were attached by a tendon at the shoulder and below the elbow to the forearm. They tried to move the door on its hinges by a string attached in a way similar to the attachment to the biceps and found it was very difficult to do. They thought that it was queer the arm should be attached in a way so difficult to move. They are now making models to work at each of the different classes of levers." [12]

Experiments were employed that stressed the role of theory and generalizations. The twelve- and thirteen-year-olds, for ex-

[11] Mayhew and Edwards, *op. cit.*, p. 229.
[12] Katherine B. Camp, "Science: Group VIII" (January, 1900), *op. cit.*, p. 26.

ample, studied photography as a basis for understanding concepts in the physical sciences. This led to a series of experiments on light, which brought out the principles involved in the construction of an image in a convex lens. The children began by working out the laws that govern the size of a shadow. A further study of light emphasized the history of the various scientific theories about its nature. After theories of the ancient Greeks and the sixteenth century corpuscular theory were stated, they were put to various scientific or experimental tests. The composition of light was demonstrated by experiment. A brief study of spectrum analysis and recent discoveries made by its use were included. The group saw that the solar spectrum had provided more knowledge of the constitution and temperature of the sun.

In the physical sciences, studies were made of gravity, heat, light, and electricity. The goal was to build in the child's mind, over a period of years, a mental image of the physical and biological processes of change and growth as a continuous round of freeing and utilizing energy. The nature of solution, evaporation, crystallization, and precipitation was studied through experiments so that the child might become thoroughly familiar with solids, liquids, and gases. Many topics were pursued in a spiral fashion. The lower groups raised questions in one form, and later these same problems were studied more systematically.

The oldest children (ages fourteen to fifteen) explored special aspects of chemistry and physics. It was considered that these children were approaching an adult level of interest. "They were beginning to see science as knowledge logically arranged (or possible of such arrangement) for the purpose of searching out more knowledge." [13] Although Dewey acknowledged the legitimacy of a move toward the logical organization of study at the secondary level, he argued that the central obligation was still that of general education; ". . . scientific method, in its largest sense is the justification . . . of science teaching, and the formation of scientific habits of mind should be the primary aim of the science teacher in the high school." [14] The physics teacher rightly should be concerned with techniques of measurement and experimentation, but the concentration on these skills as ends in them-

[13] Mayhew and Edwards, *op. cit.*, p. 219.
[14] John Dewey, "Symposium on the Purpose and Organization of Physics", *School Science and Mathematics* (March, 1909), v. 13, pp. 291–292.

selves should come later, when the task is to train scientific specialists. "The methods of experimental inquiry and testing which give intellectual integrity, sincerity and power in *all* fields rather than those which are peculiar to his specialty, are what the high school teacher should bear in mind." [15] Students should learn, for example, that scientific "laws" do not mark fixed limits to thinking, but represent instrumentalities for introducing continuity and order in experiences that otherwise are discrepant. The secondary school teacher becomes a partner, then, in creating a *"new type of mind"* that gradually develops under the influence of scientific methods. Dewey also held that the physics teacher should teach with an eye to showing the technological and social consequences that have resulted from the elaboration of the concepts of modern physics.

The aim of the elementary school was to develop attitudes that would lead children to view science as an intrinsic part of the evolution of man's mind. Having grasped this view adequately, the child would be ready for a systematic study of botany, zoology, astronomy, chemistry, and physics at the secondary level and beyond, without feeling that these were isolated "school subjects." The approach was to establish the concept that the sciences are unified in that they are manifestations of man's effort to understand and to come to terms with the whole of his world. The child, through a multitude of direct experiences, would be taught that the habits of inquiry are a natural part of man's striving. He would come to see that more complex problems and interests require progressively refined and disciplined skills and techniques; that specialization is a necessary extension of the need to pursue inquiry in depth. At the same time, the theory held that specialization could become sterile unless it was combined with an understanding of the interrelation and interdependence of fields of knowledge. The task of secondary and higher education was to work on the combined problem of specialization and interrelation.

We may note here that such approaches required teachers who were thorough students of science, who had a clear grasp of fundamental concepts and principles, and who were trained in experimental methods. The teachers of science were experts.

[15] *Ibid.*, p. 292.

But, in accord with Dewey's image of the teacher, they also had to be students of "the child's mind"—sensitive to the kinds of experiences appropriate for children at different ages, and imaginative in their efforts to get children to feel the excitement in scientific inquiry. They did not assume that the *program for instruction* could be found intact in bodies of knowledge. They had to be professional in the sense that they continued to be students of the process of teaching. The curriculum rationale was to provide the general direction; flexibility was to be employed on the specifics. It seems fair to add that the kinds of methods and materials utilized in the Dewey school could not be transferred to mass education enterprises where similar resources were lacking. We must remind ourselves that Dewey insisted that the primary function of his school was to project educational procedures consistent with his theory. He took the stand that conditions had to be provided in the Laboratory School that would enable it to demonstrate what an excellent education could be like. The records seem to show that in general there was one master teacher for every eight or nine students; with the inclusion of graduate assistants, there was one adult for every four or five children. No pretense was made that the school's procedures could be employed in other school systems where quite different conditions prevailed.

SUMMARY OF SCIENCE TOPICS STUDIED—WINTER 1900 [16]

*Group IV* (*Age* 7)    Study of metals
Construction of a kiln for making charcoal
Smelting
Molding copper weights

*Group V* (*Age 8*)    Tanning rabbit's skin
Currents
Gravitation
Comparisons of weights and measures
Experiments to show relation of movement of
earth to sun

[16] Summarized from the *Teachers' Reports of the University School*, 1899–1900. (Note the absence of reports for the oldest children [Group XI]. This is typical of the paucity of evidence about features of this last and important level.)

SUMMARY OF SCIENCE TOPICS STUDIED—WINTER 1900
## (*continued*)

|  |  |
|---|---|
|  | Weight and pressure of air |
|  | Making compasses |
| *Group VI (Age 9)* | Formation of the earth |
|  | The Appalachian Mountain Range |
|  | Beginning of rivers in the mountain region of Virginia |
|  | Erosion of rivers as affecting the Appalachians |
|  | Study of river systems in the United States |
|  | Comparison of land and water upon the globe |
|  | Interpretation of landscape pictures |
|  | Study of pewter |
|  | Experiment with antimony |
|  | Comparison of weight of mercury and water |
| *Group VII (Age 10)* | Finding proportions of soluble albumen in wheat flour |
|  | Experiments with the lever |
| *Group IX (Age 11–12)* | Making alloys |
|  | Experiments with oxygen and carbon dioxide |
|  | Experiment concerning changes from liquid to solid to gas |
|  | Visit to Armour Institute in connection with study of electricity |
| *Group X (Age 13)* | Theories concerning light |
|  | Polarization |
|  | Use of the interferometer |
|  | Study of ether |
|  | Study of color |
|  | Effect of length and tension of string upon vibration |
|  | Velocity of sound |
|  | Spectrum analysis and absorption of light |
|  | Study of the spectrum and the spectroscope |

# CHAPTER TWELVE

## Communication and Expression (Language, Mathematics, the Arts)

The third curriculum area was called "Communication and Expression." It included reading, writing, literature, foreign languages, number work and mathematics, and the arts. Rather than trying to recount the details of each part, we shall concentrate on a description of the rationale that held together this disparate group of studies.

The thematic idea that made it possible to see unity in such a range of content was derived from Dewey's theory of the social origins of knowledge. He saw rough parallels between the way that learning developed and the evolution of civilized experience.

Dewey had argued that where the child is concerned there are four basic impulses on which to build: [1] (1) the social impulse, rooted in the need to communicate something about a social situation, (2) the constructive, (3) the investigative, and (4) the expressive (with the latter two growing out of the first two). It was held that the child has a basic need to express himself in activity and to share and tell the results of his activity. The young child might express himself in various ways—by means of daubs of color on paper, a figure made of clay, a house of blocks, or by recounts of his day's doings. Under the stimulus of the desire to *communicate*, he searches out and welcomes all means of letting others know what he has done, felt, and experienced. He seeks ways of expressing himself more effectively. The optimum psychological time to teach him the techniques of communication is when his need for them is compelling.

[1] Katherine C. Mayhew and Anna C. Edwards, *The Dewey School* (New York, Appleton-Century-Crofts, 1936), pp. 336–337.

READING AND WRITING

One of the hypotheses was that the skills of reading and writing could be taught most effectively when the child was ready and saw the need for them. In Dewey's school, teachers did not begin by teaching four- and five-year-olds to read and write. The children were provided with activities that gave them a chance to engage in creative play, to construct, to explore media of expression, to raise questions, to extend their experiences through planned excursions, to engage in simple dramatic reenactments, and to communicate ideas in story and discussion.

From the occupations as a center, they were led to raise questions and engage in types of studies described in the sections on history and science. Dewey assumed that traditional approaches promoted negative attitudes toward learning and, in general, were wasteful. The child's mind was dulled by premature, unrelated drill; time was wasted on formal techniques, which were important, but which prevented the child from being introduced to more positive subject matter. The move toward more formal study of reading and writing came as children had to make these resources part of their own equipment. As we have seen, the theory held that the general time for sharpening techniques and skills was at the approach of the second stage (ages eight to nine).

Dewey advocated a basic change in attitudes toward the school child.[2] Instead of seeing him as someone to be instructed, educated, or amused, he was to be viewed as a young human being with genuine interests and questions of his own; willing and able to explore his world in a variety of ways. The job of the teacher and school was to clear out what Dewey called "saw dust" and provide the child with things that he could take seriously. If the school provided the young child with opportunities for sensory-motor pursuits and a rich range of exploratory activities, the child would have no difficulty in taking an interest in reading, writing, and number work. These skills would simply

[2] John Dewey, "The Results of Child-Study Applied to Education," *Transactions of the Illinois Society for Child Study*, Vol. 1, No. 4 (January, 1895), p. 18. Cited in Mayhew and Edwards, *op. cit.*, pp. 474–475.

be additional and necessary tools for adequate expression. To master them would require the same kind of care and practice needed to refine the control of tools in the shop.

Laura L. Runyon, before she became an outstanding teacher in the Laboratory School, described a portion of her first visit.

"I met one of the teachers in the hall and besought her to tell me about the school: whether they had days or hours when they really used books: whether Dr. Dewey believed children ought to learn how to read, write and cipher, or whether the new education was a preparation for Tolstoy's socialism. She said that Dr. Dewey believed the time spent in an elementry school on reading, writing, and arithmetic could be more profitably spent; that an average child could learn these in doing other things." [3]

Mastery of typical readers and the ability to print one's name were not first-month goals of the school, but language, as a means of social communication, operated in the school from the child's first day. Students were encouraged to share their experiences, report on their projects and activities, and relate information accurately and distinctly. They were coached informally in diction, enunciation, projection, etc. Inhibitions were eradicated early by giving the students frequent opportunities to report orally before the class and to participate in school assembly programs.

An example from the *Teachers' Reports* may serve to illustrate some of the techniques used and to indicate the attitudes the teachers employed in analyzing the results.

"The materials for the reading lessons for this group have been taken chiefly from their history with occasional changes to other subjects. . . .

"Their lessons have been presented for the most part on the blackboard with some typewritten leaflets. It has been found to be much easier to hold their attention to the blackboard work than to the other. Their interest in each other's work as that of the group as a whole is very slight, so that when each has the whole lesson in his own hands it is difficult for them to respect each other's claims upon the attention of the teacher and the

[3] Laura L. Runyon, "A Day with the New Education," *The Chautauquan*, Vol. 30, No. 6 (March, 1900), pp. 590–591.

group. With blackboard work the constant sense of expectation due to the frequent erasure of one set of sentences in order to make room for another helps to keep up their interest in something beside their individual opportunities for reading aloud. In order to insure alertness of attention, they are sometimes asked to watch while work is put upon the blackboard and then after it has been quickly erased, tell what it said. This is of service also in guarding against the danger of mere word-calling into which their reading constantly tends to degenerate. For a similar reason there has been only a sparing use of phonics, new words being associated instead with as vivid an image as possible of the realities for which they are the symbols. The work of this group confirms the results of former experience—the conviction that the effort to make out words by sounding during the first months of reading is likely to result in a fatal division of attention. For instance, a few days ago one of the brightest children in the group, after being allowed to 'sound' the new words in a sentence six words long, was unable to look away from his paper and tell what he had read until the fourth or fifth attempt.

"Comparatively little writing has been done, the reason being lack of blackboard room and of proper conditions for the use of paper and pencils and also the fact that the children tire very quickly. The general tendency seems to be towards very fine writing with a correspondingly cramped position of the fingers. An effort has been made to overcome these faults by encouraging them to write large letters that can be seen across the room and by showing them that the writing takes less muscular effort if the chalk is held lightly. One child was so delighted with this discovery that he insisted on erasing all his work and doing it over in the new way.

"A notably successful lesson was the result of a talk about the making of their looms. Sentences were put on the blackboard by the teacher as the children gave them and read and reread by the class. A list was made of the new words, chiefly names of tools, and a drill upon these was given by acting out the uses of the various tools, individual children being chosen to direct the action by pointing to certain words or to find on the blackboard the name of the tool which the others were using. The children were delighted with the lesson. The next day they were eager to write the new words and spent the entire period at the black-board without signs of fatigue. They called this writing 'putting tools into their shop,' and one boy insisted upon buying each tool from the teacher before he wrote its name,—gravely proferring imaginary money and insisting that the tool be wrapped up in paper and duly delivered." [4]

It is difficult to say just how effective these approaches were. The reports and examples of work produced indicate that many of the children were facile and creative in verbal expression. We must remember that these were children from professional families and that their academic accomplishments would be influenced by that fact. Although they read widely, some of them had the conventional difficulties in spelling and in using correct gram-matical expression.

There are fair questions that could be asked: Did the theory tend to cause teachers to be reluctant about introducing children to formal instruction in reading until later than necessary? How effective was the formal instruction and drill when it was given? People with the professional training required to make judgments on such matters would need to examine the records. It would have to be recognized, too, that this was a genuine pioneer effort. It is obvious that the emphasis on the importance of enriching and utilizing the child's experience as a basic factor in learning the three R's has become an intrinsic part of modern methods.

## NUMBER WORK AND MATHEMATICS

The approach to the study of numbers and mathematics was determined by the theory of the role of mathematical symbols in the evolution of the mind of the race, and of the child.

At the preprimary and primary level, work in arithmetic was designated as "number work." [5] Numbers were seen as symbols for handling aspects of the world and as a means of communica-tion. The preschool child lives in a world where simple counting

[4] Margaret Hoblitt, "Reading: Group IV," *Teachers' Reports of the University Elementary School*. Unpublished (March, 1900), pp. 301–303. In the archives of the University of Chicago Laboratory School.

[5] Mayhew and Edwards, *op. cit.*, pp. 339 ff.

is necessary. This is reinforced by nursery rhymes, such as "One, Two, Buckle my Shoe." When the four-year-old comes to school he has had a background of experience in the language of number, although he is not familiar with the more technical forms of unit measurement. The psychology of number was seen as similar to the psychology of language, as both are forms of communication in which conventionalized symbols are used to express ideas. Both arise out of the need to get ideas across about something important in the physical or social world. The school was to provide a series of situations that demanded the use of number symbols. Because of the fundamental character of mathematics, its development was one of the main concerns of the planners of the curriculum.

During the early stages, the problem was to see that children had many occasions to use numbers as a way of getting order and effectiveness into their activities, games, and constructions. In cooking, for instance, the child first had to count out spoons and forks. Later he learned that one cup of flaked rice took one cup of water. He found, through experimentation, that other cereals required four times as much water for proper cooking. In planning meals, he then had to work out the amounts of water needed for different cereals. He could do this only with numbers, and in making comparisons, he was dealing with the idea of ratio. Concrete manipulations of quantity, including comparisons of weights and distances, were followed by practice in more definite uses of enumeration and relation in order to control results. Units of measurement were introduced in the work of the shops and garden. It was assumed that in carpentry, cooking, sewing etc., the child would realize that the language of number provides a means for rendering many activities orderly and effective. Thus, he could gain insight into the ways men employ numbers in social life.

The theory assumed an analogy between the child's progressive experience with number, and the origin and development of number in human history. The hunter had to count his game, or the herder his flocks. Territory had to be measured off in primitive agriculture and track kept of changes in the seasons, the movements of the sun and moon. More refined tools required more precision in the use of them.

"The growing accuracy and precision as applied to the particular facts of experience, leads to number, in the form of more counting and aggregation. The definite laying off of materials and selection of energy, leads to a more refined form of counting known as measurement. Here, in other words, we have the beginnings of mathematical science: its function being, on the one hand to inventory existing resources, and on the other hand to define these resources with references to their possible use in accomplishing some desired end." [6]

This way of viewing the nature of number was used to stimulate interest in the origins of measurements of various kinds. At the age of eight, the child, in his study of the Phoenician culture, was presented with the historical basis of alphabets and numerical systems.

It was assumed that children of this age, because of their needs, desired greater facility in handling numbers.

"They gladly submit to drill in order to attain such facility. If they are allowed to discover for themselves such things as the place of digits, tens, hundreds, etc., in our system of notation, they work out their own rules for adding and subtracting, multiplying and dividing. When a child in the school found it necessary to add $\frac{1}{3}$ and $\frac{1}{4}$ of a foot he proceeded in natural logical fashion from the known to the unknown. He knew one foot as 12 inches. He then consulted the ruler and saw that the $\frac{1}{3}$ is 4 inches and that $\frac{1}{4}$ is 3 inches, or $7/12$ of a foot . . . at this stage he was given the terms numerator and denominator and understood that the figure above the line tells the number of parts taken, while the one below tells how many of these parts there are in the unit. As the work often involved the use of fractions the child liked this new and convenient tool. . . . The ability to abstract and formulate began gradually at about nine years of age." [7]

The study of the stages of growth led the members of the school faculty to believe that the age of ten represented a peak of interest in developing skills for the sheer pleasure of manipu-

[6] Dewey, *Lectures for the First Course in Pedagogy*, No. 6, p. 4.
[7] Mayhew and Edwards, *op. cit.*, pp. 342–343.

lation. Because children of this age thoroughly enjoyed playing with numbers, this year was an important one for helping them acquire many basic skills and techniques easily. When learning the multiplication tables, they also tackled division. One student volunteered the information that if the division tables were the opposite of the multiplication tables, you could prove the answer of multiplication by dividing it by the multiplier. The children received great pleasure in checking this idea. They wanted to go on immediately to long division so that they could prove multiplication problems in which the multiplier contained more than one figure.

The hard and fast distinctions between arithmetic and algebra were broken down in various ways in order to show that algebra is generalized arithmetic. Letters were used to represent quantities when writing formulas; for example, base $\times$ rate $=$ percentage $(b \times r = p)$. In weighing, the idea of an equation was given as a way of representing the gravitational power of the earth on objects. The earth pull of weights (designated as $a + b + c$ on one side of a scale) was shown to equal, in balance, the earth pull of the unknown weight of an object $(x)$ on the other side.[8]

In later years, work in algebra included involution, evolution, the theory of exponents, and operations involving radical quantities. In geometry each member of the group worked out, for the most part independently, from twenty to thirty propositions, and wrote up demonstrations with varying degrees of care.[9]

In the second quarter of the year's work for the fourteen-

[8] Mayhew and Edwards, *op. cit.*, p. 343.

[9] In the *Teachers' Reports* one finds notations like the following by the teacher of mathematics of the twelve-year-old group.

"At the last recitation the word syllogism was introduced; some major and minor premises were introduced, and the children discovered that if they admitted these, the conclusion was inevitable. They also discovered errors in some false syllogisms which I gave them. A few of them are now struggling with the proof that a dog has ten tails. The object of all this is to introduce them to the lesson which they have today, which is to complete the following syllogisms, and to make the application to some simple problems: (1) to multiply by a fraction is to multiply by its numerator and divide by its denominator; (2) division is the ——— of multiplication; (3) therefore, to divide by a fraction is to ———. I am much interested to see if they will be able to complete and apply this argument." (M. Osborne in *Teachers' Reports*, November 1899–June 1901, p. 80. In files of Teachers

and fifteen-year-olds, students used Wills's *Essentials of Geometry* as the basis for study. The propositions of the first book and many of their related exercises were covered—about one hundred in all. The remainder of the quarter was devoted to algebra with the study of radical equations, quadratic equations, and the theory of quadratics. It was felt that it was probably a mistake to try to study algebra and geometry in the same year. Some students lacked ready command of fundamental principles and processes. Others did not study long enough to acquire familiarity with the application of the principles.[10]

When considering a systematic study of mathematics and mathematical concepts in the later school years, Dewey advocated an approach similar to that in history—the genetic approach. In *The Psychology of Number*, Dewey said that the only way to answer a question like "What is a triangle?" is to find out how the triangle came to be.

"I venture the statement that (putting aside the few with the inborn mathematical instinct) higher and secondary mathematics is to the majority of students a practical riddle with no definite *intellectual* content in itself. What meaning it possesses it has got by way of attained practical facility in solving problems; or through its applications to other sciences or engineering. It will hardly be denied that the educational value of mathematics is not realized until its concepts and methods have a definite intellectual content of their own. Can this be secured save that the methods of instruction follow the evolution of the process out of its cruder psychical forms to the more finished?" [11]

Morton White theorizes that "Dewey took the constructivist theory of mathematical concepts . . . and worked it into a genetic or evolutionary approach." [12]

This is illustrated in an early article, "How Do Concepts

College Library, Columbia University.) See also John Dewey, "The Psychological and the Logical in the Teaching of Geometry," *Educational Review*, Vol. 25 (April, 1903), pp. 387–399.

[10] *Ibid.*, p. 239.

[11] John Dewey, "Psychology of Number," Letter in *Science*, N. S., Vol. 3 (February, 1896), p. 288 (reply to Henry Burchard Fine's review of McLellan and Dewey's *Psychology of Number*, 1895).

[12] Morton G. White, *The Origin of Dewey's Instrumentalism* (New York, Columbia University Press, 1943), p. 68.

Arise from Percepts?" His thesis was that "the concept arises from the percept *through realizing the full meaning im*-plied, but not *ex*-plicit in the percept." [13] He used the triangle as an example. As a mere percept it is regarded wholly as a *particular* thing. Knowledge of *that* triangle would be exhausted in getting its particular dimensions, degree of angles, lengths of sides, etc.

"Suppose the mind advances beyond the particular triangle to the thought that there is a principle involved in the triangle; that the triangle, like everything in the world, is made upon a certain principle which is embodied in it; that this principle furnishes the plans and specifications according to which anything must exist in order to be a triangle at all. What shall we call this principle which constitutes the particular thing a triangle, rather than a pumpkin or a stove-pipe, is it this principle we really mean by triangle, and are attempting to know? Well, it is this principle which forms the concept 'triangle.' The concept 'triangle,' in other words, is the way in which three lines are put together; it is a mode or form of construction." [14]

Dewey concluded that the meaning of a concept can be grasped *only in and through the activity that constitutes it*. The way to get to know the concept of triangle is to go through the act of putting it together. The generality of "triangle" lies in the fact that it is a mode of action, a *way* of putting things together. Just so, a particular cotton loom consists of specific parts, but the loom in its functioning is not particular—it is the concept, loom.

So he argued that the percept is knowledge in an accidental, or limited way, while the *concept* "means complete knowledge of an object—*knowledge of its mode of genesis*, and in its relations and bearings." [15] The concept always enriches the percept. If one once sees the process by which a triangle becomes a triangle, one can apply that knowledge to each particular triangle. This really involves the ideal of every science. "Our knowledge of the individual is limited until we have got at the

[13] John Dewey, "How Do Concepts Arise from Percepts?" *The Public School Journal*, Vol. 11 (November, 1891), p. 128.
[14] *Ibid.*, pp. 128–129.
[15] *Ibid.*, p. 129 (My italics).

principle involved in it. Our knowledge of the principle is imperfect (abstract) until we see how the principle acts under the multitude of different circumstances." [16] Dewey then drew a pedagogical moral, which permeated the work of his school. The genuine way to lead students from percepts to concepts is first to present the percept in its genesis—in its origin and growth, and in its proper relations. For the child, it is not necessary that all the abstract relations be pointed out. What is important is that "the object be, as it were, *done* over and over again; let the relations in it be used; let the mind act in accordance with the principle involved; and sure ground is laid for the conscious apprehension of the concept later." The teacher's work is to see that the child's mind goes through the constructive process involved in the concept. Later the process itself can become an object of reflection. "First the process *used* by the mind; then the process consciously thought is always the normal psychological method." [17]

At the lower levels the approach to number was somewhat incidental to other activities and studies. The intention again was to move toward abstractions in specialized mathematics at the secondary level, but the kind of concern for working out the "structure of mathematics" that characterizes recent approaches was not noticeably in evidence. The "method of discovery," however, was constantly operative. To a non-expert, it would appear that the methods employed paralleled, to an extent, some of the principles involved in the "new mathematics" a half century later. One thinks, for example, of the current advice that experience with basic techniques and concepts should precede formal instruction, or of a basic dictum of a recent program: "The Project assumes that the ability to discover patterns in abstract material is one of the most essential mathematical skills—quite possibly *the* most essential skill." [18]

[16] *Ibid.*

[17] *Ibid.*, p. 130.

[18] Robert B. Davis, "A Brief Introduction to Materials and Activities" (unpublished Madison Project, Syracuse University and Webster College, 1962), p. 8.

LITERATURE

Literature, poetry, and drama were presented throughout the curriculum. Yet the records on this subject are quite scant. Literature fell less neatly into the rationale than did history or science, and Dewey wrote relatively little about the humanities. He did have ideas about the proper relations between the "two cultures." We shall analyze his position here and describe the approaches to the study of literature in the school. In Chapter Sixteen we shall indicate what we feel were basic limitations.

In the Seventh Lecture of his First Course in Pedagogy (1896) Dewey made one of his most explicit statements about literature.[19] He described it in relation to his sociological theory of history. The basic drive in man's history he argued, was the effort to increase control over his world for social ends. Broadly conceived, this could be seen as the source of the advance of experience, in science and invention, in industrial and political developments, and in moral and spiritual life. After examining the place of history in the curriculum, he asked, "What then is literature?"

"Literature is the outcome of man's social experience. It is the record of his consciousness of the value contained in that experience. There comes a time when experience is so laden with meaning that the dead weight . . . of this meaning breaks through the outer form in which that meaning is bound up. It becomes possible for men to see that their experiences have a value which goes beyond their momentary occurrence. . . . Literature is thus the expression of man's consciousness of the more permanent and enduring values of his experience. . . ."[20]

Employing the historical interpretation, Dewey maintained that at a primitive level, literature consists of tribal traditions formulated to help a society maintain its continuity and keep track of itself. It represents both a summary of past social events and beliefs and the organizing of that material for educating the young. As such, literature is as much a social institution as the forum or temple with which it is most closely associated.[21] He

[19] Dewey, *Lectures for the First Course in Pedagogy*, No. 7, pp. 3-4.
[20] *Ibid.*, p. 3.
[21] See, for example, C. M. Bowra, *Primitive Song* (New York, New

asserted that this direct connection between social life and literature is broken as social consciousness becomes more complex, but even then, literature is primarily history more idealized. The ancient Greeks deepened their social insights and therefore saw their history in a much more flexible way than did, for example, African tribes. Instead of a mere recounting of past events, the central interest for the Greeks shifted to a concern for the spirit, or inner meaning of their life. This does not mean, however, that literature was divorced from cultural life, but rather that, as an interpretation, literature served to clarify and purify the social life.

Dewey argued against an individualistic conception of literature as inspired utterances of great geniuses, speaking truth somehow or other apart from their culture.

"[It] must be insisted that the conception of literature as the interpretation of life ought to give the standard for the place of literature in education. Literature as a key to life behind it, or as a mode of interpretation, deserves all that has ever been said in its favor. But literature taken not as a mode of introduction into primary experience, but regarded as something in itself . . . is futile and forced . . . at best it is a mere luxury for those who have the leisure to devote themselves to a highly specialized cultivation of certain refined emotions; while at worst it reduces itself to sentimentalism. Between the worst and the best it always has at least a tendency, when made a thing by itself, and not an organ of interpretation, to substitute second-hand and conventional ideas for original and vital experience, and thus to substitute artificiality for reality." [22]

In Dewey's interpretation, literature is intimately connected with the fabric of cultural life, and it has indirect bonds with science and industry. Unless the individual has had rich experiences with "the fundamental activities connected with life, and has secured some insight into the conditions and processes which make this life possible, he cannot have obtained the background

American Library of World Literature, Mentor Books, 1963). Bowra studied the roots of literature in the songs of primitive peoples that reflected their lives and superstitions.

[22] Dewey, *Lectures for the First Course in Pedagogy*, p. 4.

of experience necessary to make literature pregnant with meaning." [23]

Pedagogically, literature, drama, and poetry were seen as aspects of communication and expression in which children should
be participators and creators as well as appreciators. For the young
pupils, verbal and written expression grew out of their work in
the occupations and in other studies, particularly history. Children were constantly required to formulate the meaning of their
experiences. It was argued that anyone who, in conversation or
in writing, expresses clearly his own vital experiences is an artist
—a producer, not a mere absorber of the expression of others.

The four-year-olds recounted stories of their trips and activities, and acted out the parts of stories read to them. The five-
year-olds dramatized aspects of social occupations. After a dry-
goods store had been visited, for example, the children took the
roles of the cashier, clerks, and delivery boys. Teacher and students together worked out simple reading lessons based on these
experiences. In Group IV, the seven-year-olds, in connection
with the study of primitive history, were read *The Story of Ab*.
They then re-enacted it, and supplemented the story with other
material learned from history. The story of Abraham and Lot
was read, to illustrate the character and problems of shepherd
life. The children retold the story and printed it in large type
on the school press for a reading lesson. In the study of early
civilizations, other examples were drawn from the Bible.

One year, the agricultural conditions and peasant life of early
Greece were studied through reference to Hesiod's *Words and
Days*. On other occasions, attention was turned to aspects of
Homeric society, with selections from the *Odyssey* and the *Iliad*
as foundations for study.

When the eight-year-olds studied the great explorers, they
read the best stories available on Marco Polo, Columbus, Magellan, and others. They were always making oral reports, presenting
dramatic re-enactments, and writing accounts. At one time, the
ten-year-old students wrote a textbook in arithmetic in which
they composed their own problems based on work in the shop,
in the kitchen, in science experiments, etc. The records indicate
that Group IX (age 12) became interested one year in the logic

[23] *Ibid.*

of the syllogistic statement, and composed their own examples. The write-ups of experiments in science and of the field excursions were considered an intrinsic part of work in written expression. The thinking behind this practice is indicated in the following quotation:

"Is it not somewhat artificial to make grammar and language study the chief repository of the structure of the intellect, to the neglect of that magnificent logical apparatus exhibited in modern modes of investigation and verification? Can the average child best lay hold of and realize the laws of reason through a study of a relatively dead product in language, or through their constant personal use in the discovery and statement of truth?" [24]

For the older children, the tendency to study literature in connection with other studies continued. Mrs. Dewey, who taught English, followed this approach. When the children were reading Caesar's *Commentaries* in Latin, she had them study Shakespeare's *Julius Caesar*. The play was acted out, the characters studied, and two children debated the comparative virtues of Brutus and Cassius. In the year when the study of European backgrounds in American colonization was undertaken, the study of social life in Shakespeare's time was included. An overview of English history from the Wars of the Roses to the period of the Tudors was conducted with an intensive study of Shakespeare's *Richard III*. The meaning of the Renaissance and the Reformation was studied through lives of leading personages, including Erasmus, Sir Thomas More, and Martin Luther.

Some transition toward granting literature a more independent standing at the secondary level was contemplated, but experiments in that direction had not advanced very much by the time Dewey left.

Having examined some illustrations of the teaching of literature in the Laboratory School, we may reflect briefly on Dewey's general attitudes toward literature and the humanities. In comparison to the volume of words he wrote on the role of history and of the natural and social sciences, and the enthusiasm he saw

---

[24] John Dewey, "Review of William Torrey Harris, *Psychologic Foundations of Education*," *Educational Review*, Vol. 16, No. 1 (June, 1898), pp. 13–14.

in their educational prospects, his comments about literary studies are brief and often characterized by warnings about the misuse of these studies rather than by substantive recommendations. This could be interpreted as evidence of hostility. A closer reading, however, reveals that Dewey was stressing another kind of point. Actually he was opposed to certain kinds of teaching for *both* the humanities *and* the sciences. His real search was for a way of relating them to each other so that they would be educationally significant for the children of a new industrial, democratic society.

In this context he conceived the chief responsibility in the teaching of the sciences to be humanistic. Dewey's perspective of the evolution of human experience led him to conclude that the emergence of the scientific temper of thinking opened up possibilities for helping men to attain new insights into both the natural and social world. This in turn made it possible for men to gain a kind of control and a kind of direction that would make the fruits of intelligence available to the hitherto depressed majority of men. There was the *possibility* of a working relationship between the scientific mind and an industrial, democratic social order that justified the hope that life in the urban complexes could be humanized.

Whether the sciences in the school curriculum supported such objectives or not depended on *how* they were taught. Dewey argued that for educational purposes, the natural sciences, for example, could be taught in such a way as to provide insight into the processes of nature and their consequences for human affairs,—and give insights about the natural setting of social life. He denied that the scientific and technical studies were necessarily less humanistic than literature.

"To be aware of the medium in which social intercourse goes on, and of the means and obstacles in its progressive development is to be in command of a knowledge which is thoroughly humanistic in quality. One who is ignorant of the history of science is ignorant of the struggles by which man has passed from routine and caprice, from superstitious subjection to nature, from efforts to use it magically, to intellectual self-possession." [25]

[25] John Dewey, *Democracy and Education* (New York, The Macmillan Co., 1916), p. 267.

A dichotomy between the sciences and humanities was provided, however, when the sciences were viewed as providing mere factual information about the physical world. This would fit the wrong-headed notion, said Dewey, that science was to give information about physical things while the humanities were the sole repositories of knowledge about man. This created the impression that there were two different worlds, each of which was to be the province of a separate realm of discourse. His treatment of this issue in *Democracy and Education* is representative of his position. In the teaching of the humanities, Dewey feared an esoteric approach. This derived, he thought, from the historic role of the humanities as a specialized interest of a leisured aristocratic class. He charged that

"The older humanism omitted economic and industrial conditions from its purview. Consequently it was one sided. Culture, under such circumstances, inevitably represented the intellectual and moral outlook of the class which was in direct social control. Such a tradition is . . . aristocratic; it emphasizes what marks off one class from another, rather than fundamental common interests. Its standards are in the past; for the aim is to preserve what has been gained rather than widely to extend the range of culture." [26]

When humanistic studies were pitted against the study of nature and urban industrial realities, the tendency was "to reduce them to literary and linguistic studies, which in turn tend to shrink to 'the classics,' to languages no longer spoken." [27]

Dewey affirmed that since "Greek and Roman art and institutions had made such important contributions to our civilization there should always be the amplest opportunities for making their acquaintance, but to regard them as *par excellence* the humane studies involves a deliberate neglect of the possibilities of the subject matter which is accessible in education to the masses, and tends to cultivate a narrow snobbery: that of a learned class whose insignia are the accidents of exclusive opportunity." Then Dewey added the generalization that characterized his definition of liberal or humane studies. "Knowledge is humanistic in quality

[26] *Ibid.*, pp. 337–338.
[27] *Ibid.*, p. 268.

not because it is about human products in the past, but because
of what it *does* in liberating human intelligence and human sympathy. Any subject matter which accomplishes this result is
humane, and any subject matter which does not accomplish it
is not even educational." [28]

If a cultist attitude prevailed, the humanities would be taught
as subjects with content remote from the experiences of the
masses of urban children then crowding into the schools. Teachers
of literature and the arts would be guilty of that "isolation"
which Dewey censured so frequently.

We may understand this stance by noting the approaches in
the schools that Dewey opposed. Oscar Handlin has provided
a picture of the teaching of literature and arts of the time, based on
a study of the professional journals. As Handlin puts it, teachers
were assigned the task of softening and ennobling their charges—
especially the "uncultured" immigrant children. They were to
bring "added culture and refinement" into children's nature.

"It was not enough to teach children who lived in slums that
a 'healthful, beautiful location, good construction, perfect drain-
age, perfect plumbing, and perfect sanitary conditions generally,
are indispensable to the house beautiful'; or to illustrate the proper
mode of dining with quotations from Homer, Plutarch and Bos-
well. It was essential, in addition that the student's tastes be bent
toward desirable . . . goals. . . . That end could be attained
through the development of an appreciation of the higher aspects
of culture. Domestic science, for instance, led to an awareness
of the artistic elements in decoration and to an understanding
of the beauties of English, French, German, and Italian furniture.
Students were thus to be exposed to the noble, gentle styles of
life so different from their own." [29]

In music the approach was one of moral uplift. The subject
matter of singing was held to be important because it dealt with

"such subjects as Love of Country, Home-loving, the Golden
Rule, etc. Teachers were told that songs like these will develop

[28] *Ibid.*, p. 269.
[29] Oscar Handlin, *John Dewey's Challenge to Education.* (New York,
Harper and Row, 1959), p. 29.

'like sentiments in the children who sing them' and 'the habitual use of vocal music by a family is an almost unfailing sign of good morals and refined tastes.' " [30]

The emphasis on the need to exert "good influences" envisaged the school as cut off from and battling against the cruder currents in the out-of-school life of the child. As Dewey saw it, this made for ineffectual teaching.

This aversion to the "isolation" of literature is expressed in a more fundamental way in an earlier article by Dewey on "Poetry and Philosophy" (1891).[31] He grappled directly with the question of the relations of science, philosophy, and the humanities (here represented by poetry). His main points were made through an analysis of the work of Matthew Arnold.

Dewey quoted Arnold as representing the conviction that ancient assurance and authority have been corroded by the onslaughts of modern science. Arnold recommended poetry as a last resort for consolation. Dewey said that Arnold's feeling of regret stemmed from his sense of a twofold isolation of man— isolation from both nature and his fellowmen. He admitted that Arnold's feelings were understandable, but he could not follow Arnold to his conclusions. Dewey agreed that it is easy to disparage science and to laugh at philosophy with its "reasoning about causation and finite and infinite being."

"Both are remote enough from our immediate spiritual and ethical interests. Face to face with the supreme question regarding the right ordering of life they seem ludicrously insufficient. But, after all, science means only knowledge—philosophy, only love of wisdom, only the essay of reaching the meaning of this experience of ours. I cannot believe that the attempt to know truth, to grasp the meaning of experience, is remote from conduct, from the ideals and aspirations of life. . . . Imagination rests upon belief; it is from belief that it gets its cue to stay, to

[30] A. D. Mayo, "Methods of Moral Instruction," National Education Association, *Addresses and Proceedings*, 1872 (New York, 1873), p. 21, quoted in Handlin, *op. cit.*, pp. 29-30.

[31] John Dewey, "Poetry and Philosophy," *The Andover Review*, Vol. 16 (August, 1891), pp. 105-116.

interpret, its consolation. If there is belief in the high and serious values of the universe, with what glory shall not the imagination portray and inspire life, what consolations shall not issue from it! But let intelligence lose this belief in the meaning and worthiness of experience, and poetry is but the tricking out of illusions, the devising of artifices. I can well comprehend that poetry may deliver truth with a personal and passionate force which is beyond the reach of theory painting gray on gray. Indeed it is the emotional kindling of reality which is the true province of poetry. . . .

"Thus do I conceive of poetry. The graceless, rigid, dark facts of science, of philosophy, pass through the atmosphere of personality, of the hopes and fears of a human soul, and issue illumined and illuminate. Without the basis of fact, of fact verifiable by science, our light is a will-o'-the-wisp, a wandering flame generated in the stagnant marshes of sentiment." [32]

Dewey took the position that poetry can be illusory in its consolations unless the vision it contains is warranted by what critical investigations reveal to us of the reality of things. He saw Arnold's pessimistic view of science as representing a revolt against the mechanistic English philosophy of his day. In sensing the inadequacy of such a philosophy, Arnold "sought refuge in the unnamed, unprofessed philosophy of the great poets of England and of all time." [33] Dewey seems to be saying that the frame of reference of science and philosophy (as illustrated in British empiricism) may be limited, too, and then the poet may reach intuitively for dimensions of truth not expressed in a limited perspective of science. Dewey expressed the hope that a more adequate philosophy and concept of science would make it possible for the poet and the scientist to complement each other's work.

"Here, indeed, is just our problem. We must bridge this gap of poetry from science. We must heal this unnatural wound. We must, in the cold, reflective way of critical system, justify and organize the truth which poetry, with its quick, naïve contact, has already felt and reported. The same movement of the spirit,

[32] *Ibid.*, p. 107.
[33] *Ibid.*, p. 116.

bringing man and man, man and nature, into wider and closer unity, which has found expression by anticipation in poetry, must find expression by retrospection in philosophy." [34]

Although Dewey was in a period of transition from the Hegelian orientation at this time, there is basic continuity with his later position. Poetry had to be more than ornamental or escapist. It had a legitimate office to "kindle emotions" and to "illumine," but it had no warrant to turn from reality. Nor need it do so. Here we encounter Dewey's own basic faith in the fruits of scientific inquiry. Such inquiry did undermine some traditional supports. It did provide insights into a nature that contained desirable and disagreeable features. But, in the final analysis, it revealed a world containing those conditions that support the view of life as a gift and those that make it possible to advance the quality of life; such insights provided legitimate grounds for celebration and reassurance. The limits imposed by nature and its life-destroying features could not be denied, but Dewey chose not to assign these the front-stage position. He was content to approach life from the faith of a natural piety—and to claim neither more nor less than that position warranted.

In Dewey's recommendations for the schools we find him asking that the child be given a view of literature and the arts that would make them intrinsic to the everyday world as the child knew it. The child could bring literate and aesthetic expression into his efforts to make sense of his world. In the general curriculum Dewey sought to overcome the problem of isolation by defining literature as an expression of cultural life; thus there was room for materials on classic Greek and Roman civilizations.

This solution has merit but limitations also. Dewey constantly emphasized the danger of literature being "mere individual expression," but never clearly presented his views on the legitimacy of literature as sheer entertainment or even as self-confrontation. When a man wrestles with his inner conflicts and fights for personal integration in writing, we can learn something about ourselves by being permitted to share his revelations. In

[34] *Ibid.*

the final analysis, this observer does not feel that Dewey's view rules out this role of literature, but it is given little attention, and the main thrust of Dewey's writings points in other directions.

## FOREIGN LANGUAGES

Foreign language study began in the Elementary School with Group VII. The children studied Latin and French, and a few of them, German. The method employed would now be described as the direct, conversational approach. The children were taught to understand the meaning of words by recognizing their connections with objects or actions rather than by knowing their English equivalent. They learned the Latin words for the parts of their bodies and for other objects in their environment. After a sufficient number of nouns had been mastered, a few active verbs were taught, with the teachers performing the appropriate actions. Fables and stories, such as "Pyrrhus" and "Regulus," were read and reread to attune pupils' ears to the sounds of words and the cadence of word combinations in sentences. Miss Margaret Hoblitt, teacher of Group VIII, reported:

"In taking up a new story the children first learned the new words, each being associated so far as possible with the appropriate object, action, or quality. For instance, verbs were acted out for them and nouns presented in connection with the corresponding object. The new words were put into their notebooks, and their spelling learned in spelling matches. By means of writing from dictation, answering in Latin questions on the story, etc., the children grew familiar with the Latin before they attempted to translate it into English, and in some cases were able to tell the story in Latin without having made any conscious effort to commit it to memory." [35]

Primary importance was attached to visual and oral experiences with the language. This provided the basis for the study of grammar, declensions, and conjugations. As a grammatical example arose in reading and conversation, the children spent time studying and trying to understand the rule that governed it be-

[35] Margaret Hoblitt, "Group VIII," *The Elementary School Record*, Vol. 1, No. 3 (April, 1900), pp. 93–94.

fore continuing the lesson. Another report of Miss Hoblitt illustrates the approach:

"In Latin, after a review of the stories in the previous year, the children took up the study of parts of the sentence, work in Latin and in English going hand in hand. The children learned quickly to distinguish the subject, predicate, and object, calling the subject the 'actor' and the verb the 'action' word. Some time was spent in making clear by means of illustrations the idea that some verbs require an object, or word to show the person or thing that receives the action. The next step was to indicate the value of the Latin inflection. Simple Latin and English sentences were put upon the blackboard in the natural and the inverted order, until the children discovered that, while in English the change of order—for instance from 'The girl loves the doll' to 'The doll loves the girl'—involves also a change in meaning, in Latin this was not true. Applying their recently acquired knowledge of the parts of the sentence, they discovered that in words like *puella* the final *a*, when short, indicates the 'actor' case, and *am* that of the object. . . ." [36]

At one time, the same person taught Latin and English so that correlative study of word derivations and problems of syntax and grammar could be made. Formal study of English grammar was coordinated with foreign language study.

The more advanced classes, before reading Caesar's *Commentaries*, read his biography from *Viri Romae*. In connection with the study of the Gallic Wars, a detailed examination of the outstanding men and the social, intellectual, and political events of Caesar's time was made. As we previously noted, Caesar's *Commentaries* were also read in conjunction with the study of Shakespeare's *Julius Caesar*.

There is almost nothing in Dewey's writings or in the literature of the school that indicates a comprehensive case for the inclusion of foreign languages. Their inclusion in the curriculum and the imaginative approaches employed in teaching them testify to the fact that value was attached to them. We know that a school like Dewey's would have experienced pressures from college-oriented parents, but he was not one to concede much

[36] *Ibid.*

on these grounds alone. On one of the family's trips to Europe, Mrs. Dewey became impressed by the facility with which a foreign language is learned when there is "a need for it as a means for getting things done." [37] All that we really have are the actual accounts of how the languages in fact were taught.[38]

## THE ARTS AND THE AESTHETIC

"Art is not an outer product nor an outer behavior. It is an attitude of spirit, a state of mind—one which demands for its satisfaction and fulfilling a shaping of matter to new and more significant form. To feel the meaning of what one is doing and to rejoice in that meaning, to unite in one concurrent fact the unfolding of the inner life and the ordered development of material conditions—that is art." [39]

The Dewey school provided a wide range of materials and experiences in the arts: the visual arts ("fine" and practical), music, drama, and literature. In conception, however, the aim was not to develop skills in these areas as isolated activities.

"The ideal of the school was that the music, the literary and dramatic efforts of the children, and their artistic expression whether in design, in wood, metal, or fabric, in the graphic or plastic arts—all should represent the culmination, the idealization, the highest point of refinement of all the work carried on." [40]

In order to understand this kind of goal, one must turn to Dewey's theory of art and aesthetics. In the 1890's, his ideas on the subject were not formulated with the clarity and detail that characterized his later *Art as Experience* (1934).[41] One senses a

[37] Frances L. Davenport, *The Education of John Dewey* (unpublished thesis, Ed. D., University of California at Los Angeles, 1946), p. 122.

[38] For accounts of the foreign language program, see Mayhew and Edwards, *op. cit.*, pp. 198, 240–241, 354.

[39] John Dewey, "Culture and Industry in Education," *The Educational Bi-Monthly*, Vol. 1, No. 1 (October, 1908), pp. 1–9. Quoted in Mayhew and Edwards, *op. cit.*, pp. 347–348.

[40] Mayhew and Edwards, *op. cit.*, p. 361.

[41] John Dewey, *Art as Experience* (New York, Minton, Balch and Co., 1934). (Paperback reprint: New York, Capricorn Books, G. P. Putnams' Sons, 1958).

struggle for expression in the early writings, but the basic themes of his later theory are present.

The task, as he saw it, was "to restore continuity between the refined and intensified forms of experience that are works of art and the everyday events, doings, sufferings that are universally recognized to constitute experience." [42] He did not want to see the aesthetic confined to the galleries and the works of the masters; he conceived art to be a dimension of experience potentially present in home, job, community, and school. It is possible to sketch only a part of his thesis here.

In his article "The Reflex Arc," Dewey described the origin of the artistic impulse as being in the basic nature of the activity of the organism. Life involves interaction with the environment; ends are pursued, continuity is broken temporarily; the effort is made to restore equilibrium as the ends are gained. Form, in a fundamental sense, is achieved whenever a new level of equilibrium is reached—an ordered relationship with the environment is reconstituted. As Dewey saw it, the germ of the aesthetic is contained in the consummatory reordering that comes after disruption or conflict in experience. [43]

One of man's first needs was to handle raw materials. An example is found in primitive jug-making. When the goal was simply to make something to hold water, a purely functional object was formed. A transformation occurred if the craftsman found in the coordination of hand and eye required to produce it an outlet for all his powers. The result then possessed beauty of form and outline as well as functional utility. [44]

Art, Dewey said, involves the processes of giving shape or form to material in a way that engages the interest—the activity of the eye and hand, the ear and voice of the individual. Art, in origin, is closely connected with constructive activities. Another dimension relates to the expression of values or ideals. It is in art that the values of a civilization are expressed. An individual attains a sense of fulfillment not only when his special abilities are expressed but also when the producer realizes that his work is related to the ideals of his society. This is one feature that dis-

[42] Ibid., p. 3.
[43] Ibid., pp. 14-15.
[44] Dewey, Lectures for the First Course in Pedagogy, No. 7, pp. 5-6.

tinguishes the mechanic as technician from the mechanic as artist. He is a technician when he produces merely for the special need at hand. He becomes an artist when he senses what his product means in terms of social value.

"In so far . . . as the one who produces does not participate in the realized values of civilization and does not carry on his own work in the spirit of those attained values, his work tends to fall to a mechanical level and to be more or less servile; but no matter how small or apparently menial the thing produced, the art element, the spirit of freedom of execution and perfection of result are sure to manifest themselves, whenever the individual producer is capable of feeling himself as a social organ, reflecting in his own work the life of the community in which he belongs and contributing to its elevation." [45]

In civilizations where this sense of social values is not relevant to work, art tends to be separated out as "fine art," while work is viewed merely as a mechanical process. In more integrated civilizations, the distinctions between the minor and the fine arts practically disappear. Dewey offered ancient Greece and the Middle Ages as examples. In these two periods the preparing of food, clothing, and shelter was executed in as artistic a spirit as the making of great temples or the production of paintings. To understand the Parthenon, Dewey said, one must remember "the bustling, arguing, acutely sensitive Athenian citizens, with civic sense identified with a civic religion, of whose experience the temple was an expression, and who built it not as a work of art but as a civic commemoration." [46]

The aim in the Laboratory School was to approach art in a manner consistent with such ideas. Dewey reversed the traditional practice of first teaching technique and then providing for artistic expression. The very young children were allowed to explore a range of materials. In the occupations, the manual arts provided a natural medium for creative expression. Teachers were to introduce more advanced techniques as the children confronted more complex problems in art.

[45] *Ibid.*
[46] Dewey, *Art as Experience*, p. 4.

At the same time, artistic expression was seen as an intrinsic goal in all the studies. In 1896 Dewey formulated a list, "Means of Developing Techniques," which illustrates the point:

"1. Incidental criticism of products of imaginative expression.
2. Drawing in connection with nature study affords excellent means for development in technical definiteness and accuracy.
3. Drawing in connection with history, architectural reproductions mark a similar normal and intrinsic demand for the correction of crudity and vagueness.
4. The aesthetic interest is strong in the child and may be taken advantage of in connection with decorative design and construction.
5. Wherever there is any kind of manual training, there is a necessary demand, in the development of the activity itself, for correct technique.
6. The child may learn much from the incidental and mainly unconscious imitation of the methods used by others." [47]

Many of the studies were cooperative ventures. When these culminated in dramatic activities, or in making murals or models, the social ideal of the school as a "community of learners" and as a place where the arts would represent "the highest point of refinement of all the work carried on" was achieved. Dewey judged that the school failed more often in this respect than in any other.[48] Artistic skills could have been developed at a higher level had the arts been handled separately, but he felt this sacrifice was justified by the effort to attain more emotional and imaginative personal fulfillment through the integrated approach.

[47] John Dewey, "Imagination and Expression," *Kindergarten Magazine,* Vol. 9 (September, 1896), pp. 67–68.
[48] Mayhew and Edwards, *op. cit.,* pp. 361–362.

# CHAPTER THIRTEEN

# Evaluation and Research

The University Elementary School was designed to be a laboratory in educational psychology. As such, it had research and evaluation functions. What kind of work in these fields was undertaken?

The research was not characterized by the kind of sophisticated scientific techniques available today. This may be accounted for, in part, by the fact that research procedures in the social sciences were undeveloped at the time. Only a part of Dewey's energies were available for directing the school. Much of his time was occupied with troublesome problems of finance and the need to administer the school with limited resources. It is also true that the definition of "laboratory" as applied to the school made a difference. The school was to be a place where the staff would try to work out educational practices and programs consistent with a philosophical-psychological theory, and where changes were to follow from examining work in progress. New ground was being broken. This meant that broad hypotheses, such as seeking to integrate school work with stages of child development, were formulated. Ideas for implementation were to be employed with intelligent flexibility rather than to be treated as blueprints to be followed in detail. Each year, practices were to be examined in terms of their consequences—unpromising ones to be dropped, others modified, and new ideas to be projected for the following year. Dewey visited the school almost daily during the first year.[1] His observations were supplemented by those of Mrs. Dewey and of members of his faculty. The teachers of the school were treated as colleagues. Staff meetings were characterized by a free discussion of successes and failures.

[1] Katherine C. Mayhew and Anna C. Edwards, *The Dewey School* (New York, Appleton-Century-Crofts, 1936), p. 382. See Ch. 18 in general.

Teachers' records were kept as a source of data. These finally became systematized in the typewritten *Teachers' Reports*,[2] under the supervision of Mrs. Laura Runyon.

The directors of departments in the school were to be trained investigators with a responsibility for compiling reports as scientific findings. These were viewed as data that should be available to other investigators in education. They also were to provide a basis for effecting changes in the school. This method of putting intelligence to work for the improvement of practice certainly was consistent with Dewey's style. And evaluation may be said to have been made if evaluation is defined as "the collection and use of information to make decisions about an educational program." [3] This differs from a customary meaning attached to evaluation as the measurement of learning by pupils exposed to a given program.

One of the more striking changes that occurred in this informal mode of evaluation involved the important matter of selecting teachers and defining their roles. From what has been said to this point, it is clear that Dewey's image of teachers included the expectation that they would be students of child behavior, capable of working in terms of psychological principles. Dewey's concern for their competence in subject matter was equally compelling. Teachers were needed who had explored deeply the meaning of their subject.

Various approaches were tried. One procedure that was attempted and abandoned was the self-contained classroom. On this point Dewey observed:

"As a result of experience, a chief modification has been with regard to specialization on the part of teachers. It was assumed, at first, that an all-round teacher would be the best, and perhaps it would be advisable to have one teacher teach the children in several branches. This theory, however, has been abandoned and it has been thought well to secure teachers who are specialists by tests and training—experts along different lines. One of the rea-

[2] *Teachers' Reports of the University Elementary School (1899–1900).* Unpublished. Available in the archives of the University of Chicago Laboratory School.

[3] Lee J. Cronbach, "Course Improvement through Evaluation," *Teachers College Record*, Vol. 64 (May, 1963), pp. 672–683.

sons for this modification of the original plan was the difficulty of getting scientific facts presented that were facts and truths. It has been assumed that any phenomenon that interested a child was good enough, and that if he were aroused and made alert, that was all that could be expected. It is, however, just as necessary that what he gets should be truth and should not be subordinated to anything else.

"The training of observation by having the child see wrong is not so desirable as sometimes it has been thought to be. The difficulty of getting scientific work presented except by those who were specialists has led to the change in regard to other subjects as well." [4]

It was recognized that there was a possible danger of swinging to another extreme. This could result in destroying a unity in the child's experience. But it was accepted as a simple impossibility that one person could be competent in all lines of work. Dewey said:

"Superficial work is bound to be done in some of them, and the child, through not having a model of expert workmanship to follow, acquires careless and imperfect methods of work. Intellectual integrity and continuity in the treatment of subject matter seemed of greater benefit than the hovering care of one person." [5]

The school sought, then, to put the various subjects of study in the charge of experts who maintained agreement and harmony through continued consultation and cooperation. The results obtained "justify the belief that the undue separation, which often follows teaching by specialists, is a result of lack of supervision, cooperation, and control by a unified plan." [6]

The fact is that no elaborate or systematic effort at an over-all evaluation was provided, although the work of the school was *described* extensively by Dewey and his staff in the *University Record* and in the nine monographs of 1900 in *The Elementary*

[4] Mayhew and Edwards, *op. cit.*, pp. 35–36. This point is elaborated in John Dewey, "The University Elementary School: History and Character," *University Record*, Vol. 2, No. 8 (May, 1897), pp. 74–75.

[5] Mayhew and Edwards, *op. cit.*, pp. 376–377.

[6] *Ibid.*, p. 36.

*School Record.* Some fragmentary statements on evaluation may be found there and in the *Teachers' Reports*, in which members of the school's staff made observations of their students' progress. One example serves to illustrate. Mr. Osborne, teacher of mathematics, made several entries about his experiences with Group X (age thirteen) in the winter term of 1901. As the work for the quarter began, Mr. Osborne noted on January 16, 1901, "Their ignorance of arithmetic is almost appalling, and it may be necessary to start afresh and begin from the beginning." But several weeks later we find him reporting that the group's interest and effort had picked up so that on February 8, 1901, he comments, "We may be able to finish the work in arithmetic in less than the time previously mentioned (this quarter), and so get back to the algebra more quickly than was expected." [7]

In addition to such remarks on very specific items, there are some undated comments by Mrs. Dewey in which she offered observations on aspects of teaching in the school. There is a certain disjointed quality about these notes but they may be worth presenting at length because they represent one of the few accounts from primary sources in which the work is appraised. We do not find cold objectivity here, but we do get an insight into the spirit of the teaching and a willingness to acknowledge certain shortcomings.

"Much was learned in the mistakes of the school . . . but we should be in danger of falling into depression if we could not forget those lost opportunities which were so often forced upon our attention during the lifetime of the school.

"Our teachers had been selected as carefully as possible with reference to their social fitness and it is scarcely probable we could have found any more suitable to the needs of our pupils. Perhaps it is true that our greatest disappointments came in the study of modern languages. In French we were fortunate in securing teachers of note but yet we could not spend enough time

[7] *Teachers' Reports,* November 1899–June 1901; entries for January 16, 1901 and February 8, 1901. In files in Teachers College Library, Columbia University. For another group Mr. Osborne noted, "I find that they do not know how to cancel and how to reduce a common denominator. So Miss Bacon has been taking some of the children at this period for drill in the work."

to acquire any thing real in conversation. In German the result was more satisfactory; but, the fact is no school can teach conversation in a foreign tongue without a great deal of help in the home, or elsewhere. In Latin we did better, the first drama acted in public in the school [was in Latin]. It consisted of a few short but decisive sentences which pictured the founding of Rome. . . . Latin was begun at nine years of age and at sixteen our children had read the literature required for college and had practiced a good deal in Latin pronunciation and composition. None of them ever showed a disposition to write to their friends or to repeat Latin poetry for their own amusement. None of them became carpenters or builders, but most of them were waked up to certain aspects of life and nature such as would have remained forever obscure or unrecognized if they had not taken courses in elementary science. All of them are now walking in professional paths similar to those of their fathers.

"The most valuable habit they gained was that of thinking for themselves. Knowing that things were not 'being put over on them,' they took the responsibility that was expected of them and they took it with zeal. Without exception they learned to work. Some harder than others but there was no premium on a dull idleness. It proves nothing for independence of character to show the teacher one did not like the assigned task because the task was usually at the choice of the pupil.

"On the whole and with trifling exceptions the question of discipline after the first year was almost a negligible one.

"The experience in cooking in this school was full of encouragement. We were convinced of its full adaptability as a social exercise, and of its special fitness to young children. Appealing as it does to the first interest in life, it forms the most natural connection between school and home; it stimulates social intercourse at the most timid age; it provides an activity well proportioned in muscular training and in intellectual demand. It can be suited to the crudest attempts and to the nicest adjustments, at all stages securing a practical result. To eat one's own cooking is an awakening experience beyond any other in the beginning of school life. . . .

"From the kindergarten up our cooking was made a complete exercise. The little ones studied the farm and the grain; along with this they cooked oatmeal or other cereal, a work not too long or difficult to be finished, with the service and dishwashing. They were taught to observe what happened in the boiling of water, what obvious change there was when the grain was put into water, under heat, etc. Along with this they planted the seeds and saw the resemblances between the two processes of growing and cooking. They began to understand why food is cooked, and to think of digestion as a process which is affected by one's acts. They saw the importance and the labor in laying a table, in caring for utensils, in leaving the room orderly after all was done, they began to look upon house servants as something other than mere machines, they were filled and thrilled by a feeling of achievement and independence. One of the pleasantest memories of the school is that of a little boy who had never put on his own coat or overshoes, who glowed with enthusiasm over brushing up crumbs, and asked as a special privilege to be allowed to wash dishes. They entertained their friends at no cost of their own self-respect such as often comes in the attempt to find a visible reason for showing one's friendly feeling.

"Out of the cooking there grew the earliest and best number work of the lower classes, the need of accuracy in measurement was proved in the pudding, and fractions were inseparable from whole numbers. Fractions were cheerfully mastered with the aid of spoons and cupfuls for the sake of one's appetite. After some months of work one began to see a relation between spoon and cupfuls and pints and quarts; systems, and tables evolved from sugar and flour and water. Tables so difficult to memorize from the page of an arithmetic were even understood when the substance of life was put on the scales and one proved the relation between pints and pounds. The picture of a Thanksgiving party at school is one to engross the feelings of parents. But to one looking on all the time the daily luncheon of a class entertaining themselves or another class's often hard struggles of preparation is a fuller demonstration of the value of so-called occupational work. Such a luncheon took place every day in the school dining room with a second in the kindergarten. Thus seven groups at a time had cooking, and studied the art of expert waiting. In some cases choice could be allowed to individuals between cooking and spinning or shop work. We saw no indications that boys wished to avoid cooking. When the four large high schools were later thrown together and the young men from the boys' schools were given a chance to elect cooking, the demand for room in the new kitchens went far beyond our possibilities.

"There remains still one aspect of work to be accounted for, and that is one of the largest, and one of those difficult to separate from the whole substance, and structure,—I mean that which we called inventive. This inventive side was cultivated not alone in the mechanics but in all the intellectual processes as well, and whenever possible. When inventions were developed in the bigger constructions such as keeping the water out of Holland, or when they repeated what had been done in earlier society, such as figuring out how men first thought of the hammer, or the bow and arrow, or how stone blocks were lifted to the top of the Pyramids,—in such cases there was not much in the way of material process to be shown to a looker on. In the course of their schooling there were few of these youngsters who did not show resources of ingenuity and use these in a way that undoubtedly contributed to efficiency later in life. Sand tables are short-lived and the most cherished constructions soon follow the course of time and make way for the new. On the whole that fact contributes to encourage effort.

"In such processes as pottery, moulding in metals, testing stress and strain in building, in spinning and weaving, children made discoveries in ways and means that remained in use to their credit for a long time. Certain children won a reputation for skill in certain lines of work and carried on a business at home in partnership with their neighbors in order to do more than school hours permitted. Such a Firm carried on a business in dyeing and experimented in the manufacture of dyes till they produced colored thread enough for a rug which they wove on a loom of their own making with a design of three colors." [8]

There were some instances of more controlled inquiry. Part of the plan for research included the idea of allowing the school to become a center for graduate study in psychology.

[8] Alice Chipman Dewey, Comments on the work of the early years in relation to educational theory. In notes in files on records of the Dewey School in Teachers College Library, Columbia University.

One assignment was to develop a sequence of school activities appropriate for the muscular coordinations of children at different stages in their growth. On the basis of discussions in weekly teachers' meetings in the first year, a sequence of activities was worked out for the different groups. Weekly time allotments were specified for gymnastics, the occupations (shop, sewing, etc.), science, history, etc. Decisions were made in terms of balancing the times allocated to intellectual study, to manual construction, and to artistic modes of expression, such as modeling and painting. Careful records were kept over the years and changes in scheduling were effected.

One of the students in Dewey's seminar, Frederick Smedley (Director of the Child Study Department of the Chicago Public Schools), joined with A. A. Wood, a graduate student in psychology, to carry out a series of measurements of the sensory and motor abilities of the pupils. These tests were planned in the University Psychological Laboratory to consider the pedagogical value of measurements in determining the right balance of various school activities. In the introduction to a published report of these tests, Mr. Smedley wrote as follows:

"[The school] is a pedagogical laboratory where the students of pedagogy are investigating such questions as the correlation of studies, the psychological bearing of the different branches, and the adaptations of the material from the different sciences to the needs of primary pupils." [9]

Smedley then gave examples of how knowledge of the defects of some of the children had resulted in different approaches by the teachers who had cooperated in the study. (For example, several girls who had been judged dull were found to have hearing problems.)

He undoubtedly reflected Dewey's orientation when he added that psychology is much more likely to be effective in the teacher's work when he has gained his knowledge "from observation and experiment with children" rather than from text-

[9] Frederick W. Smedley, "A Report on the Measurements of the Sensory and Motor Abilities of the Pupils of the Chicago University Primary School and the Pedagogical Value of Such Measurements," *Transactions of the Illinois Society for Child Study*, Vol. 2, No. 2 (1896–1897), p. 85.

books alone. Following this vein, Smedley concluded his report with the statement:

"These tests are, I believe, a suitable beginning for a teacher who is to develop an organized, assimilated knowledge of child psychology and become a trained observer of children. Let us hope that the schools of the near future will be equipped with such teachers, teachers who, better understanding the natures of the children, will better know their needs and be able to provide for them, and that in those schools pupils will not be promoted simply on account of their having remembered the words of the answers to stated questions. Instead health, strength, quickness and accuracy of intellectual activity, and the acuteness and education of the senses will determine in part at least, the child's fitness for higher and harder work." [10]

In later years, studies were made to discover the stage of growth at which self-consciousness appeared. These seemed to show that conscious differences in interests and attitudes between boys and girls, except in isolated instances, were not marked until after the age of eleven.

A modest groundwork for educational experimentation was prepared, but there was nothing to compare with the mass of statistical measurements that was employed when Charles H. Judd became Director in 1909.

[10] *Ibid.*, p. 90.

# CHAPTER FOURTEEN

# Secondary and Higher Education: A Search for Integration

Dewey wrote a brief account of the Laboratory School at the end of the first year, in which he expressed his intention to extend the work to include secondary education.

"Work in the secondary period is not as yet provided. Its main object, however, is more formal differentiation of various groups of study so that the individual pupil shall secure a well balanced introduction into the whole region of human attainment, and also knowledge of the special direction in which his own interests and abilities lie, so as to prepare him for specialization in advanced work or in actual life. The secondary period really extends to the end of the present sophomore year in college. But naturally the University School is concerned with it only during its first three years. This secondary epoch is the time for formulating in generalizations the chief principles which are fundamental to various lines of study, and for amassing the detailed stores of information which embody and illustrate the general principles. If the elementary period has been adequately lived through, so that the child has secured positive experience in all these directions, has had intellectual hunger kept alive and quickened, and has acquired working use of the main lines of investigation, there is no doubt that a very large amount of technical generalization and of special detail, can easily be acquired in a comparatively short time." [1]

[1] Dewey, "The University Elementary School: History and Character," *University Record*, Vol. 2, No. 8 (May, 1897), p. 75.

During the 1890's, two distinguished secondary schools became affiliated with the University of Chicago: the South Side Academy, founded with the university in 1892 as a preparatory school, and the Chicago Manual Training School, established in 1883, which joined the university in 1897. By the end of the decade, these were placed under Dewey's jurisdiction as he was then Chairman of the Department of Education. At first he had little direct control over them, but with the forming of the School of Education in 1901, they were united as the University High School. They were brought together in a functional way only with the opening of the new Belfield-Blaine complex of buildings in the fall of 1903. We shall say more on this subject later. Here we simply wish to note that Dewey was acquiring resources for expanding educational experimentation into the secondary level. His preoccupation with the Elementary School and his other responsibilities precluded his giving systematic attention to problems of the high school in the early years. The opportunity to turn seriously in that direction came for the first time when he began what was to be his last year in Chicago.

At the elementary level, a full-fledged school was in operation. The value of his ideas for elementary education can be measured, in part, against the performance of the school. Where secondary education is concerned, however, Dewey formulated ideas that never met the test of practice. We have a record of these in a number of printed speeches and articles he wrote during and after his Chicago work. For the most part, they concentrate on an analysis of the nature and origin of problems confronted by the high schools. Some general principles are outlined that point to hypotheses he presumably would have favored, but there is a disappointing paucity of detail. Enough is there to indicate that American education would have had a special challenge had Dewey not left the field.

In reviewing this neglected aspect of Dewey's work, we shall examine four facets: (1) Dewey's argument that the problems of the high school were rooted in the social changes transforming American society, (2) his analysis of the special problems of the relations of liberal and technical studies deriving from this fact, (3) the historical background of his own move to incorporate several aspects of secondary education into the Laboratory School, and (4) recommendations for organizing studies at the secondary level.

## SOCIAL CHANGE AND PROBLEMS OF SECONDARY EDUCATION

"The modification going on in the method and curriculum of education is as much a product of the changed social situation, and as much an effort to meet the needs of the new society that is forming, as are changes in modes of industry and commerce." [2]

Dewey referred here to education in general, but the statement has special relevance for his description of the problems of the high school and college. We are reminded of his sociological analysis of the occupations in his article "The Savage Mind," where he argued that pervasive changes in mind, character, and institutions accompany fundamental changes in the nature of man's work or mode of gaining a livelihood.

Simply put, Dewey's thesis was that a new America had come into being since the Civil War, which made the former concept of the schools obsolete and inadequate.

The expansion of capitalism together with revolutions in science and technology had transformed the nature of production and commerce. "Manufacturing was split up into a very great variety of separate processes through the economies incident upon extreme divisions of labor." [3] These drastic changes in the organization and operation of mass industry were responsible for great upheavals in the social order. Industrial specialization had its counterpart in a fragmented urban situation. While the home and village gave way to the large city as the center of production, the population center shifted markedly from the rural to the urban area. His thesis is supported by figures showing that in 1840, only one-twelfth of the American people lived in cities of 8,000 or more. By 1860, the proportion of city dwellers had grown to one-sixth, and by 1900, to one-third of the population.

[2] John Dewey, *The School and Society* (Chicago, University of Chicago Press, 1923, rev. ed.), p. 4.

[3] John Dewey and Evelyn Dewey, *Schools of Tomorrow* (New York, E. P. Dutton and Co., 1915), pp. 240–241.

Census figures indicate that nearly one-half (46.3%) of the people in the United States in 1910 lived in urban areas.[4]

Not only were native Americans forsaking their farms for employment in towns and cities, but rising demands for labor were also luring millions of immigrants to the great industrial centers of the United States. Between 1880 and 1900, nine million immigrants entered the American mainstream. With the increased growth of trusts and corporations, great wealth was concentrated in the hands of the upper echelons of the managerial and ownership groups. Within the expanding urban areas, there were depressingly low standards of housing, health, and sanitation.

Fierce power struggles accompanied these transformations, but there were also efforts to advance democratic ideals. These included efforts to attain dignity for laboring people with consequent wider access to social participation. As Dewey put it:

"The change that . . . overshadows and even controls all others is the industrial one—the application of science resulting in the great inventions that have utilized the forces of nature on a vast and inexpensive scale: the growth of a world-wide market as the object of production, of vast manufacturing centers to supply this market, of cheap and rapid means of communication and distribution between all its parts . . . population is hurriedly gathered into the cities from the ends of the earth; habits of living are altered with startling abruptness and thoroughness; the search for the truths of nature is infinitely stimulated and facilitated, and their application to life made not only practicable, but commercially necessary. Even our moral and religious ideas and interests, the most conservative because the deepest-lying things in our nature, are profoundly affected. That this revolution should not affect education in some other than a formal and superficial fashion is inconceivable." [5]

The debate over how the schools should respond to this revolution was being carried on before Dewey's work at Chicago began and it has continued without abating to the present.

[4] Charles Beard, *Contemporary American History* (New York, The Macmillan Co., 1914), p. 247. (The Bureau of the Census defines as urban any town over 2,500.)

[5] Dewey, *The School and Society*, pp. 5–6.

THE HIGH SCHOOL IN SEARCH OF A PROGRAM:
PROBLEMS OF THE RELATION OF LIBERAL TO
TECHNICAL STUDIES

Dewey described the general educational situation as one of confusion. Extension of knowledge accompanied the creation of a technological society. The schools were confronted with an expanded population clamoring for entry. As the system grew rapidly and subject matter proliferated, there were pressing demands for the addition of new offerings in the academic areas, for example, modern languages competing with Latin and Greek, natural sciences and the newer social sciences challenging classical studies. Subject matter of the more familiar type was compounded by new and more practical work—manual arts, commercial and vocational subjects at the secondary level; journalism, agriculture, forestry, engineering, etc., in the universities. Voices were raised in alarm; the schools were the target of bitter criticisms from all sides and at all levels.

In the face of continuing attacks and in the absence of any clear insight into the sources of the trouble, educators responded by giving way to one pressure and then to another.

"Consider the wave by which a new study is introduced into the curriculum. Someone feels that the school system of his (or quite frequently nowadays her) town is falling behind the times. There are rumors of great progress in education making elsewhere. Something new and important has been introduced; education is being revolutionized by it; the school superintendent, or members of the board of education, become somewhat uneasy; the matter is taken up by individuals and clubs; pressure is brought to bear on the managers of the school system; letters are written to the newspapers; the editor himself is appealed to to use his great power to advance the cause of progress; editorials appear; finally the school board ordains that on and after a certain date the particular new branch—be it nature study, industrial drawing, cooking, manual training, or whatever—shall be taught in the public schools. The victory is won, and everybody—unless it be some already overburdened and distracted teacher—congratulates everybody else that such advanced steps are taken.

"The next year, or possibly the next month, there comes an outcry that children do not write or spell or figure as well as they used to; that they cannot do the necessary work in the upper grades, or in the high school, because of lack of ready command of the necessary tools of study. We are told that they also are not prepared for business, because their spelling is so poor, their work in addition and multiplication so slow and inaccurate, their handwriting so fearfully and wonderfully made. Some zealous soul on the school board takes up this matter; the newspapers are again heard from; investigations are set on foot; and the edict goes forth that there must be more drill in the fundamentals of writing, spelling, and number." [6]

As Dewey pictured it, changes were made in a mechanical, piecemeal way with each item viewed in isolation from the rest. In the absence of some unifying philosophy, he argued that there could be no relief from this unbecoming manner of designing the curriculum. He did not claim to have a full-blown answer, but he was convinced that the chance for a more orderly procedure was dependent on insight into underlying social changes that were the source of the pressures.

Conflict and perplexity were not in themselves bad if they could be used as a spur to new resolutions. There was no virtue, however, in sheer disarray. Where secondary and higher education were concerned, Dewey directed his attention to analyzing the origins of the leading problems.

In the year that the South Side Academy and the Chicago Manual Training School were being incorporated into the School of Education, Dewey presented at the Conference of the Academic and High Schools Affiliated or Cooperating with the University of Chicago a paper entitled, "Current Problems in Secondary Education." [7]

He acknowledged that honest men were divided along two lines. One group, committed to the existing school system, held that reforms should be made within the traditional framework; others clamored for more radical changes to adapt the school to

[6] John Dewey, "The Situation as Regards the Course of Study," *Educational Review*, Vol. 22 (June–December, 1901), pp. 29–30.

[7] John Dewey, "Current Problems in Secondary Education," *The School Review*, Vol. 10 (January, 1902), pp. 13–28.

contemporary social needs. Dewey said that each stood for significant values that could not be overlooked. In order to illustrate his point, he proceeded to analyze several related problems of the high school.

The secondary school, he said, could not ignore its articulation with the elementary school and the college or university. It was the link between them. Its peculiar difficulties and responsibilities resulted from this intermediate position, for it was at the center of pulls from divergent historical traditions. On the one side, the modern elementary school represented a response to the ethical demands of democratic trends. Prior to the revolutions at the end of the eighteenth century, its aim was merely to teach the three R's to children of the lower classes so that they could be of useful service to the established order. One result of the upheavals of the eighteenth and nineteenth centuries was a profound aspiration after intellectual and moral opportunity and development, as well as political equality. Rousseau and Horace Mann were reformers who represented demands for a revision of elementary education so that it would serve human development instead of narrow utilitarian ends. The expansion of the high school, going on apace at the time Dewey spoke, was in part an outgrowth of this democratic drive. It stood, he said, as an institution in which the common man sought to realize his aspiration after a higher level of human dignity.

But the high school had been profoundly affected by other traditions, particularly by the tradition of higher culture for the learned class. As such, it represented an aristocratic ideal. The universities had been the repositories of wisdom and enlightenment of higher learning. The secondary school therefore originated as a preparatory institution for higher studies. Dewey added:

"I do not mention the tradition of learning kept up in the universities of the Middle Ages and the higher schools of the Renaissance and refer to it as aristocratic for the sake of disparaging it. Eternal vigilance is the price of liberty, and eternal care and nurture are the price of maintaining the precious conquest of the past—of preventing a relapse into Philistinism, that combination of superficial enlightenment and dogmatic crudity. If it were not for the work of an aristocracy in the past, there would be but little worth conferring upon the democracy of today." [8]

The high school was the product of the meeting of these two traditions. More than any other part of the educational system, it had the task of effecting an adjustment. The basic problem that affected all levels (but which was most acute in the high school) was how to reconcile the popular demand for more education and training with the desire to conserve the values represented in the tradition of higher learning.

A second problem was related to the first: the high school's role as a preparatory institution for the universities versus its terminal role in preparing students who left it to enter the adult world. A happy formula in the 1890's stated that the best preparation for college was also the best preparation for life. Dewey said that such slogans obscured the genuine problems. He argued that forces were at work which might bring new solutions appropriate for the society that was emerging.

*Dewey's Analysis of the Relation of Higher Education to the Elementary and Secondary Schools*

In an address to the Harvard Teachers' Association (1901),[9] Dewey referred to the educational consequences of the change from a pre-industrial society to the scientific-technological society emerging in the twentieth century. He stated that the educational system reflected the dual order of society. The masses received a rudimentary education (if any) for utilitarian purposes while a literary-classical education was the prerogative of the leisure class. When science and technology and a complex industrial-urban apparatus became the dominant order of things, profound changes in education were bound to occur. Science became the great transformer. It was inevitable that the content and methods of science would take their place in education alongside the older studies. In addition, new courses of a technical nature were demanded as the increasingly complex technology and larger bureaucratic institutions required new levels of skill that could not be acquired incidentally on the job. People

[8] *Ibid.*, p. 19.

[9] John Dewey, "Are the Schools Doing What the People Want Them to Do?," *Educational Review*, Vol. 21 (May, 1901), pp. 459–474.

with aspirations in an enlightened society desired educational experiences that would aid them to realize their capacities as individuals and that would advance them in the social system.

Dewey said that both the high schools and the colleges were reflecting these changes in 1900. The role they had played in a pre-industrial stage could not be retained under the new circumstances. He saw hope, as well as possible danger, in the situation.

In his 1902 address, he approached the issues in another way by raising the question: Which subjects are to be taught in the high school, and how much time is each to receive? How much time is to be given to mathematics, classics, modern languages, history, English, and the sciences? Dewey avoided a direct confrontation by saying, "To adjust the respective claims of the different studies and get a result which is at once harmonious and workable, is a task which almost defies human capacity." [10] For a generation the problem had been growing more vexing. But before a consensus could be achieved, urban high schools had to confront yet another question—whether commercial and manual training programs could be made an organic part of the curriculum.

Dewey suggested that the pressure of these newer practical programs, instead of aggravating the problem, might reveal the underlying social realities that were urging educational change. He ended his address with a final paragraph that was both hopeful and elusive.

"In the future it is going to be less and less a matter of worrying over the respective merits of the ancient and modern languages; or of the inherent values of scientific vs. humanistic study, and more a question of discovering and observing certain broader lines of cleavage, which affect equally the disposition and power of the individual, and the social callings for which education ought to prepare the individual. It will be, in my judgment, less and less a question of piecing together certain studies in a more or less mechanical way in order to make out a so-called course of study running through a certain number of years; and more and more a question of grouping studies together

[10] Dewey, "Current Problems in Secondary Education," p. 22.

according to their natural mutual affinities and reinforcements for the securing of certain well-marked ends." [11]

A basic issue was smouldering behind all of these problems. At the heart of the matter was the question: What is a liberal education under these new conditions? Was it to be inclusive or exclusive? Could practical or technical studies be embraced within a liberal point of view, or were the two to be seen as different in nature, to be cultivated in separation?

In his 1902 paper, Dewey merely raised these questions. We must turn to a later statement to find him trying to give answers. In 1931, he delivered, at Harvard, the Inglis Lecture on Secondary Education, "The Way Out of Educational Confusion." [12] Although this lecture falls outside the Chicago years, the thesis developed in it can be understood only in terms of the ideas developed during Dewey's earlier work.

In the Inglis Lecture, Dewey returned to the questions he had raised thirty years before. The confusion and the debate over educational policy had become endemic—at a level of intensity unparalleled in the past. Conservatives, who wanted a return to past standards and ideals, and radicals, who urged innovations and departures, agreed on only one point: they deplored the present state of things. Dewey tried again to show that the roots of the problem lay in the changing social situation. The burning question was: What should be the nature of the curriculum in the high schools and universities? During the first three decades of the twentieth century, subjects had continued to multiply both in the academic area and in the technical or vocational category. The issue still concerned the relation of liberal to technical studies. Dewey suggested one way of trying to resolve the conflict—to consider a method of organizing studies *for purposes of instruction or learning*. More specifically stated, the problem was comprehended in the question: "What is the value of the accepted and generally current classification of subjects—meaning by 'subjects' such titles as appear in any high school and in any college catalogue?" [13]

[11] *Ibid.*, p. 24.
[12] John Dewey, *The Way Out of Educational Confusion* (Cambridge, Harvard University Press, 1931).
[13] *Ibid.*, p. 4.

The titles, such as history, geography, algebra, and botany, Dewey said, are based on the assumption that the material summarized in each of these subjects provides the natural occasion for the act of studying. The name tags imply there is something fixed under each label. When the material to be "covered" grew too unwieldy (as it inevitably did), the result was fragmentation and the creation of new courses. There was no end in sight to this academic-course explosion.

When the subject of organizing material for instruction arose, Dewey admitted that the expansion of knowledge certainly had contributed to the spawning of courses. But if one examined the actual processes involved in *extending knowledge*, a significant factor was present, he said, which was overlooked by planners of school programs. Specialization was accompanied by cross references, interdependencies, and interrelations. These processes of inquiry and research went on under hyphenated headings: astro-physics, bio-chemistry, geo-physics, or terms like physiological psychology, and physical chemistry. The types of investigations pursued required the utilization of concepts and materials from related areas. Yet, in the *teaching* of subjects, teachers presented material without giving students a sense of the exciting kinds of interaction that marked the work of researchers. Knowledge and the creating of knowledge had become interdependent; studies had become isolated and independent. Thus, mathematics remained for most students a vexing set of operations and symbolic formulas apparently devised *ad hoc* with little reference to the way mathematical concepts and processes apply, for example, in physics.

Dewey had stated in another article on secondary education that:

". . . two principles are continuously at work in all human institutions: one is toward specialization and consequent isolation, the other toward connection and interaction. . . .

"A certain degree of isolation or detachment is required to secure the unhindered and mature development of any group of forces. It is necessary in order to master them in their practical workings. We have to divide to conquer. But when the proper degree of individualization is reached, we need to bring one thing to bear upon another in order to realize upon the benefits which may be derived from the period of isolation. The sole object of the separation is to serve as a means to the end of more effective interaction." [14]

He was arguing that in curriculum building, the first principle—that of specialization—was being applied to the neglect of the second—the need for connection. Students were exposed to a static organization that kept them from gaining insight into the *processes* of interaction that characterized work on the frontiers of knowledge.

"In a situation where the skills of arts and the subject-matter of knowledge have become interwoven and interdependent, adherence to the policy forming the studies of secondary and collegiate instruction on the basis of many isolated and independent subjects is bound to result in precisely the kind of confusion we have at present." [15]

The same situation applied, he said, in the industrial or practical arts.

"In operation they are often immensely specialized in detail. But back of the operations there lies a concentration of knowledge derived from many sources, an integration of many processes which originated in separate arts." [16]

Educational confusion had not been lessened by the addition to the universities of technical or practical subjects like journalism, commerce, engineering, teaching, pharmacy, agriculture, forestry, library service, domestic arts: their counterparts were included in the high school curriculum. Their intrusion had sharpened the debate between the cultural, humanistic ideal and "practical" goals and operations.

Dewey acknowledged that there were genuine differences between these new subjects and the traditional trinity of law, medicine, and theology. These, however, had originated as disci-

[14] John Dewey, *The Educational Situation* (Chicago, University of Chicago Press, 1902), pp. 53–55, see "As Concerning Secondary Education," pp. 50–79.
[15] Dewey, *The Way Out of Educational Confusion*, pp. 17–18.
[16] *Ibid.*, p. 17.

plines to turn out practitioners. And still prepared students to make a living in a competitive society. That was true, too, of liberal studies, especially in their function of preparing teachers.

The important question, however, was *why* vocational and semivocational courses had gained momentum. Did they reflect the values of a materialist society? Were they the product of secret plotters? The answer, Dewey said, was not hard to find:

"The arts and technologies by which the life of society is maintained are now so affected by and saturated with applied science that the routine apprenticeship methods of the past no longer serve. Somehow and somewhere there must be organized instruction concerning them." [17]

There is no doubt that students were attracted to them partly to "get on" in life, even though the results usually disappointed them. The fact was that subjects of this kind were *socially* necessary. Until they were planned and taught properly, students would find in them neither efficient instruction nor a liberating experience.

Many deplored the existence of these courses as diversions of attention, money, and energy from scholarship and humanistic studies. Dewey acknowledged that as far as the actual occupations of men are not affected by the values and perspectives of the liberal ideal "they will be narrow and hard, tending not merely to the 'utilitarian' in its restricted sense, but even toward the brutal and inhuman." [18]

But there was a danger, too, in adhering to a traditional concept of liberal studies in the new scientific-industrial setting. If conceived as something precious and esoteric, to be preserved and conducted apart from the main directions of modern life, they could become "genteel," and devoid of vitality. Their devotees could retreat into bitterness.

Dewey referred to remarks by President Arthur E. Morgan (of Antioch College) to summarize his point:

"In so far as the liberal arts college stands for a perpetuation of the traditional conflict between vocation and culture, it seems

[17] *Ibid.*, p. 22.
[18] *Ibid.*, pp. 26–27.

doomed to play a constantly decreasing role in education. In a day when most of the occupations of men involved little more than manual skill and the repeated application of a few rule-of-thumb formulae, the concept of vocational as illiberal may have had some basis. With the modern applications of all the sciences and arts to vocations, and the successful scientific search for principles within the operations and purposes of the vocations themselves, it is no longer true. It is rapidly becoming a fact that the study within one's vocational preparation is an important means of freeing and liberalizing the mind. This being true, the inevitable trend in education is toward the rapid thinning of the traditional educational wall between vocational and cultural. The liberal arts college will survive and render service in proportion as it recognizes this fact and brings its course of study and administrative set-up into effective conformity with it." [19]

These remarks, Dewey said, applied with equal force to the high school.

Dewey rejected the idea that there was any single and easy answer for education in the new America. He was convinced that the new technical offerings were not to be dismissed with academic curses. He was *not* defending them *in toto* in their present form. But, he argued, there was a genuine possibility of developing a humanistic, liberal outlook in connection with the practical activities of life, and through these vocational studies culture might be made truly vital for many. The real question was not whether professional and semiprofessional schools should exist as part of general education in the United States, but what such programs should contain and how they should be taught. Dewey, thus, was returning to his concept of the occupations as educational centers for social insight.

Dewey opposed vocational education that would be limited to the mere acquisition of job skills. This was inefficient, he said, because new advances in technology continually made such abilities obsolete. Besides, a limited, utilitarian approach was unworthy of self-respecting, free workers. Dewey did propose a general training that concentrated on the underlying principles of industrial processes and their social significance rather than on the

[19] *Ibid.,* pp. 27–28.

mere acquisition of skills. He saw rapid technological change and the consequent large-scale mobility of the laboring population as facts that

". . . cry aloud against any trade training which is more than an incidental part of a more general plan of industrial education. They speak for the necessity of an education whose chief purpose is to develop initiative and personal resources of intelligence. The same forces which have broken down the apprentice system render futile a scholastic imitation of it." [20]

Dewey stated that it would not be easy to present in secondary education semivocational courses that would foster a social and scientific outlook and also be significant for their liberalizing aspects. A major obstacle consisted in finding teachers for these courses. The arranging of programs that involved more than mere training required patient and thorough inquiry and testing. Impatient demands for "trained hands" that were not burdened with liberal folderol would increase the difficulties. The proper reply to this latter pressure, Dewey maintained, was to acknowledge the fact that no school can give complete technical competence. Practical details must be learned on the job. When the schools do what they can do well—give insights into scientific and technical concepts and principles, and reflection on social relations and values—"they will become more genuinely practical as well as more liberal." [21]

Liberal education, Dewey said, must renounce its nostalgic stance if it is to play a vital role in the new society. At the same time, the acceptance of a proliferation of new courses must be resisted. He maintained that the situation was so complex that there was no simple, single answer. He did suggest, however, that for *purposes of instruction*, alternatives had to be tried that were organized in a manner different from that represented in the traditional divisions and classifications of knowledge.

One alternative, he said, might be found in the so-called "project" or "problem" methods being tried in the elementary schools. He did not offer this as a panacea, for he found that

[20] John Dewey, "A Policy of Industrial Education," *New Republic*, Vol. 1 (December, 1914), p. 12.
[21] Dewey, *The Way Out of Educational Confusion*, pp. 29–30.

many projects were too trival to be educative. They failed to deepen knowledge of facts and principles. It was, however, dishonest, he felt, to seize on a few failures in order to discredit a general idea. Dewey felt that there was a genuine possibility of locating projects appropriate to the experiences of students at the secondary and college level in which there was a sufficient time span for raising questions, introducing new undertakings, and creating fresh demands for knowledge. Organization, in this case, involved drawing on materials from several fields and investigating their relationships. This came closer to the way study and learning go on outside of school, where data and principles are not found packaged under neat labels. Students would be provided with the opportunity to be more active in both an intellectual and a constructive sense. They would be forced to seek their own integrations and solutions.[22]

Dewey hastened to add, "I do not urge it [the project approach] as the sole way out of education confusion, not even in the elementary school, though I think experimentation with it is desirable in college and secondary school." [23]

Another alternative that he suggested was to retain traditional titles but reorganize content to take into account the interdependencies of knowledge with emphasis on meaning and application. As an example, he cited Julian Huxley's work on life and evolution. One finds him harking back to his own undergraduate career where the elder Huxley had set him off on an intellectual adventure that he had never ceased pursuing. Properly designed, such organizations would not sacrifice scientific accuracy and could quicken intellectual curiosity and understanding.

"After all, the period from, say, fourteen to twenty-two is a comparatively short portion of a normal life-time. The best that education can do during these years is to arouse intellectual interests which carry over. . . . If a student does not take into subsequent life an enduring concern for some field of knowledge and art, lying outside his immediate professional preoccupations,

[22] Dewey did not mention specific examples, but one such would be the Antioch plan at the college level, or work-study plans in the high school, where efforts are made to raise questions that integrate intellectual inquiry with practical experience.

[23] Dewey, *The Way Out of Educational Confusion*, p. 36.

schooling for him has been a failure, no matter how good a 'student' he was. . . .

"A reorganization of subject matter which takes account of out-leadings into the wide world of nature and man, of knowledge and of social interests and uses, cannot fail save in the most callous and intellectually obdurate to awaken some permanent interest and curiosity. Theoretical subjects will become more practical because more related to the scope of life; practical subjects will become more charged with theory and intelligent insight. Both will be vitally and not just formally unified." [24]

In sum, we find Dewey presenting the case for new ways of bringing liberal and humanistic values into the educational system of a democratic, industrial-urban society. Typical of his abhorrence of dualist solutions was his opposition to a liberal education defined merely as the abstract conservator of the values of a former social setting while vocational education would be developed in a narrow, utilitarian sense. Such definitions led to a schism that, in his view, need not exist. To isolate the two could increase the unhealthy tendencies in each, and could lead to a missed chance for each to be revitalized by the other.

Dewey's hopes for the liberalizing of professional and semivocational studies can be understood only in view of his ideas about the nature and role of the occupations in the Laboratory School. It was not the mere acquisition of saleable skills but a serious study of the nature of man's work that provided an avenue for educational experiences that could throw light on many aspects of the culture. If historical trends, technological innovations, social changes in family and community, and moral, spiritual, and aesthetic dimensions were to be understood in depth, all of the knowledge and methods of liberal and scientific studies would be required. Dewey never relinquished his conviction that the study of social life through a comprehensive analysis of work forms or occupations could revitalize liberal studies—and the quality of students' experiences in school.

"The problem is not that of making the schools an adjunct to manufacture and commerce, but of utilizing the factors of in-

[24] *Ibid.*, pp. 38–39.

dustry to make school life more active, more full of immediate meaning, more connected with out-of-school experience." [25]

It is easy to become impatient with Dewey's failure to provide concrete details on how to achieve these goals. We must remember, however, that after leaving Chicago in 1904, his role was that of a professional philosopher. The philosopher's task is to frame questions that enable men to understand their situation anew and to see the values at issue. He is not in a position to work out the practical details.

Dewey's analysis of the social situation, with its call for new approaches to integrating the liberal and the technical, might have been in error. This is a fair subject for debate. Perhaps the demands of specialized knowledge and training are such that it would be impossible to frame educational programs that were integrated. This observer feels that Dewey's analysis is cogent and still warrants serious attention. An important quality in Dewey's own writing must be remembered if this be true. Dewey did not always present alternatives in a completely objective light. In the main, however, he avoided dogmatically asserting that only a single approach offered the one true solution. He did not maintain that an idea was good because it was new. He acknowledged that innovations sometimes were mis-educative when they were shallowly conceived, or when they lacked the personnel and conditions to be executed adequately. His style was to present an analysis of the situation, and from that to develop reasonable ideas that could be tested.

## DEWEY'S PLANS TO INCORPORATE SECONDARY EDUCATION INTO THE LABORATORY SCHOOL

We have examined materials that indicate the types of emphases Dewey envisioned for American high schools and universities. However, we cannot find in his Chicago experience detailed plans as to how he would have tried to integrate the secondary school with elementary and higher education. There is available, however, an address that Dewey made in his last

[25] John Dewey, *Democracy and Education* (New York, The Macmillan Co., 1916), p. 316.

year at Chicago which contains the kinds of ideas he was projecting for future work in education.

The address was delivered to the combined Parents' Association in the academic year 1903–1904,[26] the first year that the
School of Education and its Elementary and Secondary Schools
were housed in the new Blaine-Belfield buildings on campus. All
of the aspects of work in education were now brought within
unified quarters. It was a time of new problems, but also an occasion for reflecting on the meaning of past developments and for
conjecturing about the road ahead. Since this speech is a record
of Dewey's intentions, it is worth examining in detail. Its content
becomes intelligible, however, only in terms of events that had
transpired in the history of the Elementary School since its opening in 1896. We shall preface our consideration of this 1904 paper
with an historical account of the gradual expansion of work in
education at the university. More specifically, we wish to trace
the steps taken to include components in secondary education.

In his report to President Harper (1898), Dewey said, "The
Department of Pedagogy, from the first, included in its scheme
of organization a plan for a school which should take children
at the beginning of school life, or four years of age, and carry
them into the University." [27]

Dewey had to move slowly toward the goal of including
secondary education as part of his experiment. The university's
alliance with the Chicago Manual Training School and the South
Side Academy in the 1890's was a first step in this direction.

At the turn of the century, a series of events took place that
led to a further expansion of the university's efforts in education.
This created tensions that eventually were to lead to Dewey's
departure in the spring of 1904. In 1900, Dewey's Elementary
School was four years old and a subject of national interest. At
a meeting of the National Council of Education, Dr. A. B. Hins-
dale of the University of Michigan said, "More eyes are now
fixed upon The University Elementary School at Chicago than
upon any other elementary school in the country and probably

[26] John Dewey, "Significance of the School of Education," *The Elementary School Teacher*, Vol. 4, No. 7 (March, 1904), pp. 441–453.

[27] John Dewey, "The University Elementary School," reports to the
President, in the archives of the University of Chicago, 1898, p. 232.

in the world."[28] Indeed, the school was well known; but because it was dependent on the contributions of friends, it was chronically in financial straits. At one point, in 1899, in the continuing correspondence between Dewey and Harper over financial problems, Dewey suggested that if more evidence of support from the university's Board of Trustees was not forthcoming, he favored disbanding the school.[29] Then chance intervened.

In March, 1901, Colonel Francis W. Parker's Chicago Institute, a successor to the Cook County Normal School which Parker had directed for eighteen years, was incorporated into the university as the School of Education. This was done at President Harper's invitation, at least partly to help relieve the financial problem of the university. Colonel Parker was, of course, an educational innovator who, at the level of practice, championed ideas similiar to Dewey's. The Colonel was a stormy reform figure. When the Cook County Normal School was taken over by the city of Chicago in 1896, many of his ideas came under attack and his work was threatened. In 1899, he received a million dollars from Mrs. Emmons Blaine, daughter of Cyrus McCormick, who offered to support his work in a private school to be known as the Chicago Institute. President Harper, shortly thereafter, invited Colonel Parker and his faculty to join the university. Parker accepted and brought with him the million dollars. A proviso of the Trustees of the Chicago Institute was that, in the move, Colonel Parker was to remain as head, and his program of a pedagogic school, an elementary school, and a kindergarten should remain intact.

The Dewey Elementary School now seemed threatened; and its friends, locally and nationally, exerted pressure on Harper to maintain it as a separate school with its research and experimental features intact. This was a time of conflict and friction. Personnel of the two schools felt threatened, and rumors abounded. Finally, by the opening of the academic year in 1901, Parker was installed as Director of the Chicago Institute and the School of Education. Dewey remained as Chairman of the Department of Education.

[28] Ida B. Depencier, *The History of the Laboratory Schools: The University of Chicago 1896–1957* (Chicago, University of Chicago, 1960), p. 16.
[29] John Dewey, Letter to William Rainey Harper, March 8, 1899, The President's Papers, University of Chicago.

His school, now officially to be referred to as the Laboratory School, was to be maintained alongside Parker's University Elementary School.

Colonel Parker became ill in the fall of 1901, and died in March, 1902. During this period, the Chicago Manual Training School, headed by Henry Holmes Belfield, and the South Side Academy, under the direction of William B. Owen, were amalgamated, and Dewey was assigned to coordinate these operations as the newly appointed Director of the School of Education. By 1903, the two elementary schools were united under the principalship of Mrs. Dewey. However, she was unacceptable to Parker's people, and Harper decided not to reappoint her for September, 1904. Although Dewey denied this was the reason for his resignation, it was part of the picture of worsening relations between the two men. Dewey did resign in April, 1904. He was soon to join the Department of Philosophy at Columbia University where he completed his professional career.

Gifts from Mrs. J. Young Scammon and John D. Rockefeller, Sr., in addition to the money from Mrs. Emmons Blaine, made possible the launching of a new complex of buildings in 1901 that was to eventuate in Blaine, Belfield, and Judd Halls—the quarters for the School of Education, the Elementary School, and the new University High School. After arduous planning and labor, the new quarters were ready for occupancy in the fall of 1903. The first class graduated from high school in June, 1904, the spring in which Dewey resigned.

This hasty sketch provides some background for the paper that Dewey presented to the Parents' Association in the winter of the first year of the new school.[30]

The address is revealing in two respects. First, it provides insights about the objectives Dewey would have pursued had he continued to have a major commitment in education. Second, by reading between the lines, we can see aspects of the administrative difficulties he confronted at that moment.

In many ways his new problems were the products of success. As Dewey began the academic year 1903–1904, he had finally within one complex all the elements for educational experimentation, from the kindergarten through university graduate work

[30] Dewey, "Significance of the School of Education," pp. 441–453.

that he had sought from the beginning. He also had awesome professional responsibilities. By now he was firmly established as a front-ranking American philosopher. The outlines of his instrumentalist orientation had been blocked out, and demanded elaboration. While he retained his position as Chairman of Philosophy and Psychology, with Parker's death he found himself Director also of a vastly expanded School of Education. His duties included the graduate functions of his old Department of Education, now supplemented by a sizable undergraduate Normal School operation that accrued from the addition of the Chicago Institute. He was also responsible for the administration of a precollegiate operation, which included the new Elementary School, born of the merger of his own Laboratory School and Parker's lower school, and the University High School. This operation was a far cry from the primary school which had begun with sixteen children in a private home seven years earlier, and which had been temporarily disbanded for lack of funds at the end of its first term.

Each of the precollegiate schools had been pioneers in American education. This meant they had been led by strong men who had attracted creative and independent-minded faculties. The rancor, hard feeling, and mistrust that marked the joining of Parker's program with Dewey's Department of Education verged on explosion at times. Dewey and Parker had admired each other, and shared many ideas in common, but the intellectual and value orientations of their two schools also contained sharp differences. An obvious one was Parker's emphasis on teacher training as opposed to the research dimension in Dewey's program. In addition, there were the usual concerns about faculty security and the jockeying for administrative authority that accompanies mergers. Dewey had no real stomach for these matters. Because of the many pressures he faced, his communications with the Parker faculty were, at times faulty. Mrs. Dewey's appointment as Principal of the Elementary School was a particular bone of contention, and Dewey himself had serious doubts about Wilbur S. Jackman of the Parker group who, in the reshuffling, had become Dean of the College of Education under Dewey's Directorship.

Dewey expressed confidence that he could handle these complexities. Whether this was a realistic assessment is a moot point. The present writer is willing to leave the issues of the organizational struggle to those scholars who explore these questions in detail.[31]

In view of this background, we may safely assume that Dewey's remarks to the Parents' Association were framed, in part, to promote unity. The parents themselves had strong loyalties to the several schools that were brought together. If they were to split into groups of fierce partisans of the several divisions, they could exacerbate wounds already opened. Dewey used this occasion to honor the contributions of the past, to indicate that the time was fit to bring the parts together, and to ask the parents to join him in working on a new set of problems around which they could unite. We may notice the note of diplomacy in the speech, and see the vision Dewey was projecting. He made observations on each of the schools represented and argued that their inclusion provided the reconstituted School of Education with a unique opportunity. The various elements represented the areas in which the major theoretical problems of education were present. ". . . We have right here in concrete actual institutional form all the factors which any writer on education of the present day would lay down as involved in the problem of education." [32]

He began with comments on the two divisions of the school, which he listed as first in historical order. In 1883, Colonel Francis W. Parker came to the Cook County Normal School and Henry H. Belfield had opened the Chicago Manual Training [High] School.

By describing Parker's work as part of "our" history, he was bidding for the Parker people to identify themselves with the new organization. Colonel Parker's death the preceding spring was still sharply felt by those who had stood by him in his long, harsh struggles.

The incorporation of Parker's Chicago Institute added a

[31] The details of Dewey's relations with Harper and events connected with the merger with Col. Parker's school have been carefully worked out by Robert L. McCaul. See "Dewey and the University of Chicago," *School and Society*, Vol. 89. I. (March 25, 1961), pp. 152–157; II. (April 8, 1961), pp. 179–183; III. (April 22, 1961), pp. 202–206.

[32] Dewey, "Significance of the School of Education," p. 447.

teacher training component to the new School of Education. Dewey described the congruencies between Parker's ideas and his own. Parker had seen, said Dewey, that "the training of teachers is the strategic point in the educational campaign." [33] Parker, too, had created as an organic part of his Normal School an elementary school, and in idea at least, a high school. Prospective teachers needed to experience personally a learning situation which, in its enrichment and direction, freed children for their own growth. A fundamental feature of the work of all those united in the School of Education was to give teachers a more vital conception of their profession, and the intellectual insights to realize their ideals in action.

Henry H. Belfield's Manual Training School provided another element. The school had been an innovator in its field. Although Belfield's training had been in classics, he founded the school in protest against the tendency to equate education with the training of intellect at the expense of the "executive and expressive" aspects of youth—"an education which took account of the employment of the senses upon the symbols of things, but not sufficiently of the use of touch and sight and muscular sense upon things themselves." [34] Parker and Belfield had shared Dewey's aspiration for the creation of approaches that utilized other than the verbal behavior of children—of designing programs and methods that would involve the "whole child." Dewey's theory added philosophical depth to justify the idea.

Dewey next gave his interpretation of the special role of his own Laboratory School. It was founded, he said, to apply scientific concepts and methods to school work, with the more specific aim of sponsoring research on problems connected with the psychology and sociology of education. He pointed out that with the exception of a short-lived kindergarten program at Stanford University the Laboratory School had no predecessor. His statement about the school, on that occasion, was not only a mature appraisal, but also an elaboration of his future intentions.

". . . the incorporation of the Laboratory School marks the necessity of training teachers, not only giving them inspiration, practical insight, and skill, but by giving them command of the

[33] *Ibid.*, p. 442.
[34] *Ibid.*, p. 443.

most fundamental intellectual tools of the work which they are called to do. Over and above this, it stands for necessity of making the body of thought upon which education depends something more than, upon one side, a set of abstract and general theories, reinforced by a large amount of routine and empirical devices, upon the other. It commits the School of Education to the significant task of continuous research into the principles underlying educational practice, and to continual criticism of methods that are in practical use, with a view to influencing intelligent thought and practice all over the country—a function which the Laboratory School had already fulfilled to a surprising extent, considering its short history and modest equipment.

"Speaking in terms of relationship to the University, the incorporation of the Laboratory School signifies bringing to bear the intellectual methods of which the modern university is the appropriate home and embodiment, upon all the questions of education, both elementary and secondary. To infuse lower education with the intellectual ideals which inspire university work, to show how the methods and operations of mind which are so fruitful for discovery and application in the highest flights of the mind can be made effective and operative from the very beginning of the school training of the child, is surely a fact of considerable significance. All of that significance is now embodied in the life of the School of Education." [35]

He then spoke about the South Side Academy, established in 1892 as a preparatory school at the time the University of Chicago was founded. In commenting on the Academy, Dewey observed that if the School of Education were to follow the tendency of contemporay educational innovators to concentrate on the applied aspects, or even on the scientific method in education, a serious mistake would be made. He admitted that the "new" educators tended to dismiss slow-changing higher education as "medieval." In their serious hours, however, Dewey said, they had to acknowledge that the college fosters interests in the intangible, cultural concerns that represent the values most worthwhile in life. The task of giving the information, discipline, and culture necessary for entering university work was important and honorable. Dewey and his colleagues wielded the cudgels

[35] *Ibid.*, pp. 444-445.

against the tendency for schools to become abstract and dead through the isolation of their content from the concrete, moving forces of society; but Dewey warned that the manual and practical tendencies could easily become "cramped, servile and hard" apart from the illumination of liberal culture. The inclusion of the Academy provided the values and challenges of the tradition of liberal education.[36]

Dewey then turned somewhat indirectly to the rumors of dissension. He acknowledged that there were widespread comments about the unlikely prospects of welding such disparate elements into a functioning unit. He countered with what he called the *organics* of the school. Each element could do its work well, but only with the knowledge that it was part of a larger whole. Each of the factors would act on, and in turn be affected by, all the others. The scientific and cultural, the utilitarian, and the expressive-motor dimensions—all were represented. Gathering them together was an achievement in itself. The great challenge of the years ahead would be to fuse them into a new concept of education in which "the executive and the abstract, the tool and the book, the head and the hand" [37] would be brought into fruitful relation.

He anticipated difficulties in the experimentation, and asked for the sympathetic understanding of the parents.

"It will be necessary to introduce more of the physical and manual element, more of expression in art, and of construction in the shop into the academic curriculum. On the other hand,

[36] That Dewey had been interested over a period of years in the work of the South Side Academy and in seeking ways of strengthening its ties with the work at the university is evidenced in his correspondence with President Harper. In December of 1897 he asked for an addition to his staff to "mediate between the pedagogical interests of the University and the South Side Academy" and to prepare the way for the incorporation of the Academy into the University Secondary School. (Dewey to Harper, December 6, 1897, p. 2.) In 1900, when suggesting his plans for the following year, he recommended to Harper that William Owen, Director of the Academy, join Dewey in offering a joint course in pedagogy, with Owen taking special responsibility for the secondary part while Dewey concentrated on the elementary aspect. (Dewey to Harper, February 3, 1900, pp. 3-4.)

[37] Dewey, "The Significance of the School of Education," p. 449.

. . . it will doubtless be found necessary to infuse the more direct industrial and practical education with things derived from the larger outlook of history, science, and all we mean by general culture." [38]

Within a few months, he left Chicago. Never again was he to have direct contact with precollegiate education. Many of Dewey's appointees left when he did, and the school wavered in leadership. No director was appointed until the coming of Charles H. Judd in 1909. The elementary and secondary schools eventually were operated as completely separate organizations.[39] Under Judd's leadership, 1909–1919, a new emphasis, coinciding with the fever of educational testing that was sweeping the country, came to the fore.

RECOMMENDATIONS FOR ORGANIZING STUDIES
AT THE SECONDARY LEVEL

We may try to predict more specific ideas that Dewey might have introduced into secondary education, as enough is contained in his writings, to warrant such a try. Some ideas are clearly stated; on other points we may make reasonable inferences. The record is fragmentary, and includes articles written over a period of years. Sometimes Dewey seemed to be presenting ideas that could never have been employed in practice. At other times, there are inconsistencies and a lack of clarity in details. Nevertheless we offer what seems to be a reasonably accurate summary of his positions.

Dewey often considered secondary education as an aspect of one of his larger problems: how to visualize the educational program so that there would be some conceptual unity and coherence in the whole effort from the preprimary level through to the university. As we have seen, the high school was characterized as the connecting link between elementary and higher education. Its problems at the turn of the twentieth century were compounded by the fact that it had then a dual role to play. It retained its long-time preparatory function. In addition, it had

[38] *Ibid.*, p. 450.
[39] Ida B. Depencier, *The History of the Laboratory Schools: University of Chicago 1896–1957* (Chicago, University of Chicago, 1960).

a major responsibility as a sort of "people's college," where the intellectual possessions of the public that never sees the college doors could be solidified and elevated.[40] Furthermore, the high school program was defined in a period when the nature and content of both the elementary schools and the universities were being modified by the demands of new urban-industrial realities.

In an earlier consideration of his Elementary School program, we found one theme recurring. There should be a move from relatively undifferentiated study, centering on the nature and evolution of social life in early stages, to more distinctly defined studies at the secondary level. Dewey's more detailed thesis for secondary education was that the high school is characterized by more specialization, as the child's interests and society's needs demand it. Specialization wrongly pursued, however, can lead to narrowness and monotony; therefore, the task is to emphasize the benefits of specialized work and avoid its negative aspects. Specialized study must never lose sight of the connectedness and interaction with the whole of experience, of which the subject at hand is a mere fragment. All of this would be applicable to both academic and semivocational education.

Although the term "specialization" was employed, another phrase, "differentiation and generalization," more accurately conveyed the intention for the high school. "Specialization" in the sense of concentrating in depth in an academic area, and preparation for a specific profession or vocation were tasks Dewey assigned to the university.

"The movement, however, is steady, and I believe inevitable, in one direction: the demarcation of secondary work as the period of general training and culture, thus restoring to it freshness and vitality by making it what it should be, the renaissance of the individual mind, the period of self consciousness in the true sense, of knowledge of self in relation to the larger meanings of life; and the reservation of higher institution for specific training, for gaining control of the particular body of knowledge and methods of research and verification which fit the individual to apply truth to the guidance of his own special calling in life. All of

[40] John Dewey, "The Influence of the High School upon Educational Methods," *School Review*, Vol. 4, No. 1 (January, 1896), p. 2.

us have callings, occupations—only the luxuriously idle and the submerged idle, only the leisure class of fashion and pauperism, violate this law. When education ceases to ignore this fact, when it recognizes it frankly and fully, and adapts its curriculum and methods to it, the university will be coherent in itself and also doing what the people really want done." [41]

In a 1901 address to the Harvard Teachers Association, he said of secondary education:

"It certainly means . . . that the pupil shall . . . be stimulated, on all sides; that he shall be given a survey, at least of the universe in its manifold phases. Thru this . . . coming to know both himself and the universe, he may get his orientation—his placing of himself in the larger world. With proper economy of instruction, and harmonious organization instead of blind confusion in the curriculum, this result should certainly be attained by the time the average student is twenty or twenty-one. . . . Its freshness and vitality may be restored by making it what it should be, the renaissance of the individual mind, the period of self-consciousness in the true sense of knowledge of self in relation to the larger meanings of life." [42]

Several questions had to be answered in practice: (1) how to give more time to secondary education to enable it to meet its growing responsibilities, and (2) how to reconcile the values of liberal education with the semivocational needs of students not bound for college.

On the first point, Dewey argued that secondary education required a period longer than the traditional four years—not everything could be included in the high school curriculum.[43] One of his proposals to relieve the pressure was to revitalize the elementary program. He felt that much time was wasted in the ineffective memoriter methods of teaching the three R's. The introduction of more efficient methods for this task could provide

[41] Dewey, "Are the Schools Doing What the People Want Them to Do?", p. 474.
[42] *Ibid.*, pp. 473–474.
[43] John Dewey, "Remarks on the Study of History in Schools," *School Review*, Vol. 4 (May, 1896), p. 272, at the Meeting of the North Central Association of Colleges and Secondary Schools at the University of Chicago.

positive subject matter. This could result in reducing by one year the time assigned to elementary education.[44]

". . . the introduction into the lower grades of geometry and algebra taught by rational methods, in place of the numerical contortions of the average arithmetic; the substitution of literary masterpieces as wholes for the grind of continuing to read broken off fragments after one has already known how to read several years . . . ; the extension of science work and the introduction of simple experimental and observational methods . . . ; the introduction of foreign language work . . . to that degree found to be advisable to give any child command of his own powers, whether he go to college or not." [45]

He argued that the weakest point in the educational system was in the grades four through eight. These were the years when energy was consumed by repetition of drill in reading, writing, and numbers, at a time when the child was ready to apply himself to new learnings. "The benumbing, mechanical influence which is the serious evil of the average American school today is in full operation." [46]

Dewey sometimes spoke of secondary education as extending through the first two years of college. The specific point at which he envisaged this level ending is not completely clear. What he was seeking was a large enough block of time to give the high school a chance to develop its distinctive emphases.

"A six-year period would enable the high school to face its own peculiar problem: that of opening to the mind avenues of approach to all typical phases of nature and society, and acquiring a sympathetic knowledge of these areas of life—culture, in a word. Facing its own problem without distortion from outside pressure, it would have free space and leisure in which to work out that knowledge of the universe of nature and humanity that is worth while; and that would enable its graduates to undertake

[44] John Dewey, "Remarks on Frank Louis Soldan, *Shortening the Years of Elementary Schooling*," *School Review*, Vol. II (January, 1903), pp. 17–20.

[45] Dewey, "The Influence of the High School upon Educational Methods," pp. 5–6.

[46] *Ibid.*, pp. 4–8.

later specialization in professional and research lines in an intelligent way—intelligent both as to consciousness of their own capacities, tastes, and needs, and as to the knowledge of the relations of the particular province to which they are to devote themselves to the whole federated field of life." [47]

On the question of how to organize studies and how to relate the liberal and vocational, we have already noted one principle stressed by Dewey: differentiation had to be accompanied by integration. This involved a search for concepts that would be useful for relating materials. The study of vocations or the nature of work was one such idea. Another one that Dewey considered was the use of psychology and sociology (or social ethics) as two studies around which others could be correlated:

". . . psychology as a concrete study of human nature in the individual, and sociology as the concrete study of nature in its organized forms, are the natural bases for the unification of studies in the high school, whether we look at the dominant interests and impulses of the pupil at this age, or at the material studied. This seems to me to constitute a fair basis for the claim that these studies would introduce order rather than confusion, work for ease rather than hardship in the high school economy." [48]

This coincided with the psychosocial orientation of the Laboratory School. A sociological approach to the study of social institutions and vocations in a culture and a psychological study of the nature and needs of individuals could freshen the approach to other subjects. In history, for example, there could be consideration of habit, character, purposes, and motives; science could include reflection on the processes of observation, inference, and reasoning; and the study of changes in economic institutions could form a basis for unifying work in history, geography, and the sciences.

Dewey welcomed the "broadening" of the school population in high school and college, and he welcomed the innovation of technical and practical studies as a challenge to educational tradi-

[47] Dewey, "Remarks on Frank L. Soldan, Shortening the Years of Elementary Schooling," pp. 19–20.
[48] Dewey, "The Influence of the High School upon Educational Methods," p. 11.

tions. One of the hotly debated issues was whether a dual system of high schools should be established: one academic, the other vocational. Dewey vigorously opposed this separation.

"The scheme of a split system tends to paralyze one of the most vital movements now operating for the improvement of existing general education. The old time, general academic education is beginning to be vitalized by the introduction of manual, industrial, and social activities; it is beginning to recognize its responsibility to train all the youth for useful citizenship in which each may render useful service to society and make an honest and decent living." [49]

When the University Elementary School was amalgamated with the South Side Academy and the Chicago Manual Training School in 1903–1904, Dewey welcomed the chance to work on the problems of correlating studies. The Manual Training School would then have included in enrollment children from working-class backgrounds. Just how the college-preparatory work of the Academy would have been affected is not clear. We do know that Dewey held that it was as important for the academically oriented college-bound student to become acquainted with tools, materials, and industrial reality as it was for the student bound for labor in industry to be exposed to science, history, and literature. [50] We know, too, that Dewey was a vigorous advocate of the comprehensive high school, and it is reasonable to expect that he would have sought to include some common studies and experiences for the two groups of students. [51]

[49] John Dewey, "Some Dangers in the Present Movement for Industrial Education," *Child Labor Bulletin*, Vol. 1, No. 4 (February, 1913), p. 71.
[50] John Dewey and Evelyn Dewey, *Schools of Tomorrow*, p. 181.
[51] The first announcement of the University High School (1903–1904) made the following general statement regarding the curriculum:

"The courses of study offered by the high school are arranged to include, as far as possible, all subjects that may fairly belong to a secondary school curriculum. They provide a systematic and practical training for students whose formal education ends with the work of the school, and also an adequate preparation for any college or technical school in the country. A considerable portion of the work is elective. The choice of studies is determined, in part, by the needs and future pursuits of the pupil; in part, by the natural sequence of the studies themselves. The wide range of electives

We can be somewhat more confident about his emphases in what he called the semivocational area. He argued consistently, and as late as 1944, that:

"a truly liberal and liberating education would refuse today to isolate vocational training on any of its levels from a continuous education in the social, moral and scientific contexts within which wisely administered callings . . . must perform." [52]

Technical studies, when including general principles and concepts, could have a challenging intellectual content. The changes wrought by the technological revolution assured it.

makes it possible for the student to exercise a large degree of choice. This choice, however, is subject to the approval of the Deans.

"The courses offered are the Classical and the Modern Language Course, the Scientific Course and the Technological Course. Certain subjects are common to all the courses. In addition, each course covers certain subjects that are peculiar to the particular course, and that give to it its distinctive character and name: the Classical Course, Greek; the Modern Language Course, modern language and history; the Scientific Course, the sciences; the Technological Course, shopwork and drawing. Electives are possible in each course.

"The subjects common to all courses are English, history, science, and mathematics.

"The Classical Course includes four years of English, two or three years of mathematics, one year of history, one year of science, four years of Latin, and three or two years of Greek, together with electives.

"The Modern Language Course includes four years of English, two or three years of mathematics, one year of history, one year of science, and modern languages, together with electives.

"The Science Course includes four years of English, three or four years of mathematics, one year of history, and science, together with electives.

"The Technological Course includes four years of English, three or four years of mathematics, one year of history, one year of science, and shopwork and drawing, together with electives.

"The courses are not arranged with the intention of making them exclusive of one another. It is especially to be noted that shopwork and drawing may be elected by students pursuing any one of the four courses. Languages other than English are not required for graduation.

"Courses in bookkeeping are offered for students preparing to enter business." (Quoted in David Gustafson, *The Origin and Establishment of the University High School of the University of Chicago*, unpublished M.A. thesis in Education, University of Chicago, 1927, pp. 101–102.)

[52] John Dewey, "Challenge to Liberal Thought," *Fortune*, Vol. 30, No. 2 (August, 1944), p. 156.

"Industry has ceased to be essentially an empirical, rule of thumb procedure, handed down by custom. Its technique is now technological: that is to say, based upon machinery resulting from discoveries in mathematics, physics, chemistry, bacteriology, etc. . . . as a consequence, industrial occupations have infinitely greater intellectual content and infinitely larger cultural possibilities than they used to possess. The demand for such education as will acquaint workers with the scientific and social bases and bearings of their pursuits becomes imperative, since those who are without it inevitably sink to the role of appendages of the machines they operate." [53]

Dewey used the term semivocational to indicate that no pretension would be made to turn out expert technicians. The high school should present studies that would permit the exploring of interests and capacities to youth who approached it as merely an avenue to work. A range of vocational experiences should be provided. In addition, every student, regardless of his job orientation, should be well-grounded in nonvocational subject matter. An intellectual adjustment to the political, economic, religious, cultural, and social aspects of life also had to be made. The specialization and complexity of modern industry made it ever more difficult for men to see their work in terms of the social whole. The goal he projected was an education that would equip students to emerge from the schools with a broad understanding of the nature of industry and technology, a respect for the dignity of work, and an awareness of the social implications of change. They would have some insights into the nature of the economic system, and of the roles of management and labor unions. Dewey thought that the introduction into industry of such a "new breed" of laborers would serve to elevate the position of the workingman and his role in society, and hence effect at least a partial bridging of the great gulf that separated the upper class from the lower-class wage earners.[54]

Dewey knew the difficulties in striking out in such a direction. It is safe to predict that he would have tried experiments

---

[53] Dewey, *Democracy and Education*, p. 314.
[54] Jane Addams recalled that she and Dewey discussed many times the problem of the estrangement of the children of immigrants who belonged

along these lines, for the alternative was abhorrent to him—schools where large numbers of working-class youths found themselves "sitting through" academic courses that bored them, and, on the other hand, taking narrow vocational training that might or might not enable them to "take a job"; a job, unenriched by insights, so that they would "put in time" until the clock released them.

If he had had to grapple at first hand with the problems, he might have realized, more sharply, the need for imaginative and gifted teachers to make such a program effective and also the difficulty of finding and training them. Once again, in the 1960's, we are realizing the critical need for leadership and quality in this field—and the dearth of them in practice.[55]

neither to the culture of their parents nor to that of the American metropolis. She and Dewey considered what could be done to help them.

"Could we not interest the young people working in the neighboring factories, in these forms of industry, so that, through their own parents and grandparents, they could find a dramatic representation of the inherited resource of their daily occupation. If these young people could actually see that the complicated machinery of the factory evolved from simple tools, they might at least make a beginning toward that education which Dr. Dewey defines as a 'continuing reconstruction of experience.' They might also lay a foundation for reverence of the past which Goethe declares to be the basis of all sound progress." (Jane Addams, *Twenty Years at Hull House, with Autobiographical Notes* (New York, The Macmillan Co., 1910), pp. 236–237.)

We know, too, that Dewey later had hopes for Wirt's efforts, in the Gary plan, to relate the work of the schools to the realities of an industrial community; and through adult education programs to promote communication between the generations, and between the cultures of the Old World and the New America. (John Dewey and Evelyn Dewey, *Schools of Tomorrow* (New York, E. P. Dutton, 1915).)

[55] That Dewey had some awareness of the seriousness of the problem is indicated in his correspondence with President Harper. In 1897 he wrote a letter to Harper to which he attached a "Plan for organization of work in a fully equipped Department of Pedagogy." In the plan he included the statement that

"When the Manual Training School is definitely annexed to the University, and its location changed so as to be sufficiently in close contact with University work, it would be highly desirable to have it include a special course for training teachers in the direction of manual training. The introduction of this line of work in the public schools is hindered now more

It is difficult to assess the consequences of the fact that Dewey did not have the opportunity to extend the Laboratory School idea through the high school, and to struggle with the practical problems involved in relating differentiated study to the rationale of the elementary work. As the first half of the twentieth century unfolded, secondary education was to become the major arena of controversy and change. It may well be that Dewey's thought was misinterpreted because his stay at Chicago permitted a full working out of only that part of his theory that applied to young children.

We have stressed, perhaps unduly so, Dewey's deep respect for the role of scholarship and intellectual discipline in education, but we must not deny the emphasis that he placed on engaging the interests and present experience of the child. A genuine educational experience for each individual was the goal. In the Dewey school, however, the goal was not one of meeting needs in general. The professionals selected interests that could be beneficial to the study of civilization. Study of the curriculum materials indicates that important concepts and events in social evolution were the first aspect of study, as they were deemed essential for a child's education. There is no doubt at all that only those experiences were to be included that would lead to a knowledge of nature, society, or self that was of enduring significance.

In later progressivism, this qualification was not always given sufficient emphasis. In the child-study movement, valuable insights were gained about the needs of children. At adolescence, for example, a real concern of youngsters is with personality and appearance. Dewey's orientation did not make it defensible, however, to assume that location of a need was a sufficient ground for making it a formal subject of study. Hence, matters of "personality and appearance" or "hobbies" might be legitimate "needs," and educators could relate to children more effectively as possessors of knowledge in these areas, but this, *per se*, would not earn them a place in the curriculum. There were questionable trends in later curriculum development, which included the fail-

by the lack of properly trained teachers than by any other one thing. . . . The New York Training School for Teachers is the only college of rank now making a speciality of this matter." (Dewey to Harper, January 8, 1897.)

ure to work in terms of the "civilizational criterion," and to move toward more systematic study at the secondary level.

Dewey's own psychosocial theory tried to reconcile tensions between the values involved in meeting the needs of individuals and those contained in accumulated cultural experience. Dewey was convinced that these could be brought into a viable and fruitful relationship.

# CHAPTER FIFTEEN

## *Education and the Ethical Life*

"A culture which permits science to destroy traditional values but which distrusts its powers to create new ones is a culture which is destroying itself." [1]

John Dewey was at heart a moralist—a moralist in a radical sense, for he felt that the primary justification for intellectual and speculative work was its role in strengthening the ethical quality of experience.

We may remind ourselves of the importance he assigned to the ethical goal by referring again to the opening paragraph of his original plan for the Laboratory School. Here he announced that the problem of all education was to coordinate psychological and social factors. The goal was to help the individual develop his full powers—in such a way as to support and advance social ends. Morals should be cultivated so that they would make an active difference in the life of the individual and his community. Moral principles were to act as guides in directing conduct. The abiding values and interests that would form the core of a unified, integrated self would be those that emerged out of the habit of reflecting critically on experience; they would be flexible in the sense that their meaning in specific or novel circumstances would have to be reassessed accordingly.

In short, Dewey rejected approaches which suggested that moral choices could be made by applying a ready-made formula. In moral choices, as in other behavior, there was no easy substitute for the habit and method of honest, realistic thinking. The argument for *reflective* morality as opposed to a *customary or nonreflective* morality was the major thesis in Dewey's work on

[1] John Dewey, *Freedom and Culture* (New York, G. P. Putnam's Sons, 1939), p. 154.

ethics written with James Tufts.[2] A reflective approach in making moral choices could only be learned through practice in social living. It is not surprising to find that where education was concerned, Dewey argued that the entire program of the school —its curriculum, its methodology, and its total climate as a miniature community—bore the responsibility for building reflective, moral character.

In order to understand his program for moral training in education, we must recall that his basic approach to ethics was conceived as an integral part of the instrumentalist philosophy he was creating as an alternative to Hegelian idealism. Essentially, the change involved a shift from a transcendental idealist orientation to an approach grounded in the spirit, methods, and values of evolutionary theory, and of science and democracy.

We cannot attempt a complete summary of his thinking on ethics. Our focus must be on the relevance of his ethical theory to education. In the remainder of this chapter, we shall attempt, first, to give examples of trends and changes in his ethical theory that seem to have particular relevance for his ideas on education, and second, to summarize his recommendations for school practice.

From the time Dewey replaced Morris as Chairman in the Department of Philosophy at Michigan through the years of his Chicago tenure, he assumed a major responsibility in the teaching of ethics. He wrote extensively on the philosophy of ethics and on ethical problems in education. We shall limit our effort to a review of several of his writings which illustrate the changes occurring in his thinking. These writings relate to three trends or characteristics of his thought: (1) the shift from a religious idealism to the social orientation of democracy and science, (2) the relinquishing of a transcendental self for a naturalistic, biosocial self, and (3) the influence of evolution on his ethical theory.

[2] John Dewey and James H. Tufts, *Theory of the Moral Life* (New York, Holt, Rinehart and Winston, 1960), from Part II of Dewey and Tufts, *Ethics*, rev. ed., 1932.

THE TRANSITION FROM IDEALISM TO
DEMOCRACY AND SCIENCE

"Christianity and Democracy" (1893) and "The Ethics of
Democracy" (1888) were two essays that Dewey wrote while
still under the influence of idealism. They contain the seeds of
ideas that were to characterize his later thoughts, and indicate
the intense intellectual struggle Dewey endured in his prolonged
passage to a thoroughgoing instrumentalist position.

In the first essay, originally delivered at a meeting of the
Student Christian Association in March, 1892, there is evidence
of growing fusion between the religious and social motives in his
thinking. It marks the shift from his early religious idealism to
his final position on the social orientation of democracy. As
noted in the first chapter, Dewey, in his early years at Michigan,
shared the neo-Hegelian orientation of his mentor, George S.
Morris. In a nondogmatic sense, this position was supportive of
the general theological teachings of Christianity. Dewey's religious interests were reflected, too, in the active part he took in
the Student Christian Association and the Bible Institute on campus, and his teaching in the Bible Classes of the First Congregational Church. However, in the final years at Ann Arbor, his
interests were shifting rapidly toward a social approach to ethical theory. When he moved to Chicago, he did not transfer his
church membership.

In "Christianity and Democracy" [3] Dewey rejected the usual
tendency to define religion in terms of a cult with dogmas and
religious practices. In a manner consistent with his favored genetic method, he sought to locate the essence of religion in its
origins and historical development. All religions, he argued, origi-
nate in the social and intellectual life of a community. Religion
expresses the social relations of the community; its ideas, rites,
dogmas, and mysteries are symbolic expressions of the relations
of a people to their world. In time, the social and intellectual

[3] John Dewey, "Christianity and Democracy," *Religious Thought at the
University of Michigan* (Ann Arbor, The Inland Press, 1893), pp. 60–69.
Address delivered before the Students' Christian Association, University of
Michigan, Sunday morning, March 27, 1892.

significance of religion becomes less evident and the rites and doctrine become ends in themselves and are separated from the reality of life. Religion, therefore, seems to be decaying, but "in reality, the very life, the very complexus of social and intellectual interactions which gave birth to these forms, is already and continuously at work finding revelation and expression in more adequate relations and truths." [4]

In considering Christianity, Dewey argued that Jesus did not come to impose a cult or a rite, or specific acts in the name of religion. What was the essence of his teaching? "If *any* man will *do* his *will*, he shall know of the doctrine." "Ye shall know the truth and the truth shall make you free." Dewey added, "The only truth Jesus knew of as religious was Truth. There were no special religious truths which he came to teach; on the contrary, his doctrine was that Truth, however named and however divided by man, is one as God is one; that getting hold of truth and living by it is religion." [5] Christianity, then, is essentially revelation. The revelation of truth must meet the test of facts and any attempt to define Christianity in terms of fixed religious truth is self-contradictory. The revelation of truth must continue as long as life has new meaning to unfold. If any organization attempts to prescribe the content of Christianity, it means that the real Christianity is working outside and beyond it. Revelation is occurring in wider and freer channels.

Dewey then turned to the nature and significance of democracy. Jesus, he said, taught that the kingdom of God is within or among us. It is revealed through intelligence and, therefore, antagonism toward reason is unwarranted. But man lives and acts in social settings that color his understanding of religion. Jesus taught that the individual was free to seek the truth, but his message was announced in a social world permeated with social and intellectual slaveries. His teachings, under these conditions, could not be understood in their direct and natural sense.

As Dewey saw it, the significance of democracy is that it enabled man to learn truths in a practical, everyday fashion. Democracy is essentially a spiritual fact and not merely governmental machinery. If God, as Jesus taught, is incarnate in men,

[4] *Ibid.*, p. 61.
[5] *Ibid.*

then freedom in democracy has a spiritual meaning. Freedom means giving the truth at the heart of things a chance to show itself.

"Democracy, as freedom, means the loosening of bonds; the wearing away of restrictions, the breaking down of barriers. . . . Through this doing away with restrictions, whatever truth, whatever reality there is in man's life is freed to express itself. Democracy is, as freedom, the freeing of truth." [6] But truth is not a matter of individual possession. "It is in the community of truth . . . that the brotherhood which is democracy, has its being." [7] Democracy involves both the breaking down of barriers that hinder pursuit of truth, and the creating of conditions that permit its positive attainment and distribution. It is no accident that the growth of democracy coincided with the rise of science and its commitment to advance truth through inquiry. Democracy provides the social setting in which truths can be won at new levels. It furnishes the conditions for further revelation.

There is no indication as to how Dewey's address was received. We are not concerned here with assessing the persuasiveness of his argument. We may note several features. Although the idealist mode is still clearly evident, Dewey was now arguing that a genetic method is the fruitful one for understanding the origin of ethical and religious concepts. By equating the free search for truth with the religious one, he laid the groundwork for science and democracy as means for new advances in ethical living. Emphasis on the critical role of the social setting in building character led to the concept of a moral, social self emerging out of community living.

This is perhaps the last time that Dewey employed such religiously oriented language. As his interests and ideas shifted to biological-psychological-social modes of analysis, he became a thoroughgoing naturalist. However, although he relinquished an orthodox religious orientation, he insisted on the prime importance of the spiritual and religious quality of experience. He remained concerned with the nihilism that could accompany the corrosion of belief, as well as with the evils of dogmatic coercion. He took his stand with the values of science and democracy,

[6] *Ibid.*, p. 66.
[7] *Ibid.*, p. 67.

but, as this early essay indicates, sought a concept that could encompass an ethical-spiritual dimension.[8] This consisted essentially of supporting those values and actions that gave the human spirit room to grow. However unconvincing his thesis may have been to those who remained within a traditional framework, his position remained "religious" for himself. His interest in the religious quality of education was evident at the very end of his Chicago stay. He became a member of the Religious Education Association, and delivered one of the major addresses at its first annual convention. The title was "Religious Education as Conditioned by Modern Psychology and Pedagogy." [9] The theme was that the content of religious education should be planned on the basis of an understanding of the stages in the development of children. His concluding sentences illustrate the juxtaposition of scientific and religious study that he was seeking to effect.

"The title indicated that it is possible to approach the subject of religious instruction in the reverent spirit of science, making the same sort of study of this problem that is made of any other educational problem. If methods of teaching, principles of selecting and using subject-matter, in all supposedly secular branches of education, are being subjected to careful and systematic scientific study, how can those interested in religion— and who is not?—justify neglect of the most fundamental of all educational questions, the moral and religious?" [10]

In "The Ethics of Democracy" [11] (1888), Dewey took up the task of clarifying principles that should guide social reform. In the spirit of the social liberals of the time, and within the Hegelian orientation, he took aim at eighteenth-century atomistic liberalism, which envisaged society as an aggregate of isolated

[8] His mature statement on the subject is contained in John Dewey, *A Common Faith* (New Haven, Yale University Press, 1934).

[9] John Dewey, "Religious Education as Conditioned by Modern Psychology and Pedagogy," *Proceedings of the Religious Education Association*, 1903, pp. 60–66, read at the first annual convention at Chicago in February, 1903.

[10] *Ibid.*, p. 66.

[11] John Dewey, *The Ethics of Democracy*, University of Michigan Philosophical Papers, Second Ser., No. 1, 1888. Lecture delivered at the University of Michigan.

individuals, externally related. Dewey subscribed to an organic theory of society, in which men are not isolated atoms but become men only through intrinsic relations with others. They are bound together by common purposes and ideals. Society exists to assure the fullest realization of individual personality. The individual can realize himself only by participating in the life of a free community. A democratic social order provides these conditions. Democracy is seen as essentially an ethical idea. It is not the giving to individuals of unlimited rights of self-aggrandizement without considering the effects of their behavior on others, nor is it a mere political device involving numerical head-counting. It is a matter of creating the conditions for the maximum realization of the capacities incorporate in every man. The ethical concept of democracy, he says, will not be realized until it includes industrial as well as civic and political life. This would mean that industry must be viewed as a social function, serving the interests of all, ". . . all industrial relations are to be regarded as subordinate to human relations, to the law of personality." [12] But, he says, this does not imply socialism, which might destroy "individual responsibility and activity which are at the very heart of social life." [13]

His social philosophy and his analysis of democracy were to be developed, in the main, after he left Chicago. Characteristic themes appear, however, even in these earlier years. In Dewey's view, the fundamental issue was between the values, modes of thought, and social living of an emerging democratic-scientific-urban culture and the modes of a prescientific-aristocratic era. The advent of the twentieth century saw revolutionary change under way. Methods of production and distribution were being altered radically; the nature of work and leisure were being transformed; class, racial, and ethnic lines were restructured in the new urban centers; relations between nations were becoming radically different; intellectual outlooks were changing under the impact of science; and schooling was becoming available to the masses. As Dewey commented some years later,

"There was never a time in the history of the world when human relationships and their accompanying rights and duties,

[12] *Ibid.*, p. 26.
[13] *Ibid.*

opportunities and demands, needed the unremitting and systematic attention of intelligent thought as they do at present." [14]

As he saw it, an imperative task of philosophy was to bring prescientific assumptions and methods of thought under scrutiny. Formulations, consistent with scientific knowledge and insight and with the values of a democratic social order, had to be worked out. Ethical theory had to be included in such a general reappraisal.

In the 1890's, he was seeking to lay the groundwork for a new unity of thought within the concepts of evolutionary biology and functional psychology. A social philosophy, based on the values of democracy and science, was to become part of a broad evolutionary frame of reference.

Reconstruction of ethical theory required several key intellectual efforts: first, the formulation of a concept of self and character consistent with the interactionist, bio-social point of view of functional psychology (as an alternative to idealist and empiricist concepts of self); second, the formulation of a theory of the ethical-spiritual dimension of human experience that would square with a general evolutionary point of view.

## THE ABANDONMENT OF THE TRANSCENDENTAL SELF

As the decade of the Nineties opened, Dewey's thought was stimulated by his encounter with the biological, interactionist interpretations of behavior in James's *Psychology*. His close relations with Mead at Chicago helped him to extend this conception to include the critical, *social* components involved in self, character, and reflective thought. His concentration on the psychological implications of this position became a major professional preoccupation. The gradual development of the concept of a bio-social self, formed through interaction with the natural-social setting, provided a path for departing from the transcendental self of idealism, which Dewey and his colleagues were finding untenable. The transition was not abrupt. As Morton White has pointed out, there were many continuities between Dewey's idealism and instrumentalism. Both share features of activism,

[14] Dewey and Tufts, *Theory of the Moral Life*, p. 21.

organicism, and opposition to formalism.[15] But the difference was being sharpened in the early Nineties. The moral end, Dewey now argued, is still self-realization, but not in the sense of "filling in the blank scheme of some undefined purely general self." [16]

The alternative idea of a bio-social self had profound implications for Dewey's theory of the nature of morals in human experience. The details of the formulation are complex. We can attempt only a sketch of the main elements.

When Dewey came to Chicago, the large question occupying his attention was, "What is the meaning of life?" In more specific terms, the question was, "What is the meaning of life in the perspective of evolutionary theory?" He came to believe that growth is the prime characteristic of life. In human life the critical dimension is growth in experience—growth through change in our way of seeing the world and of acting in it effectively. The process of growing is the essence of the process of becoming educated. Hence his famous dictum that education is all one with growing. Growing is part of a natural process, resulting from continual interaction with the physical and social world.

The ideas represented in his essay "The Reflex Arc" provided the biological base on which his system could be built. As we have seen, Dewey criticized the disjointed analysis of the reflex arc into separate, mechanical, entities of sensation-idea-movement. Dewey and his colleagues approached the problem of growth with their attention centered on continuity of function. In searching for a unifying principle, they developed the concept of "coordination" within the unity of the human act. They contended that we cannot understand the living unity which is a child by separate study of sensation, movement, emotion, etc. As the genetic method underscores growth in the continuity of experience, the proper subject of study is the human being in the process of becoming a self in social life—not his mere physiological reactions and movements. The idea may be clarified by turning to Dewey's working hypothesis of stages in the processes of the child's growth from infancy onward. The critical item was

[15] Morton White, *The Origins of Dewey's Instrumentalism* (New York, Columbia University Press, 1943), p. 111.
[16] John Dewey, "Self-Realization and the Moral Ideal," *Philosophical Review*, Vol. 2 (November, 1893), p. 664.

a conception of the act: "The principle of coordination or of sensory-motor action supplies us with . . . a centralizing principle—a principle which can be employed equally on the physiological and the psychological side. In popular language this unit is an act, whether of greater or lesser complexity." [17] On the biological side, sensation is one element in a coordinated sensory-motor adjustment or act. But the distinctively human aspect of the act emerges with the use of *ideas* within the act. Ideas can occur only with language and language is possible only where there is social life with shared communication.

In the genetic development of the infant, three periods may be traced. The first involves the relatively independent physical maturing of eye, ear, and hand. The second period is gradually ushered in as these cease to act in isolation and their actions become parts of coordinated behavior. When what is *seen* means something for *reaching* and *handling*, then one experience points to another. Seeing the rattle and simultaneously reaching for it become parts of a coordinated act. This capacity to make cross references is the basis for the development of intelligence. In the third period, these coordinations are developed to the extent that the child gains *new* experiences. Practice in coordinating the skills required in seeing, reaching, and seizing becomes the center of interest and development for a time, and then is extended into other interests. The child may discover that rattling brings smiles and attention from the mother, or he extends his physical coordinations to master control over new toys.

"The difference between the lower animals and man is that in the former this co-ordination is predetermined quite specifically, while in man only the very general lines are laid down, thus leaving room for great variation and experimentation—implying possibility of new combinations, and thus the performance of new acts almost without limit. The acts, which to the animals are well defined ends, are, in the human structure, freed from their adjustment to predefined ends and made flexible instruments for a large number of different and much more complex ends.

[17] Katherine C. Mayhew and Anna C. Edwards, *The Dewey School* (New York, Appleton-Century-Crofts, 1936), pp. 450–453 *et passim*. Quoting from John Dewey, "Principles of Mental Development in Early Infancy," *Transactions of the Illinois Society for Child Study*, Vol. 4, No. 3.

The *definite* coordination of acts is thus, with man, not a *datum* but a *problem*.

"Each impulse in its expression tends to call up other impulses; and it brings *into consciousness* other experiences. A child puts forth, by natural impulse, his hand towards a bright color; his hand touches it and he gets new experiences—feelings of contact; these, in turn, are stimulus to a further act; he puts the thing in his mouth, and gets a taste, etc." [18]

Dewey held that the laws governing the earliest developing coordination of infants were the same as the laws at work in building more complex coordinations and in producing growth of experience. The individual is seen as one who is growing in "coordination" throughout his life-span. He progressively obtains a wider command of both his body and his environment as tools for thinking. The emergence of language and conceptual behavior creates new possibilities for extending and reshaping experience. The expanding interests that occupy the child's attention and action form the core of selfhood. They deepen and broaden as his capacity for more complex interaction with his world develops.

A distinctive feature of Dewey's position was the critical role assigned to ideas or intelligence within the human act. He challenged the later concept of behaviorism, in which stimulus and response are related to each other only externally.

In his view, the act was seen as a unified trinity involving sensory-motor stimulus, *idea*, and motor-response, with an emphasis on the interpretative function of *idea*. The inclusion of ideas or intelligence *within* the act provided an explanation for conscious behavior—behavior guided by deliberate purpose as distinct from automatic and unreflective action. *Meaningful* activities are those in which actions are guided by an idea or aim. Such activities are genuine expressions of the self. Ideas are clarified and developed in the course of action. Afterwards, reflection on the completed act can clarify the meaning of the experience. Ideas reconstituted in this process can be employed in new forms

[18] John Dewey, *The Study of Ethics: A Syllabus* (Ann Arbor, George Wahr, 1897), p. 14, printed originally in 1894 with the imprint: Ann Arbor, Register Publishing Co.

of action and in modification of environment and self. This is the nature of the process of human growth.

This abbreviated description of the principle of growth, as occurring within the act-guided-by-idea, gives us a basis for understanding Dewey's analysis of the psychological character of *moral* acts and character. The summary principle is this: *the moral act is the consciously completed act which expresses the unified self.* The trinity of factors in the act—feeling, thinking, and muscular response—is part of a coordinated functioning. Action begins with impulse. But when the impulsive act meets resistance, it divides into competing tendencies. Ideas are born in this situation as each conflicting possible course of action is represented as an idea. These ideas are examined and weighed in deliberation. In reflection, we pursue each possible course to its end and imagine the actual event and its consequence. Thinking thus becomes a substitute for overt conflict or impulsive action. In thought, the ideas may be considered and a harmonious coordination effected. A choice or decision is made, and out of such choices the self is formed. Dewey took the position that conduct and character are morally one and the same thing.

"The first effect of every mediation of an impulse is to check or arrest that impulse. Reflection means postponement; it is delayed action. Through this delay the impulse is brought into connection with other impulses, habits and experiences. Now if a due balance is kept, the result is that the original impulse is harmonized with the self, and, when expressed, it realizes not only its own partial nature but that of the whole self; it becomes the organ through which the whole self finds outlet. The moral criterion for an act proceeding from anger or from benevolence is whether only a part of the self or the whole character moves outward in the act. The bad act is partial, the good organic. The good man 'eats to live,' that is, the satisfaction even of the appetite of hunger is functional to the whole self or life; if we say the man who 'lives to eat' is bad, it is because he is sacrificing much of himself to one partial expression of himself. . . .

"The good man, in a word, is his whole self in each of his acts; the bad man is a partial (and hence a different) self in his conduct. He is not one person, for he has no unifying principle.

(Compare the expressions 'dissipated, gone to pieces, shaky, unstable, lacking in integrity, duplicity, devious, indirect, snaky,' etc.)" [19]

Dewey made the point more succinctly as follows: "Some acts tend to narrow the self, to introduce friction into it, to weaken its power, and in various ways to disintegrate it, while other acts tend to expand, invigorate, and harmonize, and in general organize the self." [20] The first may be judged as immoral, while those that expand and coordinate the self are moral.

Dewey agreed with Aristotle by holding that the goodness of a good man shines through his deeds. "The self reveals its nature in what it chooses." [21] Dewey was to insist again and again that the key to a correct theory of morality is recognition of the unity of the self and its acts.

The self, like the organism to which it is closely related, is active. The good self is the one that is unified and integrated. At the core is the set of interests or ends one has chosen to pursue. The self is integrated when choices have been made that enable one to realize one's powers, and to continue to grow. The individual must have cultivated the ability to practice a reflective morality, in which wise choices are made on the basis of a judicious examination of the consequences for the self he will become. This is also the mark of the responsible, free self as opposed to the one that is capricious or crippled by blind impulse or habit. There is congruence, so far, with Jean Paul Sartre's injunction "I am what I choose."

But the self is not an individual entity. Selves and characters cannot arise and exist apart from human relations and community. "One's conduct calls forth certain reactions from others—reactions as natural as those called forth when one comes in contact with physical force. The individual lives as truly in a social as in a physical environment. . . ." [22] The values and interests that have grown out of social experience are learned and incorporated into self. The quality of the moral life cannot be considered apart from the quality of social life. If social life is

[19] *Ibid.,* pp. 22–23.
[20] *Ibid.,* p. 73.
[21] Dewey, *Theory of the Moral Life,* p. 150.
[22] Dewey, *The Study of Ethics,* p. 125.

defective and limiting, individual self and character will be crippled. This means that social institutions must be judged in terms of whether they support the conditions for sound growth of mind and character.

This led Dewey to criticize features of the existing social system and eventually to elaborate the values of a democratic social order that would provide the conditions for human growth and moral development. The school, as a miniature community within a larger one, should be constituted so as to nourish the kinds of selves which, in turn, could aid in regenerating an industrial-urban society. For this purpose, the school's program should embody the values represented in science and democracy: respect for the integrity of the person as a self in process of becoming; the use of reflection in choosing ideals to direct conduct; and social relations based on responsible cooperation and communication that would mutually enrich the persons involved.

Mayhew and Edwards, who developed their account of the Laboratory School in collaboration with Dewey, give the following answer to the question "What are the implications for education contained in this position?"

". . . *the child* as a growing person was the first concern. How could *he* find the best expression for that which in *him* lay, that which *he* wanted to do, to say, and to be? How could *he* develop *his own* working ideals by which *he* could go into action, moment by moment, hour by hour, and day by day, and thus build within *himself* habits of moral behavior and advancing ideals and goals? How could *he* be given the manna that would be of use to *him* in the fashioning of such ideals? And what was the environment in which this could best be done?

"Two working principles stand out among the many educational implications of this theory, one of which is a corollary of the other: first, to foster the development of the child's own inner self, and second, to foster its development in social relationships. The first of these must be in order that the second may be, but neither can be considered apart from the other, for both must grow together. From this previous analysis, he who runs may read at the heart of this theory the belief in responsibility for consequences, for constant recognition by every person that he is not alone in a physical world, but that he lives in a world of men. Responsibility, therefore, lies in the process of deliberation and choice, of estimating and constituting value (to others as well as to himself), of proving and approving the worth of the deed. As ability to estimate value increases, so increases the demand for revision or 'mediation' of the plan of action. Hence, as the plan develops, responsibilities increase. The self must be true in thought and will in order that the deed may also be true.

" 'In a moral act, the will, the idea, and the consequences are all placed inside of the act, and the act itself only within the larger activity of the individual in society.' This was a twofold commandment for those who held this theory: to guide the child in the making of his deeds so that they become better and better deeds and, at the same time, more helpful deeds. A moral act is thus seen to be a social act. The school must be a place where individual activity can be social also in character, where the child by working on and in his physical environment can develop his individual powers and at the same time use them in furthering the larger activities of his group. The supplying of every available aid to this process constitutes the function of any system of moral education, for Mr. Dewey's conception of education is identical with moral education thus conceived. Certain assumptions are always implied. The growth of an individual implies and depends upon a developing society which in turn is constantly changed by the contributions of the individuals who constitute it. Growth of an integrated personality, however, necessitates freedom from undue social pressures during the maturing process. Rhythmic periods of solitude are essential that the individual may develop his own ideas and ways of bettering and adjusting his actions to the activities of his group. *This rhythm the school must provide.*" [23]

The insistence here is that the school must provide occasions for the child to develop his own individuality. At the same time, it is held that the development of integrated selfhood is dependent on the quality of community or social life. The individual needs to be free from "undue social pressures" so that the social

[23] Mayhew and Edwards, *op. cit.,* pp. 457–459.

unit may profit from his unique contributions. At the same time, the individual must become a person who lives from a sense of responsibility to his community. It may be argued that this position makes the work of the educator too complex (although to this writer the task of working out a tensional balance between the claims of the individual and the claims of the community is, indeed, both the difficulty and the glory of the free society). The position does not deserve the charge, however, that "in spite of Mr. Dewey's fine defense of individualism, his moral ideal is really that of the 'good mixer.' " [24]

## EVOLUTION AND ETHICS

The recurring problem in Dewey's work in ethics was to seek a unitary view of human experience, including the moral or ethical quality, that would agree with evolutionary theory. He came to feel that such a connection could be established. His recommendations for ethical education in the schools stemmed from the analyses he made. Some of his main arguments were set forth in two important papers: "Evolution and Ethics" (1898) and "The Evolutionary Method as Applied to Morality" (1902).

In "Evolution and Ethics," Dewey presented a reply to Professor Thomas Huxley's Romanes lecture (1893), which had profoundly disturbed those who had hoped to find a unified view within evolutionary thought. Huxley, in pointing out some differences between what he called the cosmic and the ethical processes, seemed to see a dualistic separation between animal and human life. Dewey gave his interpretation of Huxley's position with the contradiction he thought it contained:

"The *rule* of the cosmic process is struggle and strife. The rule of the ethical process is sympathy and cooperation. The *end* of the cosmic process is the survival of the fittest; that of the ethical, the fitting of as many as possible to survive. Before the ethical tribunal the cosmic process stands condemned. The two

[24] See Lawrence A. Cremin, *The Transformation of the School* (New York, Alfred A. Knopf, 1961), p. 126.

processes are not only incompatible but even opposed to each other." [25]

He then gave his own detailed refutation, which centered on the proposition that the *ethical* process is not opposed to the general cosmic process. On the contrary, ethical development was seen as part of an emerging psychosocial stage in evolution.

He used, as an example, the gardener struggling to maintain his plants against the incursion of weeds and other natural enemies. The methods of insight and reflection the gardener employs to achieve his ends are, Dewey said, those that have emerged within evolutionary development. Man uses one part of nature to control another. The gardener, through *intelligent selection*, introduces conditions of sunlight and moisture to which the untended plot is unaccustomed. The employment of intelligence to support cultivated crops as opposed to weeds permits life conditions to be determined by one set of "natural" conditions as opposed to another.

When considering the concept of fitness for survival, Dewey argued that it is critical to realize that with the advent of human social life the environment itself has changed. What is "fit" must be fit to survive in a natural world which now includes the human-social dimension. Animal instinct and impulse are not absolutely opposed to social life, but in the new conditions they become good in certain ways and bad in others. So that human life may be maintained, behavior characterized by courage, persistence, patience, initiative, and self-denial become "fitting" ways. Some animal acts, appropriate at a prehuman stage, become unfitting at the human level. The ethical "struggle" involves the need to re-adapt behavior necessary to sustain human life in co-ordination with other life forms. Habits that represent survival of outworn conditions demand reconstitution, and such a process is accompanied by pain. "Growth always costs something. It costs the making over of the old in order to meet the demands of the new." [26] Man has the possibility of freeing himself from mere impulse and instinct. Through intelligent foresight, he maintains institutions; he remakes them to serve changing condi-

[25] John Dewey, "Evolution and Ethics," *The Monist*, Vol. 8 (April, 1898), p. 323.
[26] *Ibid.*, p. 333.

tions. The consequence of maintaining them unchanged is "death, fossilization," or as Dewey put it, in slightly different terms:

"The problem is the reconciliation of unbridled radicalism and inert conservatism, in a movement of reasonable reform. Psychologically the tension manifests itself as the conflict between habits and aims—without habits, we can do nothing. Yet if habits become so fixed that they cannot be adapted to the ends suggested by new situations, they are barriers to conduct and enemies to life. It is conduct with the end or ideal which keeps the habit working, a flexible and efficient instrument of action." [27]

Just as the relative antagonism between habits and aims is necessary to their final co-adaptation, so is strain between impulse and ideal necessary for the ethical process. It is exactly there, Dewey felt, that the tension between the natural and the moral is located. Men, through public opinion and education, may constantly repress and punish certain forms of action while they stimulate and encourage others.

"In man we have [the] power of variation and consequent discovery and constitution of new environments set free. . . . The difference between man and animal is not that selection has ceased, but that selection along the lines of variations which enlarge and intensify the environment is active as never before." [28]

In Dewey's view, then, "selection"—as "fitness" and "struggle for existence"—is found in the ethical process just as it is in the cosmic, and it operates in the same way. The important fact is that man is conscious of the cosmic process: what was instinct in animal is conscious impulse in man; what was "tendency to vary" in animal is conscious foresight in man; what was unconscious adaptation and survival in animal is, with man, conscious deliberation and experimentation.

"I question whether the spiritual life does not get its . . . most ample guarantees when it is learned that the laws and conditions of righteousness are implicated in the working processes of the universe; when it is found that man in his conscious struggles,

[27] *Ibid.*, p. 335.
[28] *Ibid.*, p. 340.

in his doubts, temptations and defeats, in his aspirations and successes, is moved on and buoyed up by the forces which have developed nature; and that in this moral struggle he acts not as a mere individual but as an organ in maintaining and carrying forward the universal process." [29]

Dewey's philosophy of education rests largely on the ethical concept expressed here. Before turning to his ideas about ethics and education, we shall take a closer look at some of Dewey's specific ideas on the evolutionary method as related to morality.

### ETHICS AND GENETIC METHOD

Some years after his article on "Evolution and Ethics," Dewey again elaborated certain themes in a lengthy two-part article, "The Evolutionary Method as Applied to Morality." [30] The detailed exposition is elaborate and complex. At the risk of distortion, we shall try to focus on a single concept especially relevant to his work in education.

Dewey argued that there was need for a method to understand and interpret moral conduct. He referred to his proposal interchangeably as the evolutionary method, the historical method, or the genetic method. [31] His aim was to show that the genetic method threw light on the nature of the individual and society; that it enabled us to substitute a scientific statement on the relations of personality and society for an unsatisfactory metaphysical one. Essentially, it was a method for tracing the natural history of moral principles. Rather than treating these as fixed precepts, Dewey maintained that a critical method of studying morals would reveal their origin and evolution in man's social experience. Such understanding could provide an instrument for deepening and extending the ethical quality of life. Such a

[29] *Ibid.*, p. 341.
[30] John Dewey, "The Evolutionary Method as Applied to Morality," 1. "Its Scientific Necessity," *Philosophic Review*, Vol. 11 (March, 1902), pp. 107–124; 2. "Its Significance for Conduct," Vol. II (July, 1902), pp. 353–371.
[31] For a commentary on this vein of thought see Morton G. White, "Dewey on the Genetic Method," Part IV of "The Attack on Historical Method," *The Journal of Philosophy*, Vol. 42, No. 12, pp. 328–331.

method could provide insight into what was to be preserved and strengthened, and what was to be modified or changed.

He contrasted the admittedly controversial approach that he was proposing with two general alternatives—which he labeled intuitionalism and empiricism.

His reference to intuitionalism recalls the school of Scottish intuitionalism, which he had rejected when a student at the University of Vermont. He now broadened the term to include a variety of philosophical "schools." He had little sympathy or patience with this position. Intuitional theories of morals, he said, hold that conscience is a peculiar faculty which gives men, directly and immediately, knowledge of principles, or rules of right. This leads to the swamp of subjectivism and rationalization. It provides, as J. S. Mill had argued, for the conservation of established opinion. Each creed and institution can resist challenge by the simple assertion, "I represent an eternal and necessary intuition." [32] Dewey respected intuitions as hunches to be checked and verified against experience—but the intuitionalists were not satisfied with such modest claims.

He also judged crude empiricist and utilitarian approaches to morals to be unsatisfactory. He respected some contributions of empiricism. It had helped, he said, to show that intuitions were mere emotional sanctifications of customs, prejudice, and class interest. In rejecting genetic considerations, however, empiricism tended to hold that ideas arise as mere reflexes of some existing object of fact. Beliefs are generated by repetition or accumulation —with similar ones hanging together in reinforcement and others fading away. Dewey argued that empiricists who described moral beliefs as mere accumulations through repeated associations provided no criterion for direction or selection—no "working instrumentalities." As empiricism is essentially devoid of *ideals*, and is critical and destructive, it leads men to return to intuitionalism in order to rescue ideals.

The weakness in these alternatives, as seen by Dewey, made the historic or genetic method all the more important. Its value was that it revealed a process which is operating continuously. If the nature of the genesis of morals was understood, it was possi-

[32] From an earlier criticism of the same topic, John Dewey, *The Study of Ethics: A Syllabus*, p. 85.

ble to bring under intellectual and practical control facts that resisted general speculation or mere introspection. The historical view revealed the conditions under which moral practices and ideas had originated.

After a detailed argument about the similarities of the experimental methods of the natural sciences to genetic or historic methods, he announced that his thesis was that there is an identity

"between what the experimental method does for our physical knowledge, and what the historical method in a narrower sense may do for the spiritual region: the region of conscious values. [The] aim is to show that the historical method reveals to us a process of becoming, and thereby brings under intellectual and practical control facts which utterly resist general speculation or mere introspective observation." [33]

It does this, in part, Dewey said, by presenting in a simplified form earlier elements in an historical development. This makes it possible to detach and grasp elements that get obscured in the complexity of more mature phases. Where morals are concerned, we can grasp, comprehensively and analytically, *factors that have counted,* this way or that, in the moral development of man.[34] Ideals and purposes can be brought under critical judgment by examining the consequences that follow from acting on them. Moral judgments then may be seen as "judgments of ways to act, of deeds to do, of habits to form, of ends to cultivate." [35]

Dewey weighed the question of whether the historic approach to morals, as opposed to a view of morals as eternal precepts, would have any destructive effect. He concluded that the reflective method would not destroy distinctively ethical values. On the contrary, ethical principles of abiding value would be supplied with added meaning and sanction, and would be provided with means for careful expansion and modification.

The genetic method, in contrast to the intuitionalist or empiricist theories of morals, was held by Dewey to have special value at a time when men are experiencing rapid change. It pro-

[33] *Ibid.,* p. 113.
[34] *Ibid.,* p. 371.
[35] *Ibid.*

vided an alternative to nihilistic debunking and to unconvincing demands that we cling blindly to past modes of conduct.

Its great strength, Dewey felt, was that it makes human relationships clear and understandable. It unites the present situation—with its accepted customs, beliefs, moral ideals, hopes, and aspirations—with the past. It sees the moral process as a whole, and yet in perspective. What can be learned from a study of the past is also available in an analysis of the present. The genetic, or historic method provides a tool of inquiry, interpretation, and criticism regarding present assumptions and aspirations. As such it can aid in eliminating or reducing mere "survivals," emotional reactions, and rationalizations.

It takes but a moment's reflection to recall that the total design of the curriculum of the Laboratory School was centered on such a genetic principle, especially in history and the sciences. The effort was made to plan the curriculum around critical events in the evolution of human experience. The qualities of mind, character, and conduct that had abiding value—or that presented new possibilities for growth—were to receive special attention. Early stages in the evolution of civilized experience were selected because they could provide insights into human behavior in a simpler situation. The hope was that students, so equipped, could see more clearly aspects of a complex present.

It is not surprising that the instrument of genetic analysis, which Dewey employed in all aspects of his speculation—psychological, logical, social, and ethical—should be prominent in his educational design. In his role as educator, Dewey hoped to work out the consequences for social practice of his philosophical theory. We turn now to his recommendations for teaching ethics.

## ETHICS AND EDUCATION

Dewey's ideas about ethics and education originated in his own experiences with students and schools as well as in his philosophical work. Dewey had developed an interest in elementary and secondary education during his visits to schools as a member of the University of Michigan Investigating Committee for Accreditation. While a member of the Michigan Schoolmasters

Club, Dewey began to turn his attention to the correlation between achievements in high school and the training received in grade school. His observations and studies of the lower schools convinced him that the methods employed were not in keeping with what newer investigations in psychology revealed about the normal processes of learning in children.

The trouble began with the kind of psychology taught in the normal schools. Dewey indicated his objections in a review of a book that represented the generally accepted view of psychology: *Elementary Psychology, with Practical Applications to Education and the Conduct of Life.* His review included criticisms typical of those he later made of methods of moral teaching. The text, he said, was lacking in any unified psychological theory. The mind in general was viewed as an entity for metaphysical self-activity. Here and there, isolated items from the realm of cerebral physiology were referred to without being integrated to the mind-entity concept. An unconvincing effort was made to be scientific, safe summaries of the usual "pedagogy" of the teachers' institutions and some platitudinous moral injunctions were offered. In Dewey's view, the book belonged more in the realm of "popular science" than in that of science proper. Morals were treated as verbal abstractions, and no attempt was made to connect mental processes with the activity or growth of children. The remoteness of schoolwork from the behavior and interests of children was the result of this kind of confused theoretical basis. Dewey was thus laying the groundwork for creating a psychological theory that would be rooted in scientific investigation and that would relate more convincingly to the normal behavior of children. With this he would seek to rescue ethical teaching from formal, verbalized "moralizing."

Dewey made a statement on moral education that appeared in *The Popular Science Monthly* under the title "The Chaos in Moral Training." [36] This was a report on his own experiences in teaching ethics to undergraduate students. As a teacher of ethics, Dewey wished to avoid a mere academic review of the ethical theories of various philosophers. He wanted to include in dis-

[36] John Dewey, "The Chaos in Moral Training," *Popular Science Monthly*, Vol. 14 (August, 1894), pp. 433–443.

cussions an analysis of actual motives and behavior. Dewey had asked his students to describe some early moral experience with honesty or truthfulness, and to recall their reasons for following the virtue in question. In general, he was impressed by the stilted quality of their replies. The students had learned what they ought to say. They avoided analyses that expressed personal feelings. Generally, motivation was rooted in the desire to avoid punishment, religious or temporal; many made simple assertions that one should "do right."

Dewey drew several conclusions from this experience. One was that in ethical training there was a divorce of theory from actual conduct. Various theories of ethics agree, he said, that conduct is not moral except as its motive is pure—free from reference to personal fear of punishment of hope of reward. Yet his students showed a near absence of any approach to moral choices on other than a crude reward or punishment basis. Confidence was placed in the assertion of platitudes without awareness that they sometimes contradicted each other. Little use was made of principles that could explain motives and methods. He criticized the approach to the teaching of ethics that lay behind such behavior. Current practice, which preached about right and wrong —which simply told a child what to do, while discouraging his natural interest in understanding the reasons for or meaning of behavior—was in Dewey's eyes "a sign of depravity."

"To continue the present method of holding, on one side, that a child is so irrational that he cannot see for himself the significance of his conduct, while on the other, with regard to these self-same acts, the child is punished as a *moral* delinquent, and has urged upon him, on *moral* grounds, the necessity for doing them, is the height of theoretical absurdity and of practical confusion." [37]

This article, appearing in the year Dewey went to Chicago, contained clues as to the methods he felt should be used in instructing children.

There is further indication of the proposals Dewey was to advocate in ethical teaching in another article of the period,

[37] *Ibid.*, p. 441.

"Teaching Ethics in the High School." [38] Again he made a vigorous protest against the assumption that character and behavior could be improved by the inculcation of moral rules. Memorizing maxims was as influential in building character as would be the teaching of astronomical formulas. Dewey's goal was to help students to develop insights into how ethical choices resulted in certain consequences in actual human relations.

"Ethics, rightly conceived, is the statement of human relationships in action. Therefore, any right study of ethics means that a student is not studying fixed rules for conduct; he is studying ways in which men are bound together in the complex relations of their interactions. He is not studying, in an introspective way, his own sentiments and moral attitudes; he is studying facts as objective as those of hydro-statics or of the action of dynamos. They are subjective, too, but subjective in the sense that since the pupil himself is one who is bound up in the complex of action, the ethical relations have an interest and concern for him which no action of fluid or of dynamo can possibly have." [39]

He underscored his opinion that ethical subject matter should be taught from the lowest grades to the highest; but he chose to illustrate an approach that was most appropriate at the secondary level. His proposal was that students should be confronted with concrete situations in which moral choices had to be made. They might be confronted, he said, with a current case of human misery. The question to be considered would be *whether* to relieve it and, if so, *how* to relieve it. This should be done without preliminary dwelling on the matter as a "moral" one. The emphasis should not be on citing moral precepts but on getting students into the habit of visualizing scenes of human interaction and of analyzing them in terms of what to do. Dewey warned against letting children argue at the level of general abstraction. If instruction in the theory of morals was to have any practical value, it would have to be in helping the child to realize the nature of the practical situations in which he would find himself placed. If

[38] John Dewey, "Teaching Ethics in the High School," *Educational Review*, Vol. 6 (November, 1893), pp. 313-321.
[39] *Ibid.*, p. 314.

some suggestions were the product of impulse, these were to be brought under critical reflection. Sympathy and other emotions did have a proper role in human relations, but, if not checked by reflection, they could lead to unfortunate consequences. In the analysis of specific instances of human relations, the two factors of ethical action—impulse and intelligence—and the multitude of relations that were the result of any human action had to be taken into account.

This author recalls an example from his own experience with a ninth grade class that might illustrate Dewey's point. Immediately after World War II, the students were sponsoring CARE packages for homeless children in France. One student suggested that more good could be done by sending cigarettes that could be sold in the black market. Some of the children were eager to endorse this proposal as a bright idea, but after questions were raised about the nature and causes of the black market and the consequences of such an action had been considered, they rejected the scheme.

Dewey placed his confidence in methods that forced students to confront moral choices in specific cases week by week, for example, in their schoolwork. He maintained that "the pupil who has learned what careful study of conditions and weighing of expedients is necessary to treat many a case of relief, is prepared to understand the true meaning of 'motive' in ethical discussion far better than nineteen-twentieths of our college students who have analyzed it at large." [40]

Dewey did not necessarily advocate the study of ethics as a separate subject in the curriculum. He did argue, however, that the study of *ethical relationships* in the complex changing world should be given a high priority in the entire school program.

"Where there is one reason for the ordinary student to become acquainted with the intricacies of geometry, of physics . . . , there are twenty for him to become acquainted with the nature of those relations upon which his deeper weal and woe depend, and to become interested in, and habituated to, looking at them with sympathetic imagination. And so far as the fetish of discipline, or the culture-value of studies, or anything of that sort, is

[40] *Ibid.*, p. 318.

concerned, one need have no fear that the world of ethical activities will not afford scope for all the powers of analysis, of interpretation, and of observation, of which any pupil may be possessed. The subject here is so important, the mental power brought into play in dealing with it is of such quality and kept at such pitch that, utimately, the subject-matter of ethics must furnish the measure for other studies and not vice-versa." [41]

Dewey maintained that it was impossible for pupils to get the full meaning either of literature or of history without studying ethical material within the context he had outlined. His real wish was to see a time when the central study would be human life itself.

". . . a time when science shall be less a quantity constant in itself and more a method for approaching and dealing with human life; a time when language and literature, as well as history, shall be less realms of thought and emotion by themselves and more the record and instruments of this human life." [42]

We find Dewey returning to the theme that the central study should be that of civilized human experience, both in the individual's own life and in human communities past and present. We must now consider his most comprehensive statement on ethics and education.

## MORAL PRINCIPLES AND EDUCATION

Dewey's most explicit statement on education and morals is found in his essay *Moral Principles in Education*. [43] He took the position that the resources for building moral character were (1) the life of the school as a social institution, (2) its methods of learning and of doing work, and (3) its studies or curriculum. These three, in turn, were to be grounded in the psychological theory he then held. The thesis he developed is clearly

[41] *Ibid.*, p. 321.
[42] *Ibid.*
[43] John Dewey, *Moral Principles in Education* (Boston, Houghton Mifflin Co., 1909). This is an elaboration of "Ethical Principles Underlying Education," *Third Yearbook*, National Herbart Society, 1897, pp. 7-34.

related to the practice he had advocated for the Laboratory School.

He began by saying that he wished to make a distinction between *moral ideas* and *ideas about morality*. Typical instruction, he said, is concerned with imparting ideas about morality, but in the form of memorized verbalizations, these ideas can be meaningless. Moral ideas, on the other hand, take effect in conduct and improve it. The concern of educators must be with moral ideas. Their task is to see that moral ideas are acquired in such a way that they become *"moving* ideas, motive forces in the guidance of conduct." [44] When this is the goal, the moral purpose becomes universal in the whole of instruction.

"Were it not for this possibility, the familiar statement that the ultimate purpose of all education is character-forming would be hypocritical pretence; for as every one knows, the direct and immediate attention of teachers and pupils must be, for the greater part of the time, upon intellectual matters. It is out of the question to keep direct moral considerations constantly uppermost. But it is not out of the question to aim at making the methods of learning, or acquiring intellectual power, and of assimilating subject-matter, such that they will render behavior more enlightened, more consistent, more vigorous than it otherwise would be." [45]

In turning to the question of how this could be so, Dewey took up, in succession, the contributions of the school as a community, teaching methods, and the curriculum.

## The School as a Social Community

Dewey began with the assumption that the school must be viewed as an integral part of the social life in which it functions. Viewed as an isolated entity, the school has no moral end. He argued that the United States is a democratic and progressive society. The ends of education are set by the democratic values, which means that the child must be educated for leadership as well as for obedience. He must have the skills of self-direction, "the skills of administration," and the capacity to assume re-

[44] *Ibid.*, p. 2.
[45] *Ibid.*

sponsibility. He must have the insight required to assume obligations in industrial and business life as well as in political matters. With respect to personal fulfillment, the individual must be defined as a participating member of community life, not as an isolated individual.

The school, he said, can only develop the individual for social participation by giving him a chance to engage in social life. Habits of social service cannot be taught unless the school is envisaged as an embryonic community in which the child lives and learns. The emphasis on moral training should come through positive participation rather than through remonstrances. Punishments for wrongdoing should be viewed as incidents rather than representative of basic principles for building moral conduct. The chief moral habit to be cultivated in the child should be interest in community welfare—an intellectual, practical, emotional interest in perceiving the principles and behavior that make for social order and progress, first, within the activities of the school, and, by extension, within the activities of the larger society. The total social character of the school must be the basic factor in moral education. This social character must be reflected in the school's methods and curriculum.

## Methods

When considering methods employed, Dewey judged the typical practices, based on individual absorption and competitive recitation, to be harmful for the building of socially responsible character.

"There is no opportunity for each child to work out something specifically his own, which he may contribute to the common stock, while he, in turn, participates in the production of others. All are set to do exactly the same work and turn out the same products. The social spirit is not cultivated,—in fact, in so far as the purely individualistic method gets in its work, it atrophies for lack of use." [46]

This shows up in the poor quality of oral reading when it is divorced from its genuine social function—to communicate ideas to other human beings. The child is not in a position to *give*

[46] *Ibid.*, p. 22.

something to others, but is merely repeating the words contained in the book each child is following. The child's natural desire is to share, to do, to serve, and when this desire is not fulfilled, work becomes a burden.

Since motivation based on communication and social cooperation is lacking in the schools, teachers resort to practices aimed at keeping the individual child at his studies. One of these is to teach him to win the affection of the teacher. If he does not break the rules he will be considered good and will be liked. This is not all bad, Dewey said, but the urge to win the teacher's approval can become the student's primary aim. The move should be away from reliance on such external motivation toward an appreciation of the social value of study and work. The young person should realize that he has a responsibility to more than a few individuals, such as his parents and teachers. He should develop a sense of being a responsible participant in a series of communities.

Another typical external motivation is fear—not necessarily fear of physical punishment, but fear of losing the approval of others, or of failure. As children are all presumed to be doing the same work, they are pitted against each other in endless competition and are constantly compared in terms of relative standing. The weaker students may lose a sense of their own genuine abilities and consistently accept positions of inferiority. The strong students may learn to take pride not in the use of their abilities but in the fact that they are winners. This kind of endless competition is ironic, in Dewey's view, because it is least relevant in genuine intellectual and artistic pursuits, where the laws are cooperation, participation, and communication.

Egoistic striving is related to another feature of schools—the emphasis placed on working for future goals. The motivation of later success appeals most to those who are already too egoistically oriented. Dewey felt that the opportunity for a child to develop his moral powers was lost if the child had the impression that nothing he does is worth doing for its own sake.

Dewey did not elaborate on alternative methods, except to make clear that activities should afford opportunity for reciprocity, communication, cooperation, and positive personal achievement. "Every method," he said, "that appeals to the child's active powers, to his capacities in construction, production, and creation, marks an opportunity to shift the center of ethical gravity from an absorption which is selfish to a service which is social." [47] The search should be for methods that give children a chance to engage in creative experiences that have an aesthetic quality—that present to them opportunities to give shape and form to their activities, that help them to gain a sense of their individual capacities, and also to realize their bond with others.

## The Curriculum

Dewey, when describing the role of the curriculum in ethical development, stated that in many respects the subject matter sets the tone of the school and determines the kinds of methods and discipline employed. The goal of socially responsible selves could not be achieved through an isolated set of studies. In order to make the curriculum morally defensible, Dewey advocated the principle that studies must provide progressively deeper insights into the nature of the human situation—or of "social life." This provided a criterion for judging the educative value of *information, discipline*, and *culture*. Information is educative only when it leads the student to see new relations and connections that increase his understanding. Discipline is desirable when it leads the individual to control his behavior for social ends. And culture, if it is not mere polish, "represents the vital union of information and discipline. It marks the socialization of the individual in his outlook on social life." [48]

Dewey commented on several school subjects to illustrate his statement. A first error, he said, is to accept a pigeonhole classification of subjects, such as science, history, or geography. In fact, these subjects represent different ways of approaching reality. They yield insights into the different aspects of man's relation with his world, both natural and social. Geography does not consist, therefore, of a mere list of facts and empirical classifications: in its various phases—social, physical, mathematical, and political —it deals with the dependence of man on his natural environment, and with the changes introduced into this environment by human behavior. History may be seen not as a mere col-

[47] *Ibid.*, p. 26.
[48] *Ibid.*, p. 32.

lection of facts about past events: it becomes vital or dead according to whether or not it is presented from a sociological point of view. Its ethical value may be measured by "the extent to which past events are made the means of understanding the present," [49] affording insights into the structure and workings of human society. We are reminded of the approach employed in the Laboratory School. Dewey said that the history of past cultures can be more beneficially studied because present civilization is too complex for the child to see fundamental human relations.

"But type [sic] phases of historical development may be selected which will exhibit, as through a telescope, the essential constituents of the existing order. Greece, for example, represents what art and growing power of individual expression stand for; Rome exhibits the elements and forces of political life on a tremendous scale. Or, as these civilizations are themselves relatively complex, a study of still simpler forms of hunting, nomadic, and agricultural life in the beginnings of civilization, a study of the effects of the introduction of iron, and iron tools, reduces the complexity to simpler elements." [50]

History, furthermore, is useful for teaching the methods of human progress. The study of history can reveal the significant factors involved in critical discoveries, invention, and new modes of life that have instituted important advances in human civilization. These can be analyzed in terms of the kinds of problems confronted by man and the methods he employed to resolve them, of time-honored values at stake, or of modifications of values that ensued. Students should also study the consequences of situations where men failed to make necessary adjustments. We have here, of course, Dewey's application of what he called elsewhere the genetic or historical mode of analysis.

This section of his essay was concluded with a passage that has since become famous.

"Ultimate moral motives and forces are nothing more nor less than social intelligence—the power of observing and compre-

[49] Ibid., p. 36.
[50] Ibid., p. 37.

hending social situations,—and social power—trained capacities of control—at work in the service of social interest and aims. There is no fact which throws light upon the constitution of society, there is no power whose training adds to social resourcefulness that is not moral.

"I sum up, then, this part of the discussion by asking your attention to the moral trinity of the school. The demand is for social intelligence, social power, and social interests. Our resources are (1) the life of the school as a social institution in itself; (2) methods of learning and of doing work; and (3) the school studies or curriculum. In so far as the school represents, in its own spirit, a genuine community life; in so far as what are called school discipline, government, order, etc., are the expressions of this inherent social spirit; in so far as the methods used are those that appeal to the active and constructive powers, permitting the child to give out and thus to serve; in so far as the curriculum is so selected and organized as to provide the material for affording the child a consciousness of the world in which he has to play a part, and the demands he has to meet, so far as these ends are met, the school is organized on an ethical basis. So far as general principles are concerned, all the basic ethical requirements are met. The rest remains between the individual teacher and the individual child." [51]

In closing, Dewey turned to the psychological problem of how moral principles can be incorporated in a functional way into the character and behavior of the individual. A program for moral education cannot be sound, he said, unless it is consistent with a sound psychology of child behavior and development. This means that it must encompass the child's feelings and his impulses to construct and create, as well as his intellect. "We cannot smother and repress the child's powers, or gradually abort them (from failure of opportunity to exercise), and then expect a character with initiative and consecutive industry." [52]

In order to develop powers of moral judgment, children must have opportunities to analyze, to form and test judgments—to put selections into execution, and to observe the consequences.

[51] *Ibid.*, pp. 43–44.
[52] *Ibid.*, p. 54.

"Except so far as the emphasis of the school work is upon intelligent doing, upon active investigation, it does not furnish the conditions necessary for that exercise of judgment which is an integral factor in good character." [53]

Finally, an aesthetic quality must be available in the whole of the school's work. This work must include the opportunity for free communication among children and between children and their teachers. A school that is restrictive and narrowly utilitarian cuts children off from genuinely vital experiences in their studies and in art, music, sculpture. This makes it impossible to build qualities of awareness and responsiveness.

Dewey's final plea was that ethical education was dependent on a way of visualizing moral principles. Moral principles are not arbitrary, or "transcendental." They are not the province of a separate sector of life. The moral qualities must be made to pervade the whole of community living and the habits of the individual.

"All the rest is mint, anise, and cummin. The one thing needful is that we recognize that moral principles are real in the same sense in which other forces are real; that they are inherent in community life, and in the working structure of the individual. If we can secure a genuine faith in this fact, we shall have secured the condition which alone is necessary to get from our educational system all the effectiveness there is in it. The teacher who operates in this faith will find every subject, every method of instruction, every incident of school life pregnant with moral possibility." [54]

[53] Ibid., p. 56.
[54] Ibid., p. 58.

# CHAPTER SIXTEEN

# *Postscript*

We have completed our effort to present Dewey's ideas about education when he was a practicing educator. That was the object of the study. The hope is that it may be of help in making a rational appraisal of a chapter in our educational history. Lines of continuity might be defined on which we may wish to continue to build; we may reject that which seems erroneous or no longer relevant. In closing, we indulge in some personal summations and observations, which should not be permitted to mar the reader's own evaluation of the record described to this point.

We saw that Dewey argued for a close and necessary cooperation between general philosophy and work in education. Critical to both were the questions: What is man? What might he become? It was Dewey's conviction that events were forcing men to come to terms with a new image set by the evolutionary theory formally launched in the year of his birth. This theory, in turn, was the result of the broad onsurge of modern science. Dewey felt that although man would feel the price to be heavy, he stood to profit from the reformulation. A major gain would be freedom from a whole series of prescientific dualisms, which presented man as separate from his world and which Dewey personally had felt as "inner lacerations." A critical struggle in Dewey's intellectual journey was the one to overcome these dualisms and to replace them with conceptions that would accord with the findings of scientific inquiry. We draw on examples of such dualisms in presenting our final summary.

## MAN AND NATURE

Tradition had marked man as a being apart from the rest of nature. Dewey felt that science, reconsidered, could restore a sense of unity. The new perspective did not portray a comfortable, benign world. Existentially, the beginning and end of things were shut off from view though man had a passion to know the answers. There were more specific hazards, too, but nature had provided the conditions for man's coming into existence, and it offered the resources for him to grow in experience. He could live with a sense of gratitude for the chances provided. His capacity for "minded" reflective experience was itself a natural emergent. With it he could extend his insights into the nature of things and of his own being; he could identify the behavior that fostered or disrupted his own growth; he could give a measure of control to his emerging future. His task was to take advantage of his resources, to use his capabilities wisely. This required a judicious appraisal of the past, the will to preserve what had been of enduring value and to relinquish or modify what had been limiting or destructive. To realize through action the potential in man was to bring to life both an aesthetic and a spiritual quality. As man gained surer knowledge, he acquired new responsibilities. One of these was to fashion a kind of education that would enable children to find their way with a measure of fulfillment.

This image of man might be lacking in traditional assurances. But ancient dualisms—dualisms that separated man from nature, mind from matter, thinking from emotions, and morality from behavior—could be resolved by defining man in terms of the interactions and transactions that united him with his world and his fellows.

A major challenge of Dewey's philosophy, therefore, was insistence that men come to terms with the evolutionary perspective as revealed in the various sciences. His answer was that of a scientific humanist, and was the source of major antagonism to his work. His ideas were at odds with the religious views of the majority of his countrymen.

Dewey's thinking reflected an issue still unresolved in our times: how to bring into reconciliation the perspective and values of science and the values and views of the classical-Judaeo-Christian traditions of the West. The question is compounded now by our need to confront the prescientific traditions of the non-Western world. Dewey can hardly be blamed for not working out a reconciliation. When faced with a choice he sided unmistakably with naturalistic-humanism and science. Yet he honored the spiritual-religious aspirations of men, and sought to find a place for them within the system of thought he developed.

Although evolutionary theory has been fully substantiated, the challenge to confront its significance remains. The gap between the religious and scientific traditions, running as a fissure in our culture, has not convincingly been bridged, but the need persists and efforts continue.[1] No one can predict that a widely-agreed-on integration will be effected. The Deweyan tradition stands on the side of science, but it does not represent a stance of ridicule or sophomoric scoffing toward man's religious aspirations.

Dewey insisted on relating thought about education to the large human questions. The recent style has been to push philosophical issues impatiently aside. We may be able to upgrade the mechanics of schooling by concentrating on the improvement of specifics. If we refuse, however, to raise an order of questions beyond a certain level—whether there should be three or four years of required English in the high school, and when and where phonics should be employed in the teaching of reading—we run the risk of merely tinkering about. A pluralist society cannot agree on a single educational philosophy. Without the challenge of bold philosophical vision, however, it cannot hope to create educational programs that are the products of imaginative thinking.

### EDUCATION AS A FIELD OF PROFESSIONAL STUDY

One of Dewey's appeals that may have enduring influence was his insistence that the institution of education be made the subject of disciplined inquiry and research. By the time Dewey died, at the opening of the second half of the twentieth century, it was becoming more evident that the much publicized "revolution of knowledge" was a critical factor for the survival

[1] The most notable effort in recent years from the religious side has been, of course, the work of Pierre Teilhard de Chardin in *The Phenomenon of Man*, and in other writings.

and progress of advanced societies. The time had passed when brute strength and courage, favorable geographical conditions, or sheer drive and intuitive ingenuity could make the difference. Societies had to face the fact that they had to either become education-centered or decline. Dewey had seen this fact as the century opened—at a time when American society was dominated by the titans of industry and finance. He was a leader among those who argued that it was ridiculous to introduce research techniques to the sciences and humanities, and to institutions like agriculture, government, and industry, and at the same time to bypass the generative institution, education, on which the others depended. With President Harper's support, he tried to establish a model at Chicago in which the entire field of education—administration and finance; the history, politics, and sociology of education; the psychological and philosophical theory; the study of the behavior of children; and the critical questions in methodology and curriculum—were to be brought within the scope of university research. He opposed the isolation of education from other studies. Dewey argued that the complex of questions to be considered had to be coordinated under the "rubric of education" within the university. He also assumed that the problems required a cooperative effort by a wide range of co-workers schooled in appropriate disciplines. Thus, researchers trained in the behavioral and social sciences should analyze administrative, economic, and political problems in education; those with psychological training would investigate the nature of learning and motivation, and their applications to school situations; those schooled in the techniques for making historical and philosophical inquiries would provide their kind of perspective; and the design of the content of the school curriculum would be confronted jointly by academic scholars and by educators especially knowledgeable about the schools.

The record shows that Dewey established communication with a significant number of eminent scholars at Chicago whose main interests lay in their own disciplines. They responded with a genuine interest in the problems of the schools, and gave of their time and moral support. Dewey also had distinguished scholars in his own department who worked under the label of educationist. No single pattern was established. The critical criterion was whether they had the training and competence to be effective.

Even after joining the Department of Philosophy at Columbia, Dewey twitted as Bourbons of Culture those academicians who dismissed with ridicule the idea of bringing problems of education within the purview of university study. Yet the schools of education have been slow in bringing forth fruitful results. The reasons are many. The full story of teacher education and educational research will be known only after responsible investigations have been made. When that job is done, the popular diatribes on the subject will be seen as exercises in polemics rather than serious efforts to increase understanding. We make no pretense of providing the key here, but we present several observations for consideration.

The Professors of Education must bear some of the blame heaped on them. Too often they have failed to insist on high standards of training, with grounding in tool disciplines, for initiates to their own ranks. Too often they have given way to the demand for quick answers by resorting to ideological pronouncements on matters where there was precious little evidence to support them. Their critics matched them in this respect, item for item. But even a brief reflection indicates that such a scapegoat approach obscures more fundamental factors.

Schools of Education, with hopelessly limited resources, strained to meet the demands of training a vast army of teachers. A study in Illinois showed that of every 1,000 who were trained, only 150 were still teaching after five years of experience.[2] The gap to be filled was continually growing. A well-grounded theory on which to base professional practice was also needed. It required verification and expansion by systematic research. Even if the genius and imagination to create it had been available, the time and resources were not.

The prospects are brighter, to the extent that the hostility between academicians and educationists abates. The pleasures of name-calling are limited, and may eventually be recognized by

[2] W. W. Charters, Jr., "Survival in the Profession: A Criterion for Selecting Teacher Trainees," *The Journal of Teacher Education*, Vol. 7, No. 3, September, 1956, pp. 253–255.

both sides as futile. The scholar's indifference to the problems of the schools is self-defeating, and his tendency to make pronouncements from afar is a betrayal of canons of critical thinking. Educationists and teachers, on the other hand, must realize that the very nature of the task of transmitting knowledge and thinking skills requires continuous collaboration with the producers of knowledge. The model in effect at the University of Chicago in the 1890's might be worth a second look as an alternative to some of our behavior in recent decades.

Teachers in our time are still in the process of freeing themselves from a position of second-class professional stature. Dewey's ways of defining the tasks of the teacher might help to dispel stereotypes no longer acceptable. We are now committed to exploring the nearby corners of the universe. We can hardly hope to cling to an image of teachers as ineffectual and slightly ridiculous schoolmarms and Milquetoasts. Even on the television screen Mr. Peepers had to give way to Mr. Novak in the 1960's. The too-easy use of the term "teacher-scholar" can obscure the hard labor required to produce and retain such a person, but realistically nothing less will be adequate. Here again, Dewey's portrayal of the teacher as "student of subject matter and of 'mind activity' " is appropriate. He maintained that the creation of a teaching profession required people prepared to be continuing scholars both of their subjects and of the processes of education.

For the purpose of relating theory to practice, Dewey proposed a triadic relation of professional workers:

1. Those working on the side of pure research, to clarify the nature of basic concepts like motivation and cognitive learning;
2. Middle level educational theorists, to make the classroom itself a center of inquiry for testing hypotheses;
3. Some classroom teachers, trained in observation and research skills, to be partners in verifying and generating hypotheses.

Feedback from the teachers would be invaluable to the work of their research colleagues. The Schools of Education would need the vision to train such persons, and the school boards would have to pay them what their training warranted. Imaginative and creative young people might then be recruited. They might even find that remaining in the classroom could constitute a challenging and attractive career.

Funds for serious investigations of educational problems during the first half of the century were meager. The miracle is that any good work was done at all. The Federal government and the great private foundations made available precious few resources for educational research as compared with the hundreds of millions of dollars allocated for agriculture, the military, and the sciences. Only after the midpoint of the twentieth century did the tide begin to turn. It took the Education Act of 1965, which provided $100,000,000 for the establishment of twenty regional centers for educational research, to provide a genuinely new thrust. By that time the sad condition of education in our major metropolitan centers and in backward rural areas was glaringly apparent. When this was combined with a growing realization of the importance of education for the nation's welfare, even a reluctant Congress was willing to accept the President's appraisal that the development of education had to head the list of domestic priorities. If the time has arrived for a serious, long-term commitment to the systematic study of education, Dewey's proposals may prove to be a relevant tradition on which to build.

THE PSYCHOLOGICAL THEORY

Dewey's psychological theory was closely related to the evolutionary bent of his philosophy, and it set the tone for the methodology and curriculum of the Laboratory School. His biosocial concept of mind and behavior incorporated the biological and social interactionist ideas of William James and George H. Mead. The human tasks of thinking and building selfhood and character were accounted for naturalistically. They were explained in terms of man's need to come to terms with the physical and social world. The individual and the community shared responsibility for the quality of life that emerged. Flexible habits, which provided continuity with a proven past but which also permitted creative innovation, represented the key to human fulfillment. Reflective thinking was no longer considered as being mere contemplation by an abstract mind, but was visualized instead as a matter of analyzing, "sizing up," projecting and testing hunches, observing results, making tentative generalizations, "having another try," prizing what one had come to value, amending that value as required by change or critical appraisal. This concept of "minding"—man's interaction with others and with things during his search to fulfill needs and pursue goals—enabled Dewey to wage a war on two fronts—on the tradition of viewing mind as the functioning of a reified intellect, and on mechanistic, deterministic theories.

On the one hand, Dewey was a critic of the model of thinking and learning that defined the job of teaching as that of instilling material into the abstract minds children supposedly brought to class with them. Dewey felt that this was contradicted by the way children actually approached their world. They feel it, probe it, shape and fit it, try to make sense of it, suddenly see it differently, carry into situations today what they saw in a new way yesterday. In doing all this, they gradually come to recognize the need for more knowledge, more refined generalizations and abstractions which will enable them to progress to more learning. Experiences that yield insights and a sense of new power can make the process of learning an exciting one. Satisfactions like these are requisite for the acceptance of the labor and tedium that go with mastering the difficult disciplines of scholarship.

Thus Dewey joined those who insisted that learning is an active process that involves the whole person, with his senses, feeling, and character, as well as his intellectual processes. When sentimentalized, this opinion can lead to anti-intellectualism. But it may also make us realize the superficiality that attends a single-minded concentration on coaching for College Board Examinations.

Dewey opposed, too, the mechanistic model of learning rooted in the traditions of British emipiricism and physiological behaviorism. The idea of the human being as a mere conditioned organism ignored, in Dewey's view, the distinctive human need and capacity to project purposes, pursue values, and create novel re-orderings. Dewey welcomed research in physiological psychology, but his insistence on the social and purposive aspects of human learning led him to reject models that reduced men to passive automatons. There is nothing in Dewey's pychological theory that would make him resistant to technical devices such as "teaching machines," which expedite the learning of tool skills or basic information. His writings on the inefficient use of school time for these purposes indicates that he could have welcomed opportunities posed by such technical devices. His theory, however, does lead to a vigorous rejection of assumptions that such models of learning constitute the whole of it. He argued over and over again that the most significant learning had to be self-learning, in which the individual was active in creating his own order and meaning.

Dewey's theory of the stages of child development and levels of interest was not grounded in any well-established research studies. It was an imaginative hypothesis, influenced, no doubt, by the work of people like G. Stanley Hall and the recapitulation theories of the Herbartians, but it was never an exact borrowing. Dewey and his colleagues made adaptations to fit their general theory and made efforts to check generalizations in terms of their actual experiences with youngsters in the Laboratory School. This part of the work must be estimated as a series of shrewd hunches rather than a serious scientific contribution. Nevertheless, the theory of stages of development did indicate that Dewey saw the need for a progression of school experiences that moved from direct exploratory approaches in the early years to more systematic and abstract study at the secondary level and beyond —not with a sharp break in continuity, but with a clearly distinguishable shift in emphasis.

"Learning by doing," however, was not a phrase confined to the physical and manipulative probings of the young child. It meant being self-engaged in seeking understanding and control. At mature levels, the exemplary models were to be found in the struggles of creators of literature, science, art, and philosophy. The value of critical thinking is reflected in such models, but they serve to remind us, too, of the aesthetic values which Dewey saw as consummatory. The reach for order, meaning, and quality of product requires respect for techniques and proper use of materials; it culminates in resolutions that have a sense of form or fit. Activity without this quality—frivolity, drudgery, ostentation, or narrow utility—is flat and unsatisfying.

The values of Dewey's educational philosophy were patterned

after those of communities of inquirers and productive workers. Methodologically, the rationale was inquiry-centered, with related emphasis on problem-solving, connection-seeing, relation-building. A current renewal of interest in methods of discovery and inductive learning has been sparked by the work of Jerome Bruner.[3] The reader of the account of the Dewey school will recognize the central role assigned to such approaches there. The recognition of continuities in our educational experience may therefore serve to modify our tendency to proceed by lunges and lurches—as if we believe that the New Jerusalem is to be suddenly found over here or over there. At the same time there is the need to make discriminations. A popular phrase recently has been "the structure of knowledge." To the extent that this is interpreted as implying that the content of school studies may be found intact in organized bodies of knowledge, it is in conflict with Dewey's orientation. He emphasized that the *pedagogical problem* of organizing and planning for purposes of instruction was different from the scholar's problem of presenting the outcomes of his investigations in clear, logical form. In Dewey's terms the educator's task is to develop strategies that will lead students to see their world with new meanings—to reconstruct their experiences. This is a job requiring its own kind of creativity. The planning of experiences that will be educative cannot be done apart from the insights that have evolved from the workings of the human mind, but it requires sensitivity, too, to the backgrounds and characteristics of particular students. Which ideas should be selected as pivotal, around which to plan study and work? How many? When and in what order? Why? These are questions of no mean magnitude. The answers will not be found, fully-tailored, in the books of the scholars in the library.

THE CURRICULUM

Children were active in the Dewey school, but their spontaneous interests did not dictate the course of studies. There was a well-considered curriculum design, and the unifying theme was the story of emerging civilized experience.

[3] See Jerome Bruner, *The Process of Education* (Cambridge, Harvard University Press, 1960).

A goal was to enable students to grasp the changing pattern of man's relations with his natural and social environment. Areas of concentration centered around critical junctures in man's historic development—junctures that occurred when new tools, techniques, or modes of thought changed the course of things. Thus knowledge and intellectual processes were brought down from the clouds, and were explained as outcomes of man's transactions with his environment.

The idea of the occupations was Dewey's hypothesis for unifying the curriculum. It was based on the hunch that the most beneficial way of revealing important patterns of human relations with nature and social life was to focus on the institutional forms and the styles of thinking that are developed so that life necessities may be attained. Children were directly involved in a few typically constructive activities designed to show a substructure of civilized life. Through first-hand efforts to shape various materials, they could empathize with their ancestors, and could attain some insight into the core activities about which turned so much of the bustle in the Windy City. Dewey hoped, too, that students would be led to see the contexts in which the natural evolution of intelligence could be observed. As they moved to higher levels, they would see the subject areas as examples of "the progressive organization of knowledge." A base line could be established so that children in a changing society could feel continuity with an evolving history, yet be at home with the idea that it was man's destiny to innovate in thought and technique. With this perspective, the school might escape some of its former reputation for irrelevancy.

A style of thought that predominated was the genetic or historic mode of analysis. Students were to acquire the habit of analyzing factors that led to the occurrence of a given phenomenon or event—of seeing patterns of causes and effects. It is not surprising, therefore, that the curriculum features most confidently elaborated were history, the social studies, and the sciences. These provided occasions for helping students to appreciate the periods in man's evolution when he succeeded in attaining new mastery over his environment. Examples of failures and setbacks that were the result of chance or folly might be included, but the focus was on the modes of thought and social action that had enabled man to make gains. Skill in learning to recognize background and causes of things was intended to help students make sense of their own complicated world. The unmistakable emphasis on historical analysis is clear, and it refutes the charge that Dewey's philosophy of education was superficial because it was exclusively oriented to the present.

Dewey was confident with materials that fitted the scientific or evolutionary frame of reference. He was less sure of himself in treating the humanities. A wide variety of literary works were included in the Laboratory School program which lifted reading above the bland quality of many contemporary texts. But there were problems with the rationale. Dewey's strictures against the evils of literature as "mere individual expression" and his stress on interpreting literary works as reflections of social experience enabled him to maintain consistency with his main line but at the expense of uttering a partial truth. There are qualities of literary expression in Job, the dramas of Aeschylus, Shakespeare's *Lear, The Brothers Karamazov*, and the works of Kafka and Camus that cannot be contained in a definition of literature as an "expression of cultural life."

The full context within which the human drama is lived includes other dimensions—the tragic, the demonic, the irrational— the grip of unconscious fears, anxieties, and guilts—the personal encounters with "the dark night of the soul." These were themes to be expressed in the twentieth-century writings of the Freudians and the Existentialists. The grave perplexities encountered in the Thirties and Forties and in the period since led men to respond strongly to these writers.

Dewey's meliorism led him to concentrate on defining the rational means required to improve men's chances. This focus led him to shy away from depths of experience which all men confront. Men require the catharsis of great drama and literature to help them meet personal crises. Even Dewey's sympathetic critics noted his deficiency in this respect. Thus George Geiger said,

"There is almost nothing in his writings of anxiety, loneliness, anguish. The distressing experiences of humans all seem socially determined and socially controllable. [This] . . . makes a certain thinness and unrealism in Dewey's writings." [4]

[4] George Geiger, *John Dewey in Perspective* (New York, Oxford University Press, 1958) p. 160.

And Gardner Murphy speculated that Dewey may have failed to grasp the significance of the unconscious and irrational "partly because he was born too soon to see the full flowering of psychoanalysis, partly because he feared the irrational." In their presence "Dewey passes down the other side of the road." [5]

Dewey was not a superficial optimist, and he bore to the grave the personal wounds that came from the death of two of his sons. The limitation referred to, however, is real. The definitive philosophy has not yet been written. The scientific-humanist orientation represented by Dewey can profit from the challenges of values in other traditions—the religio-humanistic, the psychoanalytic, and the existentialist. No one knows if some synthesis might yet become possible.

Those who developed the themes of alienation, meaninglessness, anxiety, and despair, however, were also expressing partial truths. We have seen these too often degenerate into hand-wringing self-pity, unsatisfying self-indulgence, and the boring malaise of self-absorption. The civil rights marchers of the Sixties were ready once again to channel their energies toward action in their society. If they could not find meaning, they could bring meaning to their world by acting in it. This was Dewey's way of approaching life.

Where the actual content of studies is concerned, Dewey has been charged with vagueness. Thus Richard Hofstadter says,

". . . he wrote a good deal about the curriculum; but it is difficult to discover from his major books on education what he thought a good curriculum should be, or rather what the various alternative curricula should be, in the American School System." [6]

Hofstadter attributes this flaw to Dewey's definition of education as growth:

". . . having insisted that education, being growth itself, cannot have any end for it save still more education, he was unable to formulate the criteria by which society, through the teacher should guide or direct the child's impulses. The teacher was left

[5] Gardner Murphy, *Freeing Intelligence Through Teaching* (New York, Harper and Row, 1961) pp. 41–42.

[6] Richard Hofstadter, *Anti-intellectualism in American Life* (New York, Alfred A. Knopf, 1963), p. 375.

with a firm mandate to exercise some guidance, to make some discriminations among the child's impulses and needs, but with no directional outposts." [7]

The charge about Dewey's *writings* is justified in part, but we are skeptical as to the alleged cause. The record, reviewed in previous chapters of this study, shows that the actual educational work in the Laboratory School contained a well-designed sequence of studies. Dewey's association of education with growth did not prevent him from establishing criteria for what should go on in his own school.

Nevertheless, the question of why Dewey shied away from more specific curricular recommendations in his published works is important and puzzling. We do not pretend to know *the* answer but can only conjecture. A more careful study of his later career may provide some clues.

At the time that Dewey was directly engaged in education, he and his colleagues defined as a major target of attack the evils of lifeless, bureaucratic prescription. If the goal was to free teaching from the memoriter method, there was an understandable reluctance to propose an alternative content that could be debased by the old methodology. The main problem was to introduce a new way of conceptualizing the experiences of learning and teaching.

We have noted a certain ambivalence in Dewey's ideas regarding the claims of "the child" and "the curriculum." But was it really that? He was resisting the notion of education as a mere matter of instilling content. He did insist that an experience became *educative* only when students saw their world with new meaning, and this could not be assured by merely building impressive course syllabi. Dewey's stress was on the quality that should characterize significant learning; he did not offer much by way of detailed outlines for a curriculum. His refusal to take a position unequivocally on either the side of the child or the curriculum was, in fact, his way of indicating the difficulties of securing something of genuine educational significance. He was warning against the temptation to promise quick answers by rushing to get something down on paper. We have learned since that even

[7] *Ibid.,* pp. 374–375.

wealthy suburban systems can construct elaborate curricula, and still may fail to win the educational commitment of large numbers of middle-class boys. (We choose boys as an example here because we are coming to realize there are more casualties among them than we care to admit.)

Dewey also had the conviction that the tempo of cultural change in a scientific-urban-industrial society required a willingness to innovate and reconceive ways of planning school studies —both liberal and technical. There would be no end to that. No expert could pose as the single source of wisdom. Dewey, with his ingrained modesty, would certainly not assume such a role. As philosopher, he confined himself to defining the underlying problems.

He also felt that the specific content of school programs should take into account the special situation of a particular community. Thus we find Dewey endorsing aspects of the Gary plan for an industry-centered city like Gary [8] and curriculum experimentation of a different sort for a blighted rural community like Jefferson County, Kentucky.[9]

We do feel that the course of educational development in the first half-century suffered from Dewey's failure to speak more forthrightly on important curriculum issues. After leaving Chicago, for example, he did not emphasize two features that characterized his own work there: the idea of levels of development with a progression of studies in the direction of differentiation and specialization, and the practice of close collaboration with scholars from substantive areas in developing curriculum designs.

It is true that Dewey had doubts about the overly permissive excesses of the child-centered sectors of the progressive-education movement. In the main, however, he muted these, perhaps because he wanted to avoid adding strength to the heavy attacks constantly made on the progressive pioneers. In 1938, in *Experience and Education*, he made his doubts more explicit when he stated that "the weakest point in progressive schools is in the matter of selection and organization of intellectual subject mat-

[8] See John Dewey and Evelyn Dewey, *Schools of Tomorrow* (New York, E. P. Dutton and Co., 1915).

[9] See Elsie Ripley Clapp, *The Use of Resources in Education* (New York, Harper and Row, 1952), Part I and Dewey's Introduction.

ter." [10] He warned against the tendency to proceed by improvisation, and said that "the basic material of study cannot be picked up in a cursory manner." He resisted the idea that progressive schools should seek to be united by a single course of studies, but said that "the problem of selection and organization of subject-matter for study and learning is fundamental . . . the underlying ideal is that of progressive organization of knowledge." As the problem was stated with such force and clarity, the reader might be led to expect some guidelines as to how to proceed. But, as John Childs once said, "He marched right up the hill and then marched right down again."

Dewey may not have been expansive about detailed prescriptions for the curriculum, but he did have convictions about general reforms that were needed. His war on separations and discontinuities led to another attack—on the disjointedness between the levels of the school system. Applying the genetic method of analysis, he described the kindergarten, elementary, high school, and university components as having originated from separate historic needs and traditions. Their programs had been developed without conscious attention to continuities and connections. Dewey and Harper hoped to replace these disjunctions by developing unifying themes and articulations between levels of study. As we have seen, they were able to win the collaboration of many of their colleagues on the Chicago campus. There are some parallels between their effort and the way the new programs in the biological and physical sciences, and in mathematics were developed in the Fifties and Sixties. But there are differences also. In Dewey's Chicago there was no backlog of bitterness, and the lead was taken by the educationist side of the partnership. The recent reform movement has consisted of innovations concentrated within subject areas, which reflects the wish of the scholars to get authentic, current knowledge into the programs of the lower schools. There has been little or no effort to effect connections between the sciences, let alone between the social sciences and humanities. Dewey, on the other hand, was making a reach for some overarching conceptions that would give relatedness to the several parts. He was not completely

[10] John Dewey, *Experience and Education* (New York, The Macmillan Co., 1938), pp. 95–104 *et passim*.

successful with this within the elementary program, and did not have a chance to get started at the secondary level. It remains to be seen whether or not the problem of seeking some unifying themes can be defined in ways to make such a unity viable. A first obstacle would be with the different languages of "the two cultures." There are many who have given up on the possibility of even a pact between the sciences and the humanities. Such a project would require the will and the capacity to see human knowledge and its meaning for students with some perspective of wholeness. Dewey made such an effort, but we have not seen such attempts in recent times. But then the unifying effort in philosophy itself—to help men to grasp the meaning of the whole of their experience—has also fallen out of favor.

Dewey's own drive to bridge the gaps in the culture led him to tackle one more formidable problem. He argued for the necessity of a new way of relating liberal and technical studies. The classical gulf between them reflected, in his view, the social class cleavages of European society. This tradition was inappropriate for a scientific-industrial democratic age.

Dewey applied his cultural-analysis method to delineate the sources of the problem. Before the advent of science and industry, European societies were in a feudal-agricultural stage. The necessities of life were produced by manual labor, and only a small percentage of the population—those in ownership and leadership roles—was freed from such back-breaking work. This type of social organization suited the conception that there are two types of men—those ruled by their sensory being and those dominated by intellect. The training considered proper for the leadership class was contained in the classical literary studies. The rest of the population, it was assumed, would be incapable of profiting from such fare even if chance made the opportunity available.

Dewey maintained that the advance of science and related events was disrupting this whole structure. Scientific knowledge and modes of thought effected change in the techniques for producing goods. With the revolution in modes of production came the possibility of freeing the masses of men from the role of beasts of burden. Both social relations and qualities of mind were being repatterned, and the content of education had to reflect this change. The scientific temper of thinking, which could so radically change human possibilities, now had to be included as a pivotal ingredient in humanistic studies. Science, in both its pure and applied forms, had to be understood by all. It was not only the content that was important. The very style of thinking —the method of inquiry in approaching problems had to become an intrinsic part of the life style of all classes. Science and technology were the critical forces of change. None could ignore them, or be ignorant of their nature and consequences.

These underlying social and intellectual changes forced a realignment of scientific-technical and humanistic studies. We had a glimpse of Dewey's own vision in his plans for the complex of schools—elementary and secondary, college preparatory, and manual training—that he had assembled by 1903–1904, at the time he left Chicago. Youth who became part of the industrial world were to be not merely "trained hands," but were also to be equipped with the new methods and principles of inquiry; they were to be given insight into the social forces creating institutional change. Social analyses were to be accompanied by reflection on social consequences and on the values at stake for a democratic society. The goal was to provide them with the knowledge, power, and sense of obligation to be fully fledged participants in defining policies that would direct the course of change. Insight could free men engaged in productive work from their ancient subservience, and could make them possessors of an earned dignity. Furthermore, they would have the opportunity to share in the humanities and arts in a way never before possible for the majority of men. If their schooling gave them the opportunity to practice the arts as well as "appreciate" them, some, at least, might become creators of art forms appropriate for the new society that was coming to birth.

The education of those preparing for higher studies, research, and administrative roles was also to be affected. It would be a personal disservice, as well as dangerous for the values of a free society, for them to have a separate education consisting of purely academic studies, or specialized knowledge about how to make money. Dewey felt that such students should have direct experiences in understanding the same scientific-technical processes that were changing the fabric of society. They should be in communication, both intellectually and socially, and through shared values, with those who would be more directly concerned with production.

It was a rationale of this nature that led Dewey and Jane Addams to hope that ancient class hatred and warfare might be reduced, and that a joining of social forces and energies might be effected so that the promises offered by the new intellectual sources of power might be realized.

A romantic illusion? Perhaps. A comparison of ensuing harsh events with the vision just sketched makes it easy to dismiss it as far-fetched. The bitter class struggles of the depression years, the yawning gap between the "culture of poverty" and the affluent sectors that has widened since the Second World War; the realization of the major handicaps in teaching basic learning to children who are raised in slums; the uncertainty that there will be any useful work at all for large numbers of our people in an automated society; the neglect of vocational and technical education, and the lack of vision to support such an education; the confusion in large sectors of the school system in general, with the consequent failure to attract talented young teachers; the shabby use of the television screen in face of its potential for enlightenment—all provide ample room for doubt.

But that is not the whole story. The means for realizing such aspirations have grown immeasurably, and we have capitalized on them in part. We have raised the level of learning of the masses of our people. The leadership at the many levels required to face an unprecedented series of social crises has been forthcoming. We managed this in the absence of any very imaginative educational vision. Our conscience has remained sensitive enough to respond to the demands to reduce injustice—and the social conflicts have produced better results than might have been expected. There has been a measure of growth reflected in the quality of enlightened self-interest, in members of the business community. The new technology has given us new leisure, and participation in the arts has flourished at the local levels as never before.

We are far from realizing the quality of life that we could attain. Dewey would have protested but not despaired. He was not a utopian who could live only with a dream perfected.

## SOCIAL PHILOSOPHY

Dewey's anti-dualist struggle were evident, too, in his social philosophy and in his concepts of selfhood and moral character. Fundamentally, he resisted an either/or choice between values that cluster about "individuality" and those that center around "community." He assumed that problems of the free society are posed by the fact that free men cherish both but that total acceptance of either one without the other is also impossible. We need the two sets of values, but each must be protected against its own excesses and against the aggrandizement of the other. The uniqueness of the *individual* accounts for values like creativity, challenge, and innovation. Yet the individual is not truly human without the nourishment of community. Unchecked, his freedom can degenerate into self-indulgence, exhibitionism, or anarchistic iconoclasm. *Community* is the source of fellowship, solidarity, hard-won knowledge, and supportive traditions. But compulsive concern with these can bring conformity, coercion, and stagnation.

Dewey tried to build into his educational philosophy provisions for both free expression and cooperative social life. Critics who centered attention on the first charged "permissiveness," and some of his followers championed it. Others who focused on the social aspect saw Dewey as an advocate of "other-directed adjustment." Passages taken out of context may be found to support either claim. To do so is to ignore Dewey's definition of the central problem: "The ultimate problem of all education is to coordinate the psychological [individual] and social factors." [11] Stereotyping can be a dodge for evading the responsibilities of wrestling with a complex problem.

Dewey, in his theory of human nature and conduct,[12] held that self and character are not givens but constructs formed in the course of living. They acquire their form and content through the individual's interactions with a series of communities and

[11] See Chapter Seven.

[12] His book, *Human Nature and Conduct* (New York, Holt, Rinehart and Winston, 1922) was a significant contribution to the budding field of social psychology.

through the consequences of his personal choices. The attainment of moral character requires that attention be paid to qualities of community life that pattern it; but the individual must learn that the choices he makes also fashion the self he becomes.

The realization of individuality required that students be given the opportunity to discover their powers, investigate their own questions, and make real choices. The community set of values contained "the funded capital of civilization," "the intellectual and moral resources which humanity has succeeded in getting together," [13] which had to be incorporated into the individual. This realization also required that learning go on through cooperative processes, which included a disciplined respect for the role of evidence, a care for craftsmanship, and a willingness to entertain diverse ideas and to share the results of study and inquiry. Dewey, therefore, upheld the values exemplified in the productive efforts of men in workshops and scientific laboratories, and opposed the distorted competitive values of a *laissez-faire* philosophy of business, which was much in evidence in the Chicago of the Nineties. He shared Veblen's bias for the virtues of productive work as opposed to the accumulation of symbols of status achievement.

Dewey's concepts of value were framed, in part, by his analysis of the special problems posed by the advent of a metropolitan-industrial culture as contrasted with the agricultural frontier of the America of his youth. Dewey saw promise in the new shift. Chances for a more widespread enrichment of personality had emerged with the "development of modes of manufacture and commerce, travel, migration, and inter-communication which flowed from the command of science over natural energy." [14] But there were distortions, too. A society driven by mere self-aggrandizement or ruthless competition for wealth and power could despoil its resources and debase the life of the masses in the cities. There was much evidence of such a society in the Chicago of Johnny Powers, "Hinky Dink" Kenna and "Little Mike" Ryan in politics; Tom O'Brien, "King of the Bunko Men," in

[13] John Dewey, *My Pedagogic Creed* (New York, E. L. Kellogg and Co., 1897), Article 1.

[14] John Dewey, *Democracy and Education* (New York, The Macmillan Co., 1916), p. 101.

"recreation"; Philip Armour in industry; and Samuel Insull and Cornelius K. G. Billings in utilities and finance.[15]

Dewey sought models for a more humane social community life. The ingredients could be found in the quality of mind and character of the effective producers of knowledge and work.

The Vermont communities of his youth provided part of the pattern. People working in conjoint task-oriented relationships directed their skills to turn out well-made, tasteful products. The truth-seeking community of scientific investigators who created knowledge through the habits and skills of critical intelligence furnished supplementary values.

If the new metropolitan centers, with their squalor and ugliness, were to be made acceptable to live in, the values from these other communities had to be incorporated in them: (1) There had to be intelligent analysis of social problems; and (2) cooperative, working communities had to be created within the institutions of megalopolis, to bring health-giving, humane values to the masses living there. The conviction that it was possible that such behavior could be fostered, to prevent the cities from becoming totally impersonal and inhuman, caused Dewey, together with Jane Addams and Robert Park, to remain among the thin ranks of American intellectuals who did not turn their backs in despair on the advent of city cultures.[16]

Dewey conceptualized democracy as a quality of community life rather than a form of government. It encompassed a way of living that could capitalize on the new diversity, multiplicity of ideas, and improved communication, so that human personality could be deepened and broadened.

"A democracy is more than a form of government; it is primarily a mode of associated living. The extension in space of the number of individuals who participate in an interest so that each has to refer his own action to that of others, and to consider the action of others to give point and direction to his own, is equiva-

[15] Ray Ginger, *Altgeld's America: The Lincoln Ideal versus Changing Realities* (New York, Funk and Wagnalls Co., 1958), Ch. 4, "The Gray Wolves and Their Flock."

[16] See Morton and Lucia White, *The Intellectual versus the City: From Thomas Jefferson to Frank Lloyd Wright* (Cambridge, The Harvard University Press, 1962).

290 Curriculum and Methodology in the Laboratory School

lent to the breaking down of those barriers of class, race, and national territory which kept men from perceiving the full import of their activity. These more numerous and more varied points of contact denote a greater diversity of stimuli to which an individual has to respond; they consequently put a premium of variation in his action. They secure a liberation of powers which remain suppressed as long as the incitations to action are partial, as they must be in a group which in its exclusiveness shuts out many areas of interest.

"The widening of the area of shared concerns, and the liberation of a greater diversity of personal capacities . . . characterize democracy. . . ." [17]

The school was to be assigned a critical role in social transformation. It should be made into a specialized environment, which would eliminate so far as possible the undesirable features of the larger society. An enlightened society should transmit "not simply the whole of its achievements," but only "such as make for a better future society." [18] The school should "balance the various elements in the social environment, and see to it that each individual gets an opportunity to escape from the limitations of the social group in which he was born, and to come into living contact with a broader environment." [19] It was to teach the habits of associated living, the skills of communication, and the habits of reflective thinking as the means by which differences would be aired and problems solved. These would then be carried over and become effective in the society at large. A society that is both democratic and progressive "must have a type of education which gives individuals a personal interest in social relationships and control, and the habits of mind which secure social change without introducing disorder." [20]

Ideas like these caused Dewey to turn to the hypothesis of the occupations in the Laboratory School. They would provide a prototype for work in society. The occupations were used as

[17] John Dewey, *Democracy and Education*, p. 101.
[18] *Ibid.*, pp. 22–24, *et passim*.
[19] *Ibid.*, p. 24.
[20] *Ibid.*, p. 115.

springboards for opening lines of intellectual inquiry, but, in addition, products were created. The children did useful work, grew carrots and lettuce in the garden, and with them made salads to be eaten at lunch. They constructed racks to hold the bicycles they rode to school. They built a clubhouse in which they held discussion groups and special interest activities.

The occupations brought the children together in task-oriented groups, and they were designed deliberately to form the kinds of habits and values Dewey judged to be needed in the metropolitan culture. Children were to gain a sense of the cooperative human effort required to meet the needs for living. Intellectually, they were to gain insight into the complex procedure of processing basic materials and into scientific principles and techniques. They were to gain conviction that intelligence was the important factor in the surmounting of problems.

This rationale and the social philosophy supporting it has been brought under criticism. A general charge is that Dewey's thought lacked relevance to the realities of twentieth-century America. Kimball and McClellan,[21] for example, maintain that Dewey's moral commitment was to the village-type community he had known in his childhood. His efforts to preserve the nineteenth-century values of democracy, freedom, and equality, by creating working communities within a metropolitan bureaucratic society were out of touch with the facts of urban life where the dominant characteristics became institutional, hierarchical, impersonal, and service-oriented. The verbal commitments to democracy, freedom, and equality became hollow in the absence of social realities to support them. This new world is described by William Whyte in *The Organization Man*. In the organization, men do not produce objects for use. They process the flow of paper and develop social skills with no other aim but that of jockeying for position within the system. Machines do the production. The phenomenon of the skyscraper white-collar factory makes the homely activities of children in the Dewey school appear to be hopelessly archaic—nostalgically based

[21] Solon T. Kimball and James E. McClellan, Jr., *Education and the New America* (New York, Random House, 1962), Ch. 5. "Progressive Education: The Transition from Agrarian to Industrial America."

on a model long since disappeared. One does not have to defend the specifics of his program to indicate that such a criticism misses the main point of his plan.

In 1896, Dewey could not have envisaged the bureaucratic complexities that the following decades would bring forth. He did expect the nature and superstructure of the work process to change fundamentally under the impact of technology, and he was not foolish enough to think that teaching a child to use a hoe or a plumbline was the way to prepare him for twentieth-century living. His point was that in the urban community individuals would be removed from direct participation in producing life's goods. In order to make sense of a world they could only experience in fragments, they would have to be helped to see it conceptually, and to understand that the intricate superstructure of specialized processes was an elaboration of means related to fundamental human needs. As always, the fulfilling of material needs—food, medicine, living and working quarters— was related to the fulfilling of man's other needs—a sense of well-being, companionship, a sense of form and order. The task was to help students to establish continuity with the human condition —past, present, and future. They should gain insight into the workings of the human mind that created the knowledge and techniques on which contemporary work operations were dependent. The new complexity was the result of man's intellectual leap forward and the present task was to become thoroughly familiar with the intellectual skills, and with the content and habits of mind that had transformed the banks of the Chicago River—and might eventually transform the face of the moon. The task of liberal education was to give the young an understanding of their place in the scheme of things. They had to be made aware of both continuity and change at an intellectual and a visceral level. Consequently, they might avoid feeling alienated by the rush of the city's streets; they might feel that they could share in the processes that were contributing to the improvement of life. Schools had to provide more than a river of information. You could drown in that. They needed to provide an angle of vision so that people would know who they were, because they knew where they had been and the direction in which they were heading. This aim—to give unity to the parts—we have called

the civilizational theme. It was the main pedagogical message of
the Dewey school.

Dewey maintained that the habits of character needed to keep
the metropolis healthy had to be provided through a myriad of
cooperative, working groups. In these, people could retain a sense
of identity in a mass culture, and they could find themselves by
putting their abilities to work. Dewey thought the schools should
provide training in this way of living, and tried to introduce it
into the Laboratory School.

Again, the charge of nineteenth-century nostalgia might be
made—this concept of community is dated in the face of the immensities of megalopolis. Yet, even Kimball and McClellan, in
their able, hard-headed analysis of the organizational society, find
some of their "models for commitment" in features like "production work teams" within bureaucracies, or United Fund Committees at the local level.

It is true, however, that Dewey, in his early twentieth-century
writings, underestimated the enormity of the task of humanizing
an urban, corporate society. The inadequacy of his analyses of the
nature of social classes and the application of power in contemporary society are cases in point.

We have seen that Dewey was antipathetic toward educational programs that perpetuated class and race lines and antago-
nisms. But in hoping that these cleavages could be overcome
through broader association and communication, and the application of intelligence, he underestimated the tough resistance from
those who were concerned with vested interests. He had little to
say by way of a concrete analysis of the realities of social class.
His conceptual tools did not penetrate sharply enough. He seems
not to have studied Marxist thought until late in his career, and
detailed studies of social classes as elaborate subcultural rounds of
life with status and power dynamics were not produced by
American sociologists until the bulk of his work was completed.
The real difficulties involved in reaching lower social-class children and in helping them to enter the mainstream of American
society were not confronted very directly or convincingly in
Dewey's writings.

C. Wright Mills has offered another criticism in his charge
that Dewey did not come to terms with the real nature of power

as it functions in a complex, interest-group oriented society. In *Sociology and Pragmatism*, Mills argued that Dewey's biologically rooted model of thinking proved to have inadequacies when applied to the social processes within bureaucracies and to the struggles between interest groups. Mills maintained that the liberal tradition represented in Dewey's thought utilizes a concept of reflection which is

"most likely to work out satisfactorily in three or four kinds of situations:

"1. In man-object situations: technician-tool, scientist-laboratory, farmer-plough.

"2. In these inter-person situations one man has 'authority' over other individuals due to his acknowledged technical superiority. We refer particularly to a professional-client type of relation; it includes teacher-pupil; social worker-client.

"3. In 'everyday situations' in which the more complex arrangements are not too much to the foreground . . ."

The social action to which Dewey overtly refers and tacitly assumes typically consists of:

"1. School teachers and administrators: school committees in Michigan, e.g., or people organizing a new type of school.

"2. Scientists in laboratories and in industries.

"3. Men in occupations in which they contact 'nature' and handle tools, e.g., farmers or hunters.

"4. Individuals in 'daily situations' as a man at a fork in the road, or lost in the woods.

"5. Professionals, but not so much those who handle paper, e.g., lawyers, as those who handle things, perhaps technically skilled groups, e.g., doctors." [22]

Mills said that such examples tend to deal with action by individuals in situations that have not been regulated by the rules of rationalized structures.

"It is conduct on the edge of social structures, such as frontier types of society that are edging out into places not hampered

[22] C. Wright Mills, *Sociology and Pragmatism* (New York, Whitman Publishing Co., 1964), p. 392.

by social organization. . . . His conceptions are anchored in a social situation whose integration can occur by means of liberal individuals heavily endowed with substantive rationality." [23]

Mills argued further that Dewey's concept of reflective behavior did not involve an adequate accounting of the functioning of power in a society of contending interest groups.

"The concept of action in Dewey obviously does not cover the kinds of action occurring within and between struggling, organized political parties. Parties, as Max Weber put it, live in a house of power. They are organizations for social fighting. Their 'theory,' e.g., platform, has to be dogmatized, not only to insure, in a time of quick mass communication, uniformity among party workers, but because they are organizations. Some party workers become functionaries, hence it is not permitted that they think through independently problems in a 'free' and 'intelligent' manner. In organized social action 'reflection' is rather quickly frozen into 'lines.' " [24]

We might quarrel with some details of Mills's criticism,[25] but we include it because we think it points to a genuine inadequacy in Dewey's social analysis, and because it illustrates the kinds of alterations of Dewey's thought that will have to be made by those who choose to work within his tradition.

A contemporary version of the Laboratory School would have to put students to work inquiring into the realities of the organization and the values at stake for those who work within it. A tough-minded consideration of the obstacles at issue when powerful groups are divided by deep-rooted conflicts also would be required.

Dewey might have been willing to accept the fitness of such criticisms. One thing he would not have done is accept the fatalistic conclusions of the nay-sayers who have concluded that man's fate is sealed. These would have us believe that the mechanized

[23] *Ibid.*, p. 393.

[24] *Ibid.*, p. 394.

[25] The Dewey who played an active role in the founding of the N.A.A.C.P., the American Association of University Professors, the Teachers Guild, and the Liberal Party, to mention only a few of his social action affiliations, can hardly be pictured as being indifferent to the role of interest groups.

monster is uncontrollable. They leave us only options of despair: to be overwhelmed by manipulative forces, to surrender to them in opportunistic adjustment, or to seek survival by the brutal application of power.

The complexities are greater than Dewey had envisaged, but his thought had a quality that made room for correctives. His plea was to face the facts, and to seek instrumentalities to keep alive the employment of intelligence and responsible communication. To deny that this is possible is to deny that free men have a chance in the world their time has created. The evidence for that conclusion is not yet in.

We deliberately choose to end on an unfinished note and with a cogent criticism of Dewey's work. His was an open-ended philosophy, one that is betrayed if frozen into dogma. It was designed to be modified and amended. If it has any staying power it should be able to prove itself in the face of the most searching criticisms.

# APPENDIX

# Plan of Organization of the University Primary School[1]

BY JOHN DEWEY

## GENERAL PROBLEM AND END

The ultimate problem of all education is to co-ordinate the psychological and the social factors. The psychological requires that the individual have the free use of all his personal powers; and, therefore, must be so individually studied as to have the laws of his own structure regarded. The sociological factor requires that the individual become acquainted with the social environment in which he lives, in all its important relations, and be disciplined to regard these relationships in his own activities. The co-ordination demands, therefore, that the child be capable of expressing *himself*, but in such a way as to realize *social* ends.

## SOCIOLOGICAL PRINCIPLES

I. The school is an institution in which the child is, for the time, to live—to be a member of a community life in which he

[1] John Dewey, *Plan of Organization of the University Primary School*, n.p., n.d., Chicago (1895(?)). Copy in the William Rainey Harper Library, University of Chicago. The fact that Dewey did not intend this to be followed as a blueprint is indicated by his note on the first page: "This is privately printed, not published, and is to be so treated. It will be understood to define the general spirit in which the work is undertaken, not to give a rigid scheme." This statement was prepared by John Dewey shortly before the Laboratory School opened. A mimeographed copy is on file in the William Rainey Harper Library at the University of Chicago. To the best of our knowledge, it has not previously appeared in print.

feels that he participates, and to which he contributes. This fact requires such modification of existing methods as will insure that the school hours are regarded as much a part of the day's life as anything else, not something apart; and the school house, as for the time being, a home, and not simply a place to go in order to learn certain things. It requires also that the school work be so directed that the child shall realize its value for him at the time, and not simply as a preparation for something else, or for future life.

II. As an institution, it is intermediate between the family and other larger social organizations. It must, therefore, grow naturally out of the one, and lead up naturally to the other.

1. As the family is the institution with which the child is familiar, the school life must be connected as far as possible with the home life. The child should be led to consider and to get some practical hold of the activities which center in the family—e.g., shelter, the house itself and its structure; clothing, and its construction; food, and its preparation; as well as to deepen and widen the ethical spirit of mutual service.

2. A consideration and command of these same activities takes the child out into the larger relations upon which they depend—e.g., the consideration of wood, stone, and food takes in a large sphere of existing social activities, and takes one back to previous states of society out of which the present has grown.

III. The school, as an institution, must have a *community* of spirit and end realized through *diversity* of powers and acts. Only in this way can it get an organic character, involving reciprocal interdependence and division of labor. This requires departure from the present graded system sufficient to bring together children of different ages, temperaments, native abilities, and attainments. Only in this way can the co-operative spirit involved in division of labor be substituted for the competitive spirit inevitably developed when a number of persons of the same presumed attainments are working to secure exactly the same results.

IV. The end of the institution must be such as to enable the child to translate his power over into terms of their social equivalencies; to see what they mean in terms of what they are capable of accomplishing in social life. This implies:

1. Such *interest* in others as will secure responsiveness to their real needs—consideration, delicacy, etc.
2. Such *knowledge* of social relationships as to enable one to form social ideas or ends.
3. Such *volitional command of one's own powers* as to enable one to be an economical social agent.

PSYCHOLOGICAL PRINCIPLES

I. The child is primarily an acting, self-expressing being, and normally knowledge and feeling are held within the grasp of action, growing from it and returning into it. This activity is neither purely psychical, nor purely physical; but involves the expression of imagery through movement.

II. The child, being socially constituted, his expressions are, normally, social. The child does not realize an activity save as he feels that it is directed towards others and calls forth a response from others. Language, for example, whether speech, writing, or reading, is not primarily expression of *thought*, but rather social *communication*. Save as it realizes this function, it is only partial (and more or less artificial) and fails, therefore, of its educative effect, intellectually, as well as morally; its complete, or organic, stimulus being absent.

III. The Intellectual Dependence upon Expressive Activity may be indicated as follows:

1. *Sense-perception.*
   a. Sensation. Save as a sensation of color, sound, taste, etc., is functionally required in order to carry on, assist, or re-inforce some outgoing or expressive activity, appeal to sense means either a deadening, a dulling, of the sense activity, rendering it mechanical because its organic stimulus is lacking; or else means distraction, dissipation, a continued demand for stimulation for its own sake, apart from its use or function. It is often forgotten that to stimulate the ear or eye without demand, must either require the organ to protect itself by simulating response in a purely mechanical

way, or else must create an appetite for such stimulus—as much in principle in case of the eye or hand as of the taste for alcohol.

b. Observation. The mind naturally selects or discriminates material with reference to expression or maintenance of its own activity. It picks out the means, the clues, the signals to carrying its own imagery. Separated from this function, observation becomes dead, and results in making mere distinctions for their own sake, a practice which is mentally disintegrating, and results in accumulating material which is either forgotten, or else carried by sheer force of memorizing.

2. *Ideas*. Separated from their stimulus by their function in action, ideas degenerate from knowledge, or appreciated significance, and become mere information, necessarily second-handed and conventional. Symbols, which have their value as economical guides to and instruments of action become, when severed, meaningless and arbitrary, and serve to confuse and distract. A consecutive expressive activity is always logical, having its own method, and demands judgment in selection of relevant material.

Summing up, we may say that the regular relationship is that sense-observation selects the *material* for farther self-expression, while the reasoning process determines the *method* for utilizing this material in expression. Hence the psychological principle that the mind always begins with a *whole*, expressing function, use, activity, and proceeds from this to matters of form, objective quality and abstract relations.

IV. The Emotional Dependence upon Expressive Activity may be illustrated as follows:

1. The *direct* appeal to feeling, in any form, whether moral or aesthetic, inevitably leads to isolating that feeling from its proper function—that of valuing and reinforcing action— and makes it sentimental.

2. The important part played by *interest* in education is generally recognized. Normal interest accompanies all self-expression; indeed, it is only the internal individual realiza-

tion of activity. Unless the child appreciates the *end* of what he is doing, unless there is some *motive* or reason realized by him for the activity, and for mastering the facts presented, real interest and attention are elsewhere, no matter how thoroughly the external appearances of interest are simulated. Moreover, the child detects by instinct whether the end or motive present is genuine, or whether it is made up as an excuse for getting him to do something. It is the absence of genuine motives, actual demands inherent in the given situation, which so often makes training of emotion and interest partial. It is, therefore, important that not only the principle of construction should be utilized, but utilized in producing things which appeal to the child as needed, as necessary.

3. In connection with this, it is important that *real wholes* should be constructed if there is to be educative interest. Interest goes along with sense of power, of accomplishment. When (as in some of the manual training systems) a child is kept making a sequence of geometrical forms, having no relevancy to his other activities, or is kept at a certain tool or certain principle of structure till he has mastered it, irrespective of producing some actual completed whole—interest (relatively) flags. It is more important that, at the outset, the child should realize he is accomplishing something, and something needed, even if the product, externally viewed, is crude, than that an external perfection should be aimed at in such a way as to keep the child at a long series of activities meaningless to him. In other words, normal interest requires that *technique*, both intellectual and practical, be mastered *within* the process of active expression, or construction of wholes, and relative to the recognized necessities of such construction. (It is not only necessary that the child should get a sense of power, of mastery, but also should realize his own limitations and weaknesses. This feeling also results when the principle mentioned is adhered to. In the recognition of the non-adaptation of his product to its intended purpose or function, the child has put before him the objectification of his own defects, and also receives the stimulus to remedy them. No such

standard of judgment exists when genuine and necessary wholes are not produced as the child's own self-expression.)

4. The principle of interest is often abused by being reduced to the concept of amusement, or making something interesting. Complete, or organic interest, is realized only when the child puts his entire self into his activity. His activity, even if comparatively trivial, objectively considered, must appeal to the child as worth while, as genuine work. (1) Work does not mean labor in the sense of disagreeable effort, but energies directed to something recognized as necessary. (2) Work in this sense is incompatible with "play" in the sense of conscious "make believe," but not in the sense of free expression, the principle of all artistic activity. When the child is *conscious* that he is only playing, he ceases to play, because interest dies out. (3) Expression, in a word, unites the ideas of an end which manifests the self, and thus is free (principle of play) and of the complete devotion of all energies to realizing this end (principle of work).

V. *Psychology of Learning.* Learning is the process intermediate between ignorance and comprehension in self. It arrives normally when an image in process of expression is compelled to extend itself and to relate itself to other images, in order to secure proper expression. The expansion or growth of imagery is the medium of realization, and this is obtained when the materials of expression are provided, and the end to which these are the means is recognized by the child. The process of learning, in other words, conforms to psychological conditions, in so far as it is *indirect;* in so far that is, as attention is not upon the *idea of learning,* but upon the accomplishing of a real and intrinsic purpose—the expression of an idea.

## EDUCATIONAL APPLICATIONS

The problem, as already stated, is the co-ordination of the social and psychological factors. More specifically this means utilizing the child's impulses towards, and powers of, expression in such a way that he shall realize the social ends to which they may be made serviceable, and thus get the wish and capacity to utilize them in this way. The starting point is always the impulse to self expression; the educational process is to supply the material and provide (positively and negatively) the conditions so that the expression shall occur in its normal social direction, both as to content and form or mode. This gives the standard for determining the entire school operation and organization, both as to the whole and as to its details.

Consequently the beginning is made with the child's expressive activities in dealing with the fundamental social materials—housing (carpentry), clothing (sewing), food (cooking). These *direct* modes of expression at once require the derived modes of expression, which bring out more distinctly the factors of social communication—speech, writing, reading, drawing, moulding, modelling, etc.

Both by themselves and in connection with the derived modes of expression (1) they lead back to *science*, the study of the materials used, and of the processes by which these materials are produced and controlled; (2) and lead on to *culture*, the recognition of the part these activities, and others bound up in them, play in society. This leads at once into the study of history—the realization of these various activities in their development from the simple to the complex. It is obvious that this movement once initiated, whether on the scientific or the historical side, demands recognition of the relations between the natural materials and processes on one side, and the human activities on the other. This brings the analysis to that set of facts usually called "geography." This gives the materials and method of the problem of correlation. It becomes obvious that the only adequate *basis* of correlation, whether upon the social or the psychological side, is the child's own activities of primary expression—*his constructive powers*. To take either "science" on one side, or "history and literature" on the other, as the basis of correlation is psychologically to attempt the impossible task of getting a synthesis in terms of knowledge, when only action really unifies; and, sociologically, it abstracts either *materials* or else *results*, neglecting, or relegating to a subordinate position, the *process* which unites and explains both materials and outcome.

The theory of correlation to be worked out in the school involves, therefore, the following features:

1. Finding the basis of unity always in a *constructive* activity, involving an image or idea (intellectual), the co-ordination of movements required to execute this idea (volitional), and the interest in the process of adjustment (emotional).
2. The three typical activities of cooking, carpentry, and sewing (taken in a broad sense) are taken as affording adequate opportunity, on the psychological side, for constructive work, while socially they represent the fundamental activities of the race.
3. The method is to analyze these activities, so far as required to give value to the work, into a knowledge of the materials and processes. Animal, vegetable life, soil, climate, etc., are studied not as mere *objects* (a psychological unreality), but as factors in action. So the *processes,* arithmetical, physical, and chemical, are studied not in themselves, but as the forms in which these materials are controlled. The knowledge of nature, or "science," results from this analysis of the *modus operandi* and the materials of individual constructive activity.
4. Further, the method is to follow out these activities into their social ramifications. Present social life, on one hand, is too complex for realization by the child, while past life, taken as *past,* is remote and psychologically inert. But through his interest in his own activity of cooking, and primitive building, the child is interested in the different forms this activity has assumed at different times. He can be led to analyze the existing complex social structure by following up the growth of the homes, foods, etc., of men, from the pre-historic cave-dweller through the stone and metal ages up to civilization, etc.
5. As the analysis of activity on the side of its materials leads to a knowledge of the environment and consideration of its various forms leads to knowledge of history, we are taken at each point to a consideration of the relation of environment to modes of human activity—geography, whether in its simplest local features or in its broadest physical aspects.
6. Both the original construction and the consideration of materials and modes of activity call, at every point, for expression in the form of *communication.* There is, then,

everywhere the demand for artistic expression—drawing, coloring, modelling, etc., speech, written records, etc. "Literature" itself is simply one form of this process of communication or artistic expression.

Moreover, we have here also a new phase of correlation. Literature, etc., while not the basis of co-ordination (that being found only in personal construction), affords the opportunity for bringing together in a common focus the variety of interests and facts which develop out of the original unity. (The ordinary theory of co-ordination fails in taking its different subjects or facts ready made, instead of differentiating them from a unity.) The images which are expressed in an artistic whole are, of necessity, intimately fused together, no matter how diverse before.

Other distinguishing features of the school have probably been sufficiently indicated. Attention may again be called to that of having the school represent a genuine community life; and to that of a study of the individual child, with a view to having his activities properly express his capacities, tastes, and needs. Attention may again be called to the principle of *indirect* training, and the consequent necessary emphasis upon initiating the proper *process* rather than upon securing any immediate outward *product*, in the faith that the proper process, once obtained, will determine, in its due season, its own products. It must be recognized that any attempt to force the result without first securing the proper psychological process can result only in undue forcing and gradual disintegration of power.

# Bibliography

Adams, George P., and William P. Montague, eds., *Contemporary American Philosophy*. New York, The Macmillan Co., 1930. See John Dewey, "From Absolutism to Experimentalism," Vol. 2, pp. 13–27.

Addams, Jane, *Democracy and Social Ethics*. New York, The Macmillan Co., 1902.

———, *The Spirit of Youth and the City Streets*. New York, The Macmillan Co., 1909.

Andrews, Katharine, "Experiments in Plant Physiology." *The Elementary School Record*, Vol. 1, No. 4 (May, 1900).

Beard, Charles, *Contemporary American History*. New York, The Macmillan Co., 1914.

Bowra, C. M., *Primitive Song*. New York, New American Library of World Literature, Mentor Books, 1963.

Brauner, Charles I., *American Educational Theory*. Englewood Cliffs, New Jersey, Prentice-Hall, 1964.

Bronowski, Jacob, *Science and Human Values*. New York, Harper and Row, 1959.

Bruner, Jerome S., *The Process of Education*. Cambridge, Harvard University Press, 1960.

Charters, W. W., Jr., "Survival in the Profession: A Criterion for Selecting Teacher Trainees." *The Journal of Teacher Education*, Vol. 7, No. 3 (September, 1956), pp. 253–55.

"Conference on Nature Study." *The University Record*, Vol. 1, No. 41 (January, 1897). Unpaged reprint, found in Teachers College Library, Columbia University.

Coulter, John, "Some Problems in Education." *University Record*. A series of articles.
1. "The Act of Teaching" (May 21, 1897), pp. 65–67.
2. "Science in Secondary Schools" (May 28, 1897), pp. 77–80.
3. "Over Production of Teachers" (June 4, 1897), pp. 90–91.
4. "The School and the University" (June 11, 1897), pp. 97–99.

Cremin, Lawrence A., *The Transformation of the School: Progressivism in American Education*. New York, Alfred A. Knopf, 1961.

Cronbach, Lee J., "Course Improvement through Evaluation." *Teachers College Record*, Vol. 64 (May, 1963), pp. 672–73.

Davenport, Frances Littlefield, *The Education of John Dewey.* Unpublished Ed. D. thesis, University of California, Los Angeles, 1946.

Davis, Robert B., *A Brief Introduction to Materials and Activities.* Unpublished, Madison Project, Syracuse University and Webster College, 1962.

Depencier, Ida B., *The History of the Laboratory Schools: University of Chicago 1896–1957.* Chicago, University of Chicago, 1960.

Dewey, [Harriet] Alice Chipman, Comments on the work of the early years in relation to educational theory. In files on records of the Dewey School in Teachers College Library, Columbia University.

Dewey, John, *A Common Faith.* New Haven, Yale University Press, 1934.

———, "The Aim of History in Elementary Education." *The Elementary School Record,* Vol. 1, No. 8 (November, 1900), pp. 199–203.

———, "Are the Schools Doing What the People Want Them to Do?" *Educational Review,* Vol. 21 (May, 1901), pp. 459–74.

———, *Art as Experience.* New York, Minton, Balch and Co., 1934.

———, "Challenge to Liberal Thought." *Fortune,* Vol. 30, No. 2 (August, 1944), pp. 155–157, 180, 182, 184, 186, 188, 190.

———, "The Chaos in Moral Training." *The Popular Science Monthly,* Vol. 14 (August, 1894), pp. 433–43.

———, *The Child and the Curriculum.* Chicago, University of Chicago Press, 1902.

———, "Christianity and Democracy." *Religious Thought at the University of Michigan.* Ann Arbor, The Inland Press, 1893.

———, "Consciousness and Experience," in *The Influence of Darwin on Philosophy* (New York, Holt, Rinehart and Winston, 1910), Ch. 10. Reprinted with slight variations from "Psychology and Philosophic Method." *University of California Chronicle,* Vol. 2 (August, 1899), pp. 159–79.

———, "Culture and Industry in Education." *The Educational Bi-Monthly,* Vol. 1, No. 1 (October, 1908), pp. 1–9.

———, "Current Problems in Secondary Education." *The School Review,* Vol. 10 (January, 1902), pp. 13–28.

———, *Democracy and Education.* New York, The Macmillan Co., 1916.

———, "Education as a University Study." *Columbia University Quarterly,* Vol. 9, No. 3 (June, 1907), pp. 284–90.

———, *The Educational Situation.* Chicago, University of Chicago Press, 1902.

Dewey, John, *Essays in Experimental Logic.* Chicago, University of Chicago Press, 1916.

———, "Ethical Principles Underlying Education." *Third Yearbook,* National Herbart Society, Bloomington, Illinois, 1897.

———, *The Ethics of Democracy.* University of Michigan Philosophical Papers, Second Ser., No. 1, 1888.

———, "Evolution and Ethics." *The Monist,* Vol. 8 (April, 1898), pp. 321–41.

———, "The Evolutionary Method as Applied to Morality." *Philosophic Review.*
1. "Its Scientific Necessity," Vol. 11 (March, 1902), pp. 107–24.
2. "Its Significance for Conduct," Vol. 11 (July, 1902), pp. 353–71.

———, *Experience and Education.* New York, The Macmillan Co., 1938.

———, *Experience and Nature.* Chicago, London, Open Court Publishing Co., 1925; New York, W. W. Norton and Co., 1929.

———, *Freedom and Culture.* New York, G. P. Putnam's Sons, 1939.

———, "General Principles of Work, Educationally Considered." *The Elementary School Record,* Vol. 1, No. 1 (February, 1900), pp. 12–15.

———, "George Herbert Mead." *Journal of Philosophy,* Vol. 28, (June, 1931), pp. 309–14.

———, "George Herbert Mead as I Knew Him." *University Record,* Vol. 27, No. 3 (July, 1931), pp. 173–77.

———, "How Do Concepts Arise from Percepts?" *The Public School Journal,* Vol. 11 (November, 1891), pp. 128–30.

———, *How We Think.* Boston, D. C. Heath and Co., 1910. (Rev. Ed., 1933.)

———, *Human Nature and Conduct.* New York, Holt, Rinehart and Winston, 1922.

———, "Imagination and Expression." *Kindergarten Magazine,* Vol. 9 (September, 1896), pp. 61–69.

———, *Individualism: Old and New.* New York, G. P. Putnam's Sons, 1930.

———, "The Influence of the High School upon Educational Methods." *School Review,* Vol. 4, No. 1 (January, 1896), pp. 1–12.

———, *Interest and Effort in Education.* Boston, Houghton Mifflin Co., 1913.

———, "Interest as Related to [the Training of the] Will." Second Supplement to the Herbart *Yearbook* for 1895, National Herbart Society, Bloomington, Illinois, 1896.

Dewey, John, "Interpretation of the Culture-Epoch Theory." *Second Yearbook*, National Herbart Society, Bloomington, Illinois, 1896.

——, "Interpretation of the Savage Mind." *Psychological Review*, Vol. 9 (May, 1902), pp. 217–30.

——, *Lectures for the First Course in Pedagogy*. Unpublished, Nos. 1–7, 1896. Copy made available to the author by Professor Frederick Eby (emeritus), University of Texas.

——, Letter of John Dewey to Jane Addams in the Swarthmore College Library, Peace Collection (January 19, 1896).

——, Letters to William Rainey Harper, President of the University of Chicago. The President's Papers, University of Chicago (May 13, 1897; December 6, 1897; June 23, 1898; February 10, 1899; March 8, 1899; December 21, 1899; February 3, 1900).

——, "The Metaphysical Assumptions of Materialism." *Journal of Speculative Philosophy*, Vol. 16 (April, 1882), pp. 208–13.

——, "Monograph No. 3—Textiles." *The Elementary School Record*, Vol. 1 (April, 1900).

——, "Monograph No. 7—Manual Training." *The Elementary School Record*, Vol. 1 (October, 1900).

——, *Moral Principles in Education*. Boston, Houghton Mifflin Co., 1909.

——, "The New Psychology." *The Andover Review*, Vol. 2 (September, 1884), pp. 278–89.

——, "The Pantheism of Spinoza." *Journal of Speculative Philosophy*, Vol. 16 (July, 1882), pp. 249–57.

——, "A Pedagogical Experiment." *Kindergarten Magazine*, Vol. 8 (June, 1896), pp. 739–41.

——, "Pedagogy as a University Discipline." *University Record*, Vol. 1, Nos. 25, 26 (September, 1896), pp. 353–55, 361–63.

——, *Philosophy and Civilization*. New York, Minton, Balch and Co., 1931.

——, *Plan of Organization of the University Primary School*. Unpublished (1895(?)). Copy in the William Rainey Harper Library, University of Chicago.

——, "Poetry and Philosophy." *The Andover Review*, Vol. 16 (August, 1891), pp. 105–16.

——, "A Policy of Industrial Education." *New Republic*, Vol. 1 (December, 1914), pp. 11–12.

—— "The Psychological and the Logical in the Teaching of Geometry." *Educational Review*, Vol. 25 (April, 1903), pp. 387–99.

——, "The Psychological Aspect of the School Curriculum." *Educational Review*, Vol. 13 (April, 1897), pp. 356–69.

Dewey, John, "Psychology and Philosophic Method." *University of California Chronicle*, Vol. 2 (August, 1899), pp. 159–79.

———, *Psychology and Social Practice*. Chicago, University of Chicago Press, 1901.

———, "The Psychology of Effort." *Philosophical Review*, Vol. 6, No. 1 (January, 1897), pp. 43–56.

———, "Psychology of Number." Letter in *Science*, Vol. 3 (February, 1896), pp. 286–89.

———, "The Psychology of the Elementary Curriculum." *The Elementary School Record*, Vol. 1, No. 9 (December, 1900), pp. 221–32.

———, "Reflective Attention." *The Elementary School Record*, Vol. 1, No. 4 (May, 1900), pp. 111–13.

———, "The Reflex Arc Concept in Psychology." *The Psychological Review*, Vol. 3, No. 4 (July, 1896), pp. 357–70.

———, "The Relation of Theory to Practice in Education." *Third Yearbook*, Part I, National Society for the Scientific Study of Education, 1904.

———, "Religious Education as Conditioned by Modern Psychology and Pedagogy." *Proceedings of the Religious Education Association*, 1903, pp. 60–66.

———, "Remarks on Frank Louis Soldan, *Shortening the Years of Elementary Schooling*." *School Review*, Vol. 11 (January, 1903), pp. 4–17, 17–20.

———, "Remarks on the Study of History in Schools." *School Review*, Vol. 4 (May, 1896), p. 272.

———, "The Results of Child-Study Applied to Education." *Transactions of the Illinois Society for Child Study*, Vol. 1, No. 4 (January, 1895), pp. 18–19.

———, "Review of Katherine Elizabeth Dopp, *The Place of Industries in Elementary Education*." *Elementary School Teacher*, Vol. 3 (June, 1903), p. 727.

———, "Self Realization and the Moral Ideal." *Philosophical Review*, Vol. 2 (November, 1893), p. 664.

———, "Significance of the School of Education." *Elementary School Teacher*, Vol. 4, No. 7 (March, 1904), pp. 441–453.

———, "The Situation as Regards the Course of Study." *Educational Review*, Vol. 22 (June–December, 1901), pp. 26–49.

———, "Some Dangers in the Present Movement for Industrial Education." *Child Labor Bulletin*, Vol. 1, No. 4 (February, 1913), pp. 69–74.

———, "Some Stages of Logical Thought." *Philosophical Review*,

Vol. 9 (September, 1900), pp. 465–89. Reprinted in *Essays in Experimental Logic*. Chicago, University of Chicago Press, 1916.

———, *The School and Society*. Chicago, The University of Chicago Press, Revised edition, 1923.

———, *The Study of Ethics: A Syllabus*. Ann Arbor, George Wahr, 1897. Printed originally in 1894 with the imprint: Ann Arbor, Register Publishing Co.

——— "Symposium on the Purpose and Organization of Physics." *School Science and Mathematics*, Vol. 13 (March, 1909), pp. 291–92.

———, "Teaching Ethics in the High School." *Educational Review*, Vol. 6 (November, 1893), pp. 313–21.

———, "The University Elementary School." Reports to the President, in the University of Chicago archives, 1898.

———, "The University Elementary School: General Outline of Scheme of Work." *University Record*, Vol. 3 (December, 1898).

———, "The University Elementary School: History and Character." *University Record*, Vol. 2, No. 8 (May, 1897).

———, "The University Elementary School, Studies and Methods." *University Record*, Vol. 2, No. 8 (May, 1897).

———, "The University School." *University Record*, Vol. 1, No. 6 (November, 1896), pp. 417–19.

———, *The Way out of Educational Confusion*. Cambridge, Harvard University Press, 1931.

Dewey, John, et al., *Studies in Logical Theory*. Chicago, The University of Chicago Press (University of Chicago Decennial Publications), 1903.

Dewey, John, and Evelyn Dewey, *Schools of Tomorrow*. New York, E. P. Dutton and Co., 1915.

Dewey, John, and James H. Tufts, *Theory of the Moral Life*. New York, Holt, Rinehart and Winston, 1960. Taken from Dewey and Tufts, *Ethics*. Part II, rev. ed., 1932.

Dykhuizen, George, "An Early Chapter in the Life of John Dewey." *Journal of the History of Ideas*, Vol. 13 (October, 1952), pp. 563–72.

———, "John Dewey and the University of Michigan." *Journal of the History of Ideas*, Vol. 23, No. 4 (October–December, 1962).

———, "John Dewey at Hopkins (1882–1884)." *Journal of the History of Ideas*, Vol. 22, No. 1 (January–March, 1961), pp. 103–16.

———, "John Dewey: The Chicago Years." *Journal of the History of Philosophy*, Vol. 2, No. 2 (October, 1964), pp. 227–53.

Eastman, Max, *Heroes I Have Known.* New York, Simon and Schuster, 1942.

Ginger, Ray, *Altgeld's America: The Lincoln Ideal versus Changing Realities.* New York, Funk and Wagnalls Co., 1958.

Gustafson, David, *The Origin and Establishment of the University High School of the University of Chicago.* Unpublished M. A. thesis in education, University of Chicago, 1927.

Hall, G. Stanley, "The Ideal School." *National Education Association Proceedings and Addresses,* 1901, pp. 474–88.

Ham, Charles H., *Mind and Hand.* New York, American Book Co., 1899 (3rd ed.).

Handlin, Oscar, *John Dewey's Challenge to Education.* New York, Harper and Row, 1959.

Harper, William R., "Ideals of Educational Work." *National Education Association Proceedings and Addresses,* 1895, pp. 987–98.

Hoblitt, Margaret, "Group VIII." *The Elementary School Record,* Vol. 1, No. 3 (April, 1900).

Hofstadter, Richard, *Anti-Intellectualism in American Life.* New York, Alfred A. Knopf, 1963.

James, William, "The Chicago School." *Psychological Bulletin,* Vol. 1, No. 1 (January, 1904).

Kimball, Solon T., and James E. McClellan, Jr., *Education and the New America.* New York, Random House, 1962.

McCaul, Robert L., "Dewey and the University of Chicago." *School and Society,* Vol. 89, I (March 25, 1961), pp. 152–57; II (April 8, 1961), pp. 179–83; III (April 22, 1961), pp. 202–6.

———, "Dewey's Chicago." *The School Review,* Vol. 67, No. 2 (Summer, 1959), pp. 258–80.

Mayhew, Katherine C., and Anna C. Edwards, *The Dewey School.* New York, Appleton-Century-Crofts, 1936.

Mead, George Herbert, "The Child and His Environment." *Transactions of the Illinois Society for Child Study,* Vol. 3, No. 1 (April, 1898), pp. 1–11.

———, *The Philosophies of Joyce, James and Dewey in Their American Setting.* Cambridge, Harvard University Press, 1930.

———, "The Relation of Play to Education." *University Record,* Vol. 1, No. 8 (May, 1896), pp. 141–45.

Mills, C. Wright, *Sociology and Pragmatism.* New York, Whitman Publishing Co., 1964.

Perry, Ralph Barton, *The Thoughts and Character of William James as Revealed in His Unpublished Correspondence and Notes together with His Published Writings.* Boston, Little, Brown and Co., 1935.

Phenix, Philip, "John Dewey's War on Dualism." *Phi Delta Kappa,* Vol. 61, No. 1 (October, 1959), pp. 5–9.

*Publications of the National Herbart Society (1895–1900). First Year-book,* Charles A. McMurry, ed., Chicago, University of Chicago Press, 1908.

Rice, Joseph Mayer, *The Public-School System of the United States.* New York, The Century Co., 1893.

Runyon, Laura L., "A Day with the New Education." *The Chatauquan,* Vol. 30, No. 6 (March, 1900), pp. 589–92.

———, *The Teaching of Elementary History in the Dewey School.* Unpublished M. A. dissertation in history and education, University of Chicago, 1906.

Schilpp, Paul A., ed., *The Philosophy of John Dewey.* New York, The Tudor Publishing Co., 1951. (Original edition in the *Library of Living Philosophers,* Vol. 1, Evanston and Chicago, Northwestern University, 1939.)

Small, Albion, "Some Demands of Sociology upon Pedagogy." *American Journal of Sociology,* Vol. 2, No 6 (May, 1897), pp. 839–51.

Smedley, Frederick W., "A Report on the Measurements of the Sensory and Motor Abilities of the Pupils of the Chicago University Primary School and the Pedagogical Value of Such Measurements." *Transactions of the Illinois Society for Child Study,* Vol. 2, No. 2 (1896–1897).

*Teacher's Reports of the University Elementary School.* Unpublished, (1899–1901). Available in the archives of the University of Chicago Laboratory School. Extensive scrapbooks from the *Reports,* organized according to subjects, may also be found in the files of the library at Teachers College, Columbia University.

Teilhard de Chardin, Pierre, *The Phenomenon of Man.* Introduction by Julian Huxley. New York, Harper and Row, 1959.

Thayer, Vivian T., *Formative Ideas in American Education.* New York, Dodd, Mead and Co., 1965.

Thomas, Milton Halsey, *John Dewey: A Centennial Bibliography.* Chicago, The University of Chicago Press, 1962.

Thomas, William Isaac, *Source Book for Social Origins.* Chicago, University of Chicago Press, 1909.

Tufts, James, "Extract from the Address by James Tufts." *University Record,* Vol. 27, No. 3 (July, 1931).

Van Liew, C. C., "The Educational Theory of the Culture Epochs." *First Yearbook,* National Herbart Society, Bloomington, Illinois, 1895.

White, Morton G., "Dewey on the Genetic Method." Part IV of

"The Attack on Historical Method." *The Journal of Philosophy*, Vol. 42, No. 12, pp. 328–31.

——, *The Origin of Dewey's Instrumentalism*. New York, Columbia University Press, 1943.

——, *Social Thought in America: The Revolt Against Formalism*. Boston, The Beacon Press, 1957.

White, Morton G., and Lucia Morton, *The Intellectual versus the City: From Thomas Jefferson to Frank Lloyd Wright*. Cambridge, The Harvard University Press, 1962.

# Index